To Ros[...]

Lydel Sims

Assignment: Memphis

Assignment: Memphis

by
Lydel Sims

Illustrations by Charles Nicholas
Introduction by William Thomas

YOKNAPATAWPHA PRESS
OXFORD, MISSISSIPPI

The essays and illustrations in this book were originally published by The Memphis Commercial Appeal.

Published by Yoknapatawpha Press, Inc.
P.O. Box 248, Oxford, Mississippi 38655

ISBN 0-916242-19-6   Library of Congress Catalog Card Number 82-60323

Printed in the United States of America
Illustration by Charles Nicholas

DEDICATION
To Gayle
Constant Collaborator
and to
Jan and Linton

Contents

CLOTHES MAKE THE MAN

IT'S US VERSUS THEM

WAY BACK WHEN

AGE OF AUTOS

PEOPLE IN HIGH PLACES

CRITTERS

THE WORLD IS FALLING APART

FOOLING AROUND WITH MOTHER NATURE

KIDS

Introduction
By
William Thomas

A MAN IS IN trouble. His watch is driving him dingy. It's a new battery-operated quartz digital watch. It tells the time, the day, the month and it plays Sousa. It's a jewel of technology. But the man can't set it. Neither can the clerk who sold it to him. Neither can digital-watch clerks in other digital-watch stores. The man is desperate. He's close to gibbering. He grabs a pencil. He writes to the one person who can help: Lydel Sims.

Although he knows nothing about digital watches—he even believes they typify the idiocy of the ages: "Who needs a watch to tell you what day of the month it is?"—Sims, for more than 30 years, has been finding answers to man's most agonizing dilemmas.

Since 1949, when he went to work for The Commercial Appeal as a daily columnist charged with laughing at the things that make the rest of us scream, Sims has dealt with backless hospital gowns, with the toe-wiggling method for keeping feet warm, with cats that back into chill chasers and set their tails afire, with the mystery of how flies land on the ceiling, and with his old archenemy, snow.

Although Sims' "Assignment: Memphis" column is probably read by more Mid-Southerners than anything since "Gone With the Wind," the readers know little of the man himself, including the fact that his first name is not Lydel at all but Linus.

Sims explains: "When my mother was a small girl, she was orphaned. A family named Lydel helped raise her, and she unloaded the family name on me. My father's name was Linus. So I became Linus Lydel. With two names like that, you can't win either way."

Maybe not. But it is a mark of Sims' art to pluck victory from the bear claws of defeat. So he took the middle name, and, despite a confused American Army that screwed up his military records with names like Linus L. and L.L. Sims, he proceeded to turn "Lydel" into a household word that is as common in these parts now as grits at the breakfast table. (By the way, he once mused, are grits plural or is they singular?)

That gritty puzzle is the sort of nagging question with which Sims wrestles at the bottom of Page 1 six days a week.

But who is he and where did he come from and how did he get that way, anyhow?

Well, Sims is a thin, quiet, careful, pleasant, patient, gentle, watchful, introspective man, 65, who somehow looks and feels like all of us who find ourselves adrift in a society that is altogether baffling and preposterous and nonsensical and wildly, madly, wonderfully absurd.

He is also an old-time newspaperman who started out at nothing-a-week and now finds himself writing under the best-known by-line in Memphis and working in a modern newsroom full of computer terminals, punch-button phones, molded plastic chairs, glass walls, cream-colored desks, lighted ceilings and orange people-dividers.

In 33 years, he has interrupted the column twice—once to manage the political campaign of George Grider and once to serve a a term as postmaster of Memphis.

He is a man of habit.

He walks into the newsroom at approximately 9:30 a.m. every day —only a few staff members are around at that time of morning, which is early for an a.m. paper—and crosses to a far corner of the room where he deposits his coat, cap and umbrella in a green wooden chair that he brought (despite official protests) from the newspaper's previous offices in an effort to save something of the past.

"I get attached to things as they get older," says Sims, who drives a 1966 Mustang that has logged 128,000 miles. "The older the car gets, the more I love it," he says. "Almost everything in it has been changed. And it's not just the car. I don't like to throw away bedroom slippers or old sweaters, either. I just like old, familiar things."

Perhaps it has something to do with the fact that Sims, who was born in Shreveport, La., in 1916, grew up in small-town America in times when things seemed to last longer and were held dearer.

The town was Hammond, La., where Sims' father was principal of the high school and later organizer and president of the junior college.

"He was the dominant man in my school life," says Sims, who was always three to four years younger than any of his classmates. He graduated from high school at 14 and from college at 18. In between, he became a regular contributor to the Hammond Daily Courier, which was edited by Hodding Carter, Sr., the man who later won a Pulitzer Prize.

"In school, I was a quick, surface learner," Sims remembers. "I learned things easily, but I forgot them right away. I went two years to Southeastern Louisiana College (where his father was president) and then graduated from Northwest Louisiana College in 1935. Then my mother wanted me to go to Harvard. I ended up going to

Nashville, first to George Peabody, then to Vanderbilt. I made good grades, but when I went in for my oral exams, they shot me down. Those were the golden days at Vanderbilt when you had to know everything."

It was the end of Sims' formal education and the beginning of his newspapering.

"I went down to the Nashville Banner and asked for a job. They didn't have any, but I persuaded them to take me on at nothing a week. It wasn't a big deal. They had a guy from the Missouri School of Journalism who was working for the same wage. Later, they took me on at $15 a week, the highest salary they'd ever given anybody to start."

Despite the lowly salaries—"our star city hall reporter got $22.50 a week and had been waiting two years to get enough money to get married"—Sims was hooked by his early days as a reporter.

From the Banner, Sims went to the Jackson Sun, where he became sports editor and met his wife, Gayle, on a blind date. They were married in 1939. In 1940, Sims went to work in the Memphis bureau of the Associated Press. He wanted to be a war correspondent, but he was drafted instead. After the war, Sims rejoined AP and in 1949 he wrote a feature about his tomcat, Caruso, who surprised them with a litter of kittens.

As a result of that story, Frank Ahlgren, who was then editor of The Commercial Appeal, offered Sims the job of writing a light daily column for Page 1. It's the only job Sims has ever done at the paper. It's also the only one he's ever wanted to do, and he takes it seriously.

"I think somebody ought to try to laugh at the insanity around us or we'd go wild," says Sims.

Although Sims frequently tees off on bureaucrats and politicians and the errant ways of our over-organized society, he frequently gets into a subject that is so earthy and so wacko that only Lydel Sims could have thought of it.

The braying mule is a case in point:

"For years, one of my most fascinating subjects was an investigation aimed at answering the question of whether a mule could bray without raising his tail. I came across the story at the library where I read about a colonel who tied down the tails of some mules during the Civil War and led them right past the Yankees and there wasn't a sound out of them.

"I threw this out in the column and it set off a controversy that went on for three or four years. Memphis was the mule capital and I heard from old mule traders, from veterinarians, from farmers, from people who had fought in the Indian wars.

"Finally, a girl from Brighten, Tenn., wrote and invited me up to experiment with her retired mule, Blue. She called him in from the pasture every afternoon to eat day-old bread and he always spread his legs and brayed when he came. She said come up and we'll see if he does it with his tail tied down.

"So I went and listened to this wonderful bray. Then we tied his tail down, chased him off, called him back and waved the bread at him. He spread his legs but just sputtered without braying. My conclusion was that it still was not certain if no mule could bray with its tail tied down, but this particular mule named Blue sure couldn't."

Although Sims deals with a considerable amount of frivolity, he does not consider the column frivolous. "After all," he says, "Shakespeare wrote a lot of frivolous plays, but there is nothing frivolous about his writing."

And Sims knows more about Shakespeare than you'd suspect.

"I'm a great fan of Mark Twain and Shakespeare," he says. Every so often I get on a Shakespeare kick, like now. I've read eight plays in the last month or so, and I proably will read them all before I'm done."

Sims also likes what he calls "good junk"—both in books and on TV, which he and his wife watch between 8 and 10 p.m. He reads at least two or three books a week and sometimes five or six. Not surprisingly, his favorite authors include the humorists James Thurber and Robert Benchley.

For years, Sims taught at Southwestern and then at Memphis State University. Sims' "Assignment: Memphis" has recently been adapted for the stage by "The Moving Line," a Memphis State touring theatre group.

A practicing grammarian, he is concerned about "the academic gobbledegook that comes out as English in the universities these days. When it comes to abuse of the language," he says, "the universities are worse than the bureaucracies."

To fellow journalists, Sims' job of coming up with a funny column day after day seems an exceptionally difficult one. "At first, this worried me, too," says Sims. "But I solved it with Sims' Law: as the day grows later, my standards grow lower. Things that didn't look at all good to me at 9 a.m., look wonderful at 11 a.m. I keep a list of stuff I have dismissed a dozen times as hopeless. On blank days, I'll take one of these ideas in desperation, go to that damn terminal, log on, watch that little light blink, start writing and see what happens. Funny thing is, one of those ideas might ring a bell where one that I thought was terrific gets no reaction."

William Thomas has been a reporter for *The Commercial Appeal* since 1964. He was named Scripps-Howard's Writer of the Year for 1981 and was co-winner of the 1967 Ernie Pyle Award for human interest reporting. Thomas has worked in the same newsroom with Lydel Sims for 18 years. His introduction first appeared as a feature article in *Scripps-Howard News* magazine.

Way Down South

N.Y.C. Discovers Iced Tea

THEY'VE GONE ABOUT as far as they can go in New York City, and that's a fact.

You won't believe what they have hit on this time.

There is this fashionable new drink, see. People sip it in places like Elaine's. Everybody knows about Elaine's.

Know what they call it?

Iced tea.

No, that's not a cute name for some new drug or anything like that. It's regular tea, but—now get this—with ice in it. And it's been discovered by what the Wall Street Journal calls the glitterati.

Yes indeed, says the noted business journal, iced tea is becoming chic. Listen to the evidence:

"Among others who have turned to iced tea from such trendy boosters as Campari-and-soda and Perrier are Richard Burton, Rudolph Nureyev and Meryl Streep."

The newspaper goes on to quote Elaine Kaufman, proprietor of Elaine's: "Tea is a stimulant. They don't realize it, but that's why it works."

That little lady seems to have put her finger right smack on the point. How come nobody ever thought of it before?

According to industry sources, says the Journal, per capita consumption of tea a decade ago was 5.6 gallons a year. Now it's about 12 gallons—and about 80 percent of it is drunk iced.

And now that it has been discovered at Elaine's, some New Yorkers have no doubt concluded, the provinces will follow along in two or three years. Who knows, some day even you and I may drink iced tea, just like the swells.

Actually, we've been drinking it all along, of course, but we didn't realize it was smart. Now we don't have to feel ashamed about it any more. If it's good enough for Burton and Nureyev, surely it's good enough for little old us.

Next time you drop some powdered tea mix into a glass, pour in some tap water and add ice, you can tell yourself: Gee whiz. This is just how the beautiful people do it.

There is one small cloud on the horizon, to be sure. The Journal story says a London resident who tasted her first glass of iced tea in an outdoor cafe in New York was outraged.

"How horrible!" she said. "How could anyone do that to an innocent cup of tea?"

Hah. What does London know these days about chic?

This news will be of little interest to some rugged individuals who
have never given a hoot about what people drink or say or do at
places like Elaine's. But others will be tremendously heartened.
Somehow it uplifts all of us. Tea-wise, we're more couth than we
ever dreamed. We have been made respectable.

It does make you wonder, though.

If New York has finally gotten around to discovering iced tea, who
knows when it will hit upon sassafras tea as well? The future for
pace-followers could be grim indeed.

Of Grits I Sing

A tiny cloud, no larger than a cracked grain of corn, has arisen over
that splendid renewed institution, The Peabody.

They got funny ideas there about grits.

At least, that's the way it might strike some people. Let me give
you an example.

During a recent dinner at The Peabody's Dux, acting on information received, I asked our splendid waiter if grits was available at
breakfast.

He said he thought so, but he would be happy to check for me.

In a short time he was back.

Yes, he said, grits was indeed on the breakfast menu. Would I like
to see a copy?

I would. What I found did not startle my wife, but it sure as
shooting startled me.

They had a lineup of breakfast combinations on there, and not one
of them included grits. Three of the breakfasts—the sort where grits
might be expected—offered hash brown potatoes.

By then, the waiter was gone.

"Look," I said. "No grits after all."

"No, you're looking at the wrong place," said my wife, who never
cared much for grits anyhow. "Look under 'Cereals.' "

And sure enough, there it was. Under "Cereals." Right alongside
Cream of Wheat and oatmeal.

Well, frankly, it shook me. At The Peabody, in whose lobby, as we
all know, the Delta begins, grits is listed along with Cream of Wheat
and oatmeal, while hash browns are offered with the breakfasts.

I had engaged in this sterling bit of investigative reporting because a woman had called earlier about the same subject.

Recently she attended a breakfast in the Continental Ballroom, she said, and instead of getting grits with her breakfast she got hash browns.

She said she asked a waiter if they didn't have grits, and he said no. She said she asked why, and he said the chef didn't know how to make grits.

I was so staggered I forgot to get her name.

So after checking for myself, and discovering that they do indeed have grits, but that they link it with Cream of Wheat and oatmeal, I called Ms. Kay Feree, director of public relations at The Peabody, and asked for the lowdown on grits.

Oh, yes, she said, the executive chef knows about grits. She said he has worked at Opryland. She said she would check further on the situation.

So the next day she told me that, as a matter of fact, they were getting ready for another special group breakfast right then, and the people had asked for grits, and grits they would get.

But that was a special breakfast. What about somebody who just walked into Dux for breakfast and wanted grits instead of potatoes on one of the regular breakfasts?

Then grits could be provided, she said.

Instead of hash browns?

Instead of hash browns.

At no extra cost?

At no extra cost.

So I suppose it's not as bad as it sounded at first. The chef does know about grits, and you can get it, even though you have to ask for it as a substitution on a combination breakfast. Still, the way things are today, that's something.

But lumping grits with Cream of Wheat and oatmeal? In The Peabody?

It's a good thing the Delta begins in the lobby and not in the restaurant.

Let's Settle the Bread Issue

Some of the finest elements of our regional heritage are slipping away from us. Do you realize an entire generation is growing up that never even heard of "light bread"?

And even those who remember the term can't seem to agree on what it means.

Oh, the bald definition is clear enough, all right. Even the unabridged Webster has that:

"Chiefly South & Midland: Wheat bread in loaves made from white flour leavened with yeast."

But that's not the point. What distinguished light bread from other bread?

A fellow I know brought up that question in a conversation the other day, and members of the group were unanimous in their disagreement.

"People talked of light bread," said one latter-day expert, "to distinguish it from whole wheat or rye. Light bread was white. The others weren't."

This appalling response was immediately challenged by someone else.

"No, no. When you said you were having light bread, it meant you weren't having biscuits."

At that point, a third authority chimed in.

"You're both wrong," he said. "Light bread meant store-bought bread."

Being a peaceable sort, I make it a point never to intervene in arguments of any kind, or even to express opinions, except in cases of extreme provocation like this. I undertook to clarify the issue as diplomatically as possible.

"You're all crazy," I explained. "If you were eating light bread, it meant you weren't eating corn bread. It was probably made at home, but that wasn't the point. The point was that it wasn't corn bread."

I was hooted down by whippersnappers.

Actually, of course, the biscuit man was not entirely on the wrong track. In the old days you were likely to get one of three kinds of bread: light bread, corn bread or biscuits.

But since the term "biscuits" was clear enough in and of itself, there was really no need there for the essential distinction that had to be made between the two kinds of bread. They were light or corn, and that was that.

Since the matter first came up, I have been questioning people at random, and the results are remarkable.

Most of those who are familiar with the term at all seem to think it meant, or means, store-bought bread—or even, in some cases, one particular brand of store-bought bread.

Hah. I will bet that most of those people aren't even old enough to remember when we had to slice our own store-bought bread.

At any rate, there is at least one honest-to-goodness authority to back up my own point of view. A friend who got involved in the debate called his 79-year-old aunt down in Mississippi, and she straghtened him out in a hurry.

Light bread, she said without hesitation, was what you ate when you didn't eat corn bread. It didn't have anything to do with store-bought.

The world is so full of stubborn, opinionated and misguided people that I don't really expect this clarification to settle the issue.

But I have done my best. Those who wish to persist in their own confusion have only themselves to blame.

Compared with Nuttin'—Not Bad

It is high time for loyal citizens of the Mid-South to do something to protect the glorious reputation of fried catfish.

I don't know, maybe it's too late already, not that you can't still find places that serve that delicacy of the gods just the way it ought to be served; you can. But you have to know where to go.

And tourists who have heard tales of the almost unbearable goodness of catfish are, in all too many cases, in for a brutal and greasy surprise. Who knows what sorrows and disillusions they take home with them, along with their indigestion pills?

This is no theoretical matter, mind you. I speak from bitter and recent experience, so recent that my stomach is still squeamish.

Let me say right now that I don't intend to get into the matter of naming bad—or even good—catfish restaurants. That's not the point. The point is that nobody, nobody should be allowed to serve sorry catfish in an area where they should be our glory rather than our shame.

But it's done. Oh, lordy, it's done.

During a brief vacation that has just ended, a group of us went to a certain area of West Tennessee said to be famous for its succulent catfish dinners. We went to the most popular of the locally acclaimed restaurants. And we ordered catfish.

Any lover of fine food will know what we expected: Platters of pan-sized catfish, fried a delicate golden brown, piping hot, the meat tender but dry, the batter thin and crispy.

Good night, that's what catfish is all about.

But what did we get?

We got what I suppose you would call catfish steaks—cross-sections whacked off the carcasses of great hulking monsters of the deep.

Now that is bad enough in itself. Large catfish are fine to look at, and it is great sport to catch them, but they leave much to be desired as food. There's too much fat on them. They have lost their youthful flavor. They are mere hunks of greasy fish, good no doubt for catfood or even for staving off starvation but completely out of consideration if you want really good eatin'.

And these, it appeared, had been marinated in grease for 24 hours before being covered in half an inch of batter and dropped momentarily into a fry pot, removed and then set on a counter to cool.

The result reminded me poignantly of a comment made by an Army buddy when we were on bivouac in Louisiana many years ago. It was bitter cold, and the two of us shared a pup tent, and our masters had issued one candle per pup tent as fuel. The idea was to crawl into the tent, button it securely, light the candle and then bask in its warmth.

As we shivered through the night, my buddy made one comment about the candle. "It's not bad," he said philosophically, "compared wit' nuttin.' "

Nuttin' was the only thing you could compare that catfish with favorably—unless it was the giant, dripping pile of noxious fried onions that accompanied it.

And this happened, let me remind you, in a part of the country where people of discrimination have been known to swoon with pure ecstasy over the sight and taste and aroma of catfish prepared as it should be prepared.

You and I know the difference. We even know, in most cases, where to go for such memorable treats. But what of the strangers in our midst? Are we to let them wander unguided and unwarned into restaurants that fling down sodden hunks of dripping batter surrounding lukewarm globs of fat identified as catfish?

By golly, if we're going to have government standards for everything else, let's have them for catfish, too. Or at least a citizens' review board or something. We must not stand idly by while fried catfish gets a bad name.

Liquid Grits

Recent talk here about old-fashioned buttermilk has reminded many Memphians of the unfortunate ignorance displayed in other sections of the country regarding milk in general.

In days past, of course, before we were forced to accommodate the weaknesses of other cultures, you never just bought "milk." After all, there are two kinds of milk. You asked for sweet milk or butter-milk.

But get out of your own neck of the woods, and people thought you were crazy. A.H. "Shorty" Addison, for example, still remembers his encounter with a waitress at Child's in New York years ago.

". . . and a glass of sweet milk," he said, completing his order.

"I beg your pardon?"

"Sweet milk."

She looked at him and sniffed. "Oh," she said, as one would speak to a person of severely limited intelligence, "you mean milk."

He said duhh, yeah, milk, and she finally brought it. But she kept her eye on him. You could tell what she was thinking. Did this nut think they served sour milk to their customers?

Which brings us around to the opposite side of the coin as reported by Martie Sullivan.

"While you are on the subject of buttermilk," he said, "I thought you might enjoy hearing my Yankee friend's first experience with the beverage.

"Entering a restaurant on the sunny side of the Mason-Dixon Line, he ordered a glass of milk with his breafast.

"The conscientious waitress asked, 'Sweet milk or regular milk?'

" 'Regular,' he told her, and received a tall, cold glass of butter-milk.

"He then beat a hasty retreat to the wilds of New York State."

In referring to buttermilk as "regular" milk, that waitress was, of course, unconsciously revealing a preference shared by many. Paul L. Kidd is among them.

"Buttermilk," Kidd assured me, "is the closest thing I know to li-quid grits."

That is about as far as a fellow can go in praising the drink, and it is high praise indeed. Kidd went on to explain that sweet milk is for babies, while sour milk is fit only for hogs.

He used to churn buttermilk himself, he added, and he remembers songs he sang to make the butter come. Being a thoughtful man, he didn't volunteer to sing any.

But he did recall a time in his youth when he undertook a great breakthrough.

"It was right after I had read a book called 'Young Tom Edison—Boy Genius.'

"I devised an electric churn. Well, not exactly. It never churned anything except a stack of freshly washed and dried dinner dishes. I was 10 at the time, and it was generally understood that I would never see 11."

So much for the tribulations of an inventor. But those of the drinker of what passes today for buttermilk can be even worse, and Kidd had a report on that, too.

Recently, he bought some of what is now called buttermilk and, for some reason, failed to finish it off at one sitting.

The next day it was spoiled.

"I was puzzled," he told me. "Back a while, we kept ours sitting in the springhouse for weeks, and it only got thicker and better."

So, he took it back to the store.

"How come it spoiled so soon?" he asked the lady.

"I guess it's that stuff they put in it," she said.

"What stuff is that?"

She looked at him, he told me, without batting an eye.

"Preservatives," she said, and Kidd slunk off in defeat.

Put This in Your Computer!

The time has come to put away frivolities like politics and inflation, and get down to a truly serious issue raised by Mitt Kilpatrick of Tupelo, Miss.

How much is a mess of turnip greens?

Or, if you prefer, how many?

Lest there be the slightest doubt what we're talking about, let us put it yet another way: Precisely what quantity is meant when a person speaks of buying or selling a mess of greens?

The question has lain dormant in his mind, Kilpatrick told me, for nigh onto 40 years—since he was a small boy in Fulton, Miss., and his father owned a grocery store.

Mitt worked in the store.

In a town that size, he said, you were usually on a first name basis with everybody, and everybody expected prompt service.

People who have grown up in the lightning-swift computer age don't understand what prompt service means, of course. Thanks to the miracles of modern technology, it now takes weeks or months to accomplish what used to be done in minutes in the old days. And can you imagine having groceries delivered when you order them?

But that's how it was in the primitive 1940s. Kilpatrick remembers it well.

The store telephone would ring, he said, and the voice on the other end would say:

"This is Mary Sue. I need a quart of sweet milk."

And then Mary Sue, who "was not one to mince words," would

hang up and young Kilpatrick would get busy. He reviewed the routine for me:

"Get the milk out of the case. Make a charge ticket to Mary Sue, 15 cents. Sack the milk. Get on your bicycle and ride seven blocks to deliver the milk. Return to store and await more phone calls."

His father, he confessed, used child labor to good advantage.

"As time passed," he said, "I became adept at receiving orders and filling them. There was one disconcerting question, however, that always caused much doubt in my mind.

"When a phone order came in, the customer would call out the items she needed and then she was likely to say:

" 'Oh law me, hon, I'm about to forget. Send me a good mess of turnip greens.' "

And there was the puzzle. How many turnip greens in a mess?

And how much difference was there between a good mess and a regular mess?

He used to worry about it, he said, and he never solved the question, and then the years passed and he almost forgot. But recently a friend gave him a book by Florence King, entitled "Southern Ladies and Gentlemen," in which the author said that a mess is "about" two pounds.

And Kilpatrick still wonders. Can you really measure a mess by the pound? If two pounds of greens makes a mess, how about two pounds of potatoes?

As a matter of fact, the word isn't a quaint Southern term at all; it has been around for centuries in England as well as America, and it means, among other things, a quantity of food, a course, or a sufficient quantity for a dish or a meal. So let us have no superior comments about the way people talk down here.

Still, nobody knows turnip greens better than we do. And it's high time we qualify the term in regard to greens.

My own answer is that a mess of greens is a whole lovely heap of 'em. But can anybody convert that to a measurement in the metric system and give Kilpatrick some relief?

On Behalf of Black-eyed Peas

A question just in from Hampton Sides can only be classifed as a cruel blow to every lover of true tradition and good food.

"In the superstitious hope of breaking ominous spells of bad luck," he told me, "millions of Americans annually grace their dinner tables on New Year's Day with a generous serving of steaming-hot black-eyed peas.

"Apparently overlooking the sheer ugliness of the vegetable itself, we credulous individuals have blindly accepted the whimsical New Year's tradition without any skepticism or questioning of its origins.

"As a New Year's resolution, I decided to bury my naive docility and attempt to track down the roots of this absurd superstition. In matters of paramount importance such as this, it is essential to hear it straight from the foremost authority. Whence this curious tradition?"

For shame, sir. How anyone, and especially any resident of the South, can mock that proud and worthy tradition is beyond me.

I must confess that I don't know precisely whence it comes, but I can blamed sure tell you whyce.

Few delicacies on this green earth can come even close to black-eyed peas, that's why. These gifts of bounteous nature to an unworthy population rank right up there with turnip greens and grits as the most sublime taste treats available to the human palate.

And as for the tradition, why, it simply stands to reason. Eat the best on the first day of the year, and you are at least off to a good start.

Not only that, but consider the cost of black-eyed peas as opposed, say, to hamburger. Before this year is over, I fully expect Black-Eyed Burger franchises to cover the country. And we'll all be better off as a result.

At my house, we didn't have a big dinner of black-eyed peas. It just didn't fit in with the plans. But ere the day had ended, we had faithfully eaten our individual helpings, and had felt better therefor. How can anyone survive the rigors of January in frozen Memphis without the thought of black-eyed peas to provide comfort?

And how in the everloving blue-eyed world could anyone speak harshly of black-eyed peas? Some day, one can only hope, Sides will learn the error of his ways.

Watermelon Salters—Stand Up

JUST WHEN EVERYBODY in town is worn out with strife and controversy, we come to an issue that makes any others seem minor:

Is watermelon better with salt on it?

I hadn't realized what an emotion-packed matter this was until Gary Coughlan told me how worked up he still gets when he remembers his Army days in California at a language school.

There he was, he said, trying to speak Korean with a Southern accent and having to put up with all sorts of wisecracks by classmates from other parts of the country, and that was bad enough, but he endured it.

They they pushed him too far.

He and a friend from Massachusetts were at a snack bar and found watermelon on the menu, so they ordered some.

"He plunged right into his slice while I paused to salt mine," Coughlan said. "He glared at me with his eyes bugged out and a look of pure disgust on his face."

But it didn't stop there. In what Coughlan described as a snarl, the fellow announced:

"You put SALT on your watermelon."

Coughlan said sure he put salt on it, didn't everybody?

"No," his companion snapped, in that dogmatic way some people have, "and nobody I know does either."

Like all good Southerners, Coughlan sought to calm the man down and reason with him. Southerners generally use salt on watermelon, he explained, "to spruce up the taste and make it tangy." Northerners generally don't use salt, his companion rasped, because they feel it spoils the natural sweetness.

Since neither was able to convince the other, they decided to poll the members of their language class.

The vote was split along sectional lines. They appealed to their Korean teachers to break the tie.

"They were no help," Coughlan reported, "because they said they would use sugar."

All that is back in the past, but Coughlan still broods over it, as well he might. What, one must ask, is the world coming to if people are repelled by the idea of putting salt on watermelon?

It is true, of course, that by now many persons have become afraid to put salt on anything, having been convinced that it causes warts, cancer, hypertension, low blood pressure, skin rashes or something. But you can say that about any food consumed by human beings.

The basic question is not, is it safe to put salt on watermelon? Instead it is, does salt improve the taste of watermelon?

Southerners, Coughlan feels, should be "ready to defend our use of the shaker." But are they? Has an appreciation of salted melon, lika a natural love of grits, gradually disappeared from the Southern scene in the course of the general homogenization, standardization and fast-foodization that has beset the nation?

One can only hope that some of the fine old traditions and principles remain unchanged. But alas, one cannot be sure. It is a depressing thought, but we must be prepared to face it.

Perhaps the South has lost its ability to appreciate salt on watermelon. Who knows, perhaps it has even faltered in its recognition that the only good cantaloupe is a peppered cantaloupe. These are troubled times. But, plague take it, a few fine old standards should be maintained.

You Ain't Seen Nothin' Yet

One great thing about our language is the variety of meanings that can be packed into the same word, depending on the accent.

Mrs. Jane Sohm was telling me about her granddaughter, Beth Safian (it is not often that someone will tell you about a grandchild, but it does happen), and the story provides a handy example.

At Beth's home they say grace before meals, and Beth has been taught to say: "God is great, God is good, let us thank him for this food. Amen." So on a recent evening, her father turned to her and asked her to say the blessing.

"God is great, God is good, let us thank him for this food," Beth recited. Then she added the emphasis as she had learned it:

"Ah meant it."

Which brings us to the question, if that is the right word, posed by Maure Lee Talley.

"I'm a Yankee trying to make it in the South," she told me.

"I'm from St. Louis, and some people consider anyone living north of Southland Mall a Yankee. Until I moved South, I always thought a Yankee was a member of the National League.

"I have learned to pronounce 'penny' as 'pinny,' 'wire' as 'war' and 'ice' as 'eye-us.'

"Instead of getting ready, nowadays I'm fixin' to go.

"I cut things half-in-two instead of just cutting them in half.

"I ask for hamburger meat, not hamburger.

"The only thing that has me confused is what happened to the afternoons. It appears that anything that occurs after noon is evening. A serviceman told me he would be out to fix something at 2 in the evening.

"Please, Unk, explain Southern time to me."

Well, now, there are a heap of different times involved when you talk about evening, and I'm not even counting Daylight Saving Time. Let us consult Webster's Unabridged.

Evening may be considered "the latter part and close of the day and early part of darkness or night." That's the definition 1a.

Another version, identified as "chiefly South & Midland," is that evening is "the time extending roughly from noon to midnight." That's definition 1b.

Strangely enough, definition 1c is almost identical: "the part of the day from noon to midnight—used in the Bible."

And finally, before Webster goes on to another set of definitions entirely, there is 1d: "The period from sunset or from the evening meal to bedtime."

Now, that's Webster. My own observation is that many people around here use "evening" to mean the period from about quittin' time until after supper.

But if somebody uses "evening" for any time from noon until midnight, then all you have to do is apply definition 1b or 1c.

So if you're fixing to worry about it, just decide instead to take all four definitions, divide them half-in-two, and use the result for guidance.

But don't let all this confusion get you down, you heah?

And anyhow, whoever said that people living in the vicinity of Southland Mall are real Southerners? Where I grew up in Louisiana, we went north to get to Mississippi. Memphis, with or without a mall, was so far north it actually had snow and eye-us in the wintertime. If you think that's the South, you ain't seen nothin' yet. Ah mean it.

Somethin' for Cottonpickin' Speech Coaches

We are enjoined to be not weary in well-doing, but I declayuh, it suah is wearisome to keep on a-tryin' and a-tryin' to tell the moviemakers how we talk daown heah.

Man and boy, for most of my lil ole life, I have wrestled with them over just two little cotton-pickin' words: Anything and everything. But hawgfry mah potlikker, it don't leastwise seem to do hardly no good at all.

So this time, even after being goaded to rise once more to the occasion, I was going to remain silent. But then Peggy Ray brought up the matter so eloquently I couldn't resist.

"Did you watch Beulah Land on television last week?" she asked.

"You were constantly in my thoughts, for anythin's and everythin's rained without mercy, like dreaded snowflakes, on the viewers.

"Usually such verbal offenses are confined to the swooning, helpless, fluttery lil ole Southern belle.

"But in Beulah Land, neither the debauched, to-the-manor-born young gentlemen nor the evil sheriff spared us.

"The dialect and regional accent coach must have worked overtime on this one, for in the final episode our heroine actually said everythin', and anythin' and the acceptable nothin' all in one sentence."

I did indeed watch that unforgettable television saga, all three murky installments, all the way through to the bitter end, which proves to what lengths a person can be driven in an election year. And my first thought was that, in an opus where everything was incredibly bad, there was little point in carping about dialects.

But Peggy Ray is right. We just have to keep calling attention to things like that. For, we are also told, in due season we shall reap if we faint not.

And anyone who could faint not after hearing the dialects in Beulah Land is entitled to do a little reaping, I can tell you that.

But let us concentrate simply on those two little words.

Just as, a generation ago, British writers believed that Americans say "I reckon" about every 15 seconds, Hollywood—and Broadway—authorities are convinced that all Southerners say "anythin' " and "everythin'."

Never mind that Southern speech is different in Mississippi, in Tennessee, in Georgia, in the Carolinas and so on. (And never mind, while we're at it, that in Beulah Land, set somewhere near Savannah in Georgia, the old plantation is visited by the Delta Queen.) Let us concentrate on two narrow specifics: Anything and everything.

There may possibly be some remote area in the South where people say "anythin' " and "everythin'," but I have never come upon it, and I never talked to anybody who did.

No, sir. We say anything, or innything, or even innythang. We say everything or everythang. But we just don't say anythin' or everythin'.

On the other hand, as Peggy Ray properly noted, we do say nothin'. And, for that matter, we also say somethin'. Which only proves that regional dialects don't follow set patterns. Why can't those cotton-pickin' speech coaches get a simple little thing like that straight?

But no. They clearly figure that, if we drop one final "g," we drop 'em all. Now, why is that?

When Walter Cronkite says "police," it comes out "pleece." Fine. Why not? But do the speech coaches then conclude that all television announcers make one syllable of all two-syllable words?

Somethin' ought to be done about it, that's for sure. Because if nothin' is done, they're goin' to go on sayin' everythin' and anythin'.

And if there's anythang that can get on a Southerner's nerves, it's to be pictured as somebody who always says anythin'. Nothin' is further from the truth.

Landing A Whopper

Save Regrets For Otis

IN ALL THE excitement about the Miss America people firing Bert Parks, the country has overlooked a far greater loss to our culture.

That would be, of course, the demise of the Burlington Liars' Club after half a century of selfless service in selecting the world's best tall tales, year after year.

Everybody's outraged about ol' Bert, who apparently will come out of the Miss America deal with more jobs than he can handle. But nobody even remembers Otis C. Hulett, who at 82 announced recently the end of the club he had headed since it was founded in 1929. So much for our sense of proportion.

There's no doubt the pageant people goofed. Only the lunacy of Parks braying his musical tribute could match the lunacy of the contest itself. And the idea of canning him simply because of his age was scarcely what you would expect from an organization dedicated to fostering such high ideals as wholesomeness, tap dancing, vital statistics and the American way of life.

No wonder the public was indignant. One critic, I understand, suggested that if the pageant people wanted a more relevant image they should replace Parks with the Incredible Hulk. Another came out in favor of keeping Parks and firing the pageant.

Fine, fine. Anything to help spread the idiocy.

But what about the ideal of creative prevarication nourished so faithfully by the Burlington Liars' Club? Isn't anybody going to hail Otis Hulett for his 50 years of service to the country?

I for one will miss him. The story told by the final winner, C.O. Laurie of Kirkland, Mo., was a sample of the gems Hulett came up with year after year. Laurie, in case you've already forgotten, said it got so cold in his neck of the woods that he actually saw a politician standing on a corner with his hands in his own pockets.

And it has been that way through the years. I still remember one of the earliest prize winners, an involved story about a stray cat adopted by the operators of a warehouse.

It turned out to be a splendid mouser, and all went well until the cat got tangled in some machinery one day and lost a leg. The friendly warehousemen made it a peg leg, but they agreed its mousing days were over. Who ever heard of a mouse slow enough to get itself killed by a peg-legged cat?

But to everyone's surprise, the cat went right on catching mice every night and leaving them for the inspection of the boss in the morning.

At last one of the workers hid in the warehouse to see how the cat managed. Well, sir, that critter would hide behind a 4-by-4 up right and watch through a knothole until a mouse came close; then it would reach out and club it with the peg leg.

Everybody was happy, the storyteller continued, but then matters went awry. The cat quit catching any mice at all.

They examined it and discovered that hours of looking through knotholes with one eye and around the corner with the other had left the animal cross-eyed. Whenever it hit at a mouse, it missed.

So they kept it on as a pet—and then, by golly, it began catching mice again. Again somebody watched to see how. And the answer turned to to be remarkably simple.

The cat simply hid until it heard a mouse, and then leaped out at it. You can guess what happened. Any mouse that saw it was being attacked by a cross-eyed cat with a peg leg would die of fright.

In my book, that story alone is worth one Miss America and three alternates, not to mention Bert Parks. Isn't it time that somebody sounded off in appreciation of Otis C. Hulett of Burlington, Wis.?

Mosquitoes Have Pot, Will Travel

We may be past the peak of the mosquito season, but a recent big-mosquito story here has set a few members of the audience itching.

Carl Kelly of Greenwood, Miss., for example, has been remembering that terrible August in Louisiana back in 1925.

The story he tells might be hard for some people to believe. But I grew up in Louisiana, and I heard the same story only a few years after he was there—and, I might add, several other times during the years that followed—so at least part of it must be true.

You think you've seen mosquitoes? Then listen to this.

At the time in question, Kelly told me, he was working as third-trick telegraph operator for the Illinois Central Railroad at Destrehan, La.

"It was very hot," he recalled. "Mosquitoes by the trillions were being blown off the marshes at the edge of Lake Pontchartrain, into the surrounding country.

"They were very large indeed, and all had voracious appetites for human blood."

Extreme measures were called for.

"It was necessary for me to wear two pairs of pants and stuff paper into my shoes and up the trouser legs.

"I also smeared pine oil on my face and hands and neck, pushed a handkerchief down the back of my neck under my tightly buttoned shirt collar, and walked as rapidly as possible from my living quarters to the depot.

"There the second-trick man, who was just going off duty, had a fire smouldering in a five-gallon paint bucket, over which was poured at intervals sawdust and an insect powder, creating a volume of smoke.

"Of course I had to continue feeding this fire until 8 a.m. when I was relieved."

But even that wasn't enough to handle the situation.

"One day the mosquitoes were so bad that the yard engine operations at Harahan Yard, just out of New Orleans, had to be suspended.

That was because the operations then were based on my hand signals only, and the switchmen were so busy fighting the insects that the engineers couldn't determine the signals."

All of that, mind you, is merely a prelude to the story at hand, but it should prepare you to face facts with an open mind. Are you ready?

One day, Kelly said, the wind off the lake was bringing in a great cloud of insects, and one unusually large swarm took after a man who lived in the vicinity.

"He rushed into his back yard trying to escape, picking up a hammer as he ran toward the cast iron family washpot.

"Quickly crawling beneath what he thought was good shelter, he found that the mosquitoes were piercing the pot with their long sharp stingers.

"He immediately set to work bradding them down against the inside of the pot with his hammer, but there were so many of them that, finally, they lifted the pot and flew away with it."

I am proud to say I can offer at least some confirmation to that story. As I say, I heard versions of it later.

The washpot couldn't be produced as evidence, of course, and nobody even discussed what happened to the man after his cover was blown. But I am sure there were some people around who saw the hammer the man used.

I don't know what further proof anybody would need. If you think we have big mosquitoes around here, you ought to go to Louisiana.

It's The Gospel

If you want to hear a really tall tale about a hunting dog, I always say, look for a minister.

I don't know why that is. Maybe fishers of men feel a community of interest with hunters of animals. Whatever the reason, you can count on the results.

There is, for example, the tale told me the other day by Ken Joines, minister of the Whitehaven Church of Christ.

He heard what he was about to tell me, he said, right here in Memphis just a short time ago. One hunter was telling another hunter what a fine coon dog he had.

And here, as Mr. Joines recounted it to me, is how it went.

"She can not only follow a trail twice as old as the average dog," the man said, "but she's got a pretty good memory to boot.

"For instance, last week this old boy who lives down the road from me, and is forever stinkmouthing my hounds, brought some city fellow around to try ol' Sis here.

"So I turned her out south of the house and she made two or three big swings back and forth across the edge of the woods, set back her head, bayed a couple of times, cut straight through the woods, come to a little clearing, jumped about three foot straight up in the air, run to the other side, and commenced to letting out a racket like she had something treed."

The connoisseur of such tales will have noted that bit about how ol' Sis jumped straight up in the air, and will also have noted that it was craftily buried in a mass of other details. There is, of course, a reason for that.

But to continue Mr. Joines' account of how the sales pitch went:

"We went over there with our flashlights and shone them up in the tree but couldn't catch no shine off a coon's eye," the fellow continued.

"My neighbor sorta indicated that ol' Sis might be a little crazy, cause she stood right to the tree and kept singing up into it.

"So I pulled off my coat and climbed up into the branches, and sure enough, there was a coon skeleton wedged in between a couple of branches about 20 feet up.

"Now, as I was saying, she can follow a pretty cold trail."

For the ordinary tale-teller, this demonstration of cold-trail-following would be sufficient. Actually, its whole function was to shake up the listener sufficiently to prepare him for what was ahead.

So, Mr. Joines went on, the owner of the remarkable dog continued his story.

"But her memory is really what sets her apart," he added solemnly.

"As we left the tree and headed back for the truck, she came to this same spot where she had jumped straight up, and she did it again.

"This fellow was still calling ol' Sis crazy until I reminded him that the Hawkinses had a fence across there about five years ago.

"That dog has some memory."

And so does Mr. Joines, who just happened to be reminded of another sales pitch he heard years ago in Kentucky, this one by an old fellow who was trying to sell his shotgun.

"This gun ain't never been hurt," he told his potential customer. "You see, it ain't never been shot up no real tall trees, just short timber."

"If I weren't a minister myself," Mr. Joines told me, "I'd think for sure that such yarns were hatched up by men of the cloth."

I sure don't know why he would say that. Shucks, I'm no minister, and I believe every word he told me.

Don't Count Your Mule Before It Hatches

One of the saddest commentaries on the decline of Memphis is the fact that we don't get good mule stories around here any more.

Time was when our city gloried in the title of Mule Capital of the World. The Memphis mule market was famous, as were the tales glorifying that magnificent creature. But now? A whole generation has grown up that doesn't even know what mules are, let alone how to tell tall tales about them.

Now and then a splendid classic is recalled by an old timer, to be sure, but that only emphasizes the point.

Shucks, people don't even argue about mules the way they used to. I can recall the time when emotions grew high if you insisted that a mule says "Haw-Hee" instead of "Hee-Haw," and tempers frayed in debates over whether a mule could bray if its tail was tied down.

Today we squabble over gas shortages instead. Is it any wonder everything is going to pot?

These glum thoughts are occasioned by a column written awhile back by a Florida newspaperman, Dick Bothwell of the St. Petersburg Times. The mule story he told—he said he got it from a psychologist—is enough to make any Mid-Southerner hide his head in shame and envy.

But perhaps it will serve as an inspiration. Perhaps, even yet, authorities on mulish lore will rise to face the challenge offered by a Florida psychologist.

Let us examine the narrative in question.

Back in the days when livestock was big business in America, the story went, two sharp Chicago operators hit on a plan to buy mules cheap from dull-witted country boys and then sell them high up North.

So they hastened down to the backwoods of Missouri and put out the word. Anybody got mules? We're buying.

But the minute they got down to trading, the country fellows realized they had a pair of plump pigeons on their hands, all ready and eager to be plucked. So they hit on an idea.

I want to be sure to get the facts exactly straight here, so I'll quote what they said just as Bothwell reported it:

"We don't have no mules right now, but we got some fine mule eggs you can buy for half price, and raise your own."

The city slickers were overjoyed at this fresh opportunity to outwit the locals, and agreed to buy a batch of mule eggs as soon as they could be rounded up.

So the country boys got some big watermelons, painted them aluminum, loaded them into a wheelbarrow and delivered them the very next morning.

Everything went well. The buyers were delighted with the size of the eggs and paid a handsome price. The sellers departed hastily.

Next came the task of getting the wheelbarrow down to the railroad station. It was a hard job, and along the way one of the mellons fell out, rolled down a slope, and smashed open in a weed patch.

The buyers looked at it in dismay.

Then a remarkable thing happened. The breaking melon had startled a jackrabbit in the same weeds, and it leapt up and lit out for distant parts.

In no time at all, the rabbit was disappearing in the distance. The men stopped, and one of them spoke. Again I cite the record.

"Aw, let him go, Jake," he gasped. "Blasted mule woulda been too fast to plow with anyways."

It's too much. If a story like that can bypass Memphis entirely and wind up in the hands of a Florida psychologist, what's the good of city planning? Maybe we need to establish a commission for the preservation of regional mule lore before it's too late.

Four-Ply Potatoes

Jay C. Jackson said the other day that there are bigger liars in Dresden, Tenn., than there are in Memphis, but I'm not sure I believe him.

Unless you count late arrivals, that is.

Jackson is a retired builder who moved from Memphis to Dresden back in August, 1977. He was telling me about the four-bushel potatoes-in-the-tires crop that he raised last fall.

In the interest of scientific farming everywhere, I think the story needs to be recorded.

"After living in your fair city and not having a garden spot for 17 years, I could hardly wait to try my green thumb after we moved here," he told me.

"I had heard a lot of advice from country fellows who had moved to the city about how to raise remarkable crops, but one thing struck my fancy more than all the rest. That was the potato-growing system.

"They told me you can raise four bushels of potatoes and then wheel them into the shed without any digging if you just follow the plan. It works like this:

"First, you cut out a potato eye and plant it somewhere in the ground. Then you wait awhile.

"After it has grown up a ways, you wheel an old tire over there and lay it flat on the ground with your potato plant in the middle. Then you fill in the circle with dirt.

"After that you wait for the plant to grow above the dirt high enough to fill another tire laid above the first one.

"You keep doing that until you have four tires, one on top of the other, with the potato growing up in the center.

"And when digging time comes, all you have to do is pick up the tires and roll them into the shed. There'll be a bushel of potatoes inside each of the tires."

I asked what about making it five tires and getting another bushel, but Jackson said no, that would be greedy, and it wouldn't work anyhow. Four tires are all one plant can handle.

All right, four tires. So how did it come out?

"As advised," he told me, "I got four old tires, planted one potato, waited for it to grow high enough, laid my first tire around it and filled in the center with dirt.

"I waited for the potato to grow high enough, just like they told me, and then added a second tire, and so on until all four tires were in place and filled.

"Each step seemed to go as it should, and the plant looked mighty prosperous coming up from the level of that fourth tire.

"I watched it closely, and as time for maturity drew near I would sit on my porch and dream about unstacking the tires and rolling them, filled with potatoes, into my shed."

"But something happened?" I asked, fearing the worst.

"You might say that. One fine afternoon, while I was sitting on my porch and dreaming, I was startled by the dangedest noises you ever heard. The next thing I knew, something hit me up side of the head and knocked me plumb off the porch. It was a while after I came to before I realized what had happened."

"You mean . . ."

"Yep, that's it. The system had worked, all right—it had worked too well. All four of those tires were swelled up so tight with potatoes that the hot sun shining on them had made them all blow out at the same time. We had so many potato chips in our yard, people passing by thought it had snowed. Farming's a hazardous occupation and don't let any city slickers tell you different."

A Cow-Magnet In Every Home

One thing you have to say for Americans, they're ingenious. And the farther west you go, the more ingenious they get.

So now Leo Merrick of Senath, Mo., is looking for one of those Wild West cow magnets.

Why? He wants to save gas, that's why. The way they say they're doing it out in Oregon and Idaho.

You never heard of cow magnets? Neither did I, but Merrick read all about the things recently in an Idaho newspaper, and he has passed the happy word along. Prepare to be amazed.

Cow magnets, according to the clipping Merrick sent me (the name of the newspaper doesn't appear, but the story's in good, clear type), are magnetic cylinders three inches long. Ranchers feed them to live stock.

The object—I'm pretty vague about the interiors of cows, so I'm just telling you what the story says—is for the magnet to lie in the cow's first stomach and collect bits of metal "such as baling wire, which could puncture the animal's lung."

All right, you got that? Now for the great inspiration that turned cow magnets into gas savers.

Some fellows over in Ontario, Ore., the story said, were discussing the merits of putting magnets on water lines as conditioners. I won't go into the details of that, but the results were said to be beneficial.

Well, sir, smack in the middle of the conversation somebody came up with an idea and they talked it over.

"They wondered if magnets could have a similar effect on gasoline by changing electrons, and decided to put their theory to test . . ."

Presto. According to the supply-house manager quoted, "they took some cow magnets, stuck them on a car's fuel line and found a noticeable decrease in gas consumption."

And since then they have kept testing and reported improvements of from four to eight miles per gallon, all on account of those magic magnets.

So now, if the story is to be credited, people out there are buying the things like crazy. In Ontario, Ore., alone, one store has sold 6,000 of them in just over a month and has another 3,000 on order. A manager of a chain of stores in Idaho Falls says sales "have sky-rocketed from about 1,000 a year to about 3,000 in the past two weeks."

And the manager said they don't even claim the things work on fuel lines.

But the newspaper quotes an auto mechanics student at an Idaho vocational school as saying: "It just seems to me that it has something to do with the molecular structure of gas. The magnets disturb the flow of the molecules."

I dont' know why anyone would want a better authority or a more convincing explanation than that.

Which brings us back to Leo Merrick. His motor home uses quite a lot of gas, he told me, and he could certainly use some of those cow magnets if they'll improve his mileage.

But on the other hand, he worries about the cows.

Suppose all the cow magnets are bought up by motorists and the cows don't have any magnets to go into their first stomachs? What happens then?

Do we have a beef shortage? A milk shortage?

Life is just plain downright complicated. You solve one problem, you create another one. But it there's any way to work everything out at once, you can count on American imagination to do it.

Think of it. All those gasoline molecules being disturbed in their flow to produce better mileage, and by a plain old cow magnet. When those OPEC countries started putting the squeeze on us, they didn't know what they were getting into.

Good Monster Hard To Find

No wonder the world is in such a mess. We have flat run out of old-fashioned monsters.

Either that or we've run out of a capacity to be scared by them. A brief item in this newspaper a couple of days ago is a good example.

Up in rural Northwest Tennessee, it said, officials are investigating a monster report. But do you think it's raising a ripple of excitement? The story might as well have been reporting a meeting of the Parent-Teacher Association.

What happened was, a fellow called the sheriff's office in Weakley County and said his son had shot at what appeared to be a large manlike creature, described by someone as a Bigfoot-type monster.

So somebody went out and checked, and no footprints were found, but there were some long, brown strands of what looked like hair from a horse's tail. And that was about it. No posses formed, no general alarms, no shrieking sirens to alert the neighborhood.

There was a time when a report like that could have had the whole country in a sweat. But no. A spokesman was quoted as saying: "This is the kind of thing that a lot of people don't believe and there probably isn't anything to it."

How far have we fallen when people can't get worked up at the prospect of a monster with a horse's tail lurking about in the darkness, just waiting to jump out and whinny at unwary night travelers?

Well, sure it could have been a horse. But who is to say it wasn't? What are we coming to?

In the good old days when the economy was booming and people had faith in the future, monster tales were more successful.

But who shivers nowadays at thoughts of the Abominable Snowman, the Loch Ness Monster, the original Bigfoot, or creatures from dark lagoons or outer space?

For that matter, how long has it been since a measurable portion of the public got worked up over little green men from Mars?

We can blame Hollywood for much of the depressing new skepticism that keeps us from taking monster stories seriously. After all, the film makers have just about worn out our credulity.

We have sat through movies in which civilization was threatened by birds, bees and blobs. Ants have overrun whole cities. Terrible tarantulas have marched relentlessly on hairy legs. Giant rats have gnawed away at mankind. Strange creatures have oozed up from murky deeps to destroy innocent swimmers.

What chance does an old-fashioned monster have with the likes of those?

Science bears part of the blame, of course. By now it's pretty clear that there aren't any men on the moon except those that are sent there occasionally by somebody on Earth, and they generally just bounce around a while and act cheerful. And if there are any creatures on Mars, they must be white-hot rather than green.

So there goes another wholesome source of terror. Orson Welles' famous "War of the Worlds" broadcast that electrified the nation back in the innocent days would fall flat on its face today.

But most of all, I think it's the politicians' fault that we have so little time for monster stories of the old sort. They've ushered in a whole new monster era.

It's especially obvious in an election year. Listen to the opposition, and what are our choices for president? A man who'll plunge us into nuclear war or a man who'll plunge us into economic chaos, that's what.

So there you are. In times like these, who can afford a shiver at the thought of a horse-tailed Bigfoot or even a man-eating chicken? No wonder the economy is dragging. We have lost faith in the American way of fantasy.

Monsters Have To Live, Too

The shocking news from Ocala, Fla., can only provide added emphasis to a need that has existed for some time now.

This country must have a Society for the Prevention of Cruelty to Monsters (SPCM).

You have read, no doubt, about Rev. S.L. Whatley, who was cutting firewood in Ocala National Forest when he looked up and saw a monster perhaps eight feet tall, staring at him from "less than a city block away."

"I went to the bed of the truck to get out my ax," he told reporters later. "Me and that creature was going to mix it up."

As it turned out, they didn't. By the time he got the ax, the creature had vanished. Another terrible case of monster-mangling had been averted.

But is this the way we wish people, let alone ministers, to treat our endangered monsters? What have such creatures ever done other than provide innocent merriment and increase tourist business? Shall tiny snail darters be cherished while mighty monsters are mangled?

The answer, for people of good will everywhere, must surely be a resounding "No!"

Think for a moment. Where would the world be without the Loch Ness Monster, without the Abominable Snowman, without Bigfoot, without even our own East Arkansas monster who turns up from time to time in river bottoms or low-budget movies?

And yet a man, a man of the cloth at that, has called his own newly-discovered monster "that sapsucker" and reported his first reaction upon seeing it was to think:

"If it thinks I am afraid of it, it's got another think coming."

You can just bet the Ocala Chamber of Commerce, if there is one, isn't thinking along those lines.

Already it must be planning to construct a Monster Mall in the heart of downtown Ocala. Bumper stickers will proclaim the message to the world: "Visit the Home Town of the Ocala Ogre." Souvenir shops will spring up all over town. Guides will conduct tours of the fabled forest, promising monster footprints.

Enthusiasm over ogres in Ocala may in time approach the enthusiasm in Memphis over plastic bubbles for the fairgrounds.

Clearly it is not the American way to go after such benefactors with axes or other tools of slaughter. Our new SPCM must see to it that people show respect. It should draw up a few basic guidelines:

It's all right to look at monsters. That's what they're there for. It's all right to track them, swim in search of them, climb mountains to locate them.

But axes are out. Traps are out. Guns are out. Monsters have to live like anything else, and it's our duty to protect them. It's the only decent thing to do. Sometime in the future, our protected monsters will rise up and call us blessed.

Who's Getting Skinned?

Mid-South investors and other dreamers of overnight riches should be warned: The old cat-ranch scam has surfaced again.

Plausible? You'll be begging to lay your money on the line if your're not careful.

An ancient copy of the pitch lies yellowing in my files, but darned if a fresh version didn't arrive in the mail only the other day from a seedy sounding promoter who inadvertently omitted his address. Now I'm sure not to succumb.

But lest you be tempted by similar offers, let me share his offer with you. In its latest version it goes like this:

"I don't know if you will be interested in this, but I thought I would mention it to you because it could be a real 'sleeper' in making a lot of money with a small investment of $50,000.

"A group of us are considering investing in a large cat ranch near Hermosillo, Mexico.

"It is our purpose to start rather small with about one million cats. Each cat averages about 12 kittens a year; skins can be sold for about 20 cents for the white ones and up to 40 cents for the black. This will give us 12 million cat skins per year to sell at an average price of around 32 cents, making our gross about $4 million a year.

"This really averages out to about $11,000 a day, including Sundays and holidays.

"A good Mexican cat man can skin about 50 cats each day, at a wage of $3.15 a day. It will take 663 men to operate the ranch, so the net profit would be over $9,200 per day. Your $50,000 investment would be recovered in 5.4 days, which beats the stock market.

"Now, the cats would be fed on rats exclusively. Rats multiply four times as fast as cats. We would start a rat ranch adjacent to our cat farm. If we start with a million rats, we will have four rats per cat per day.

"The rats will be fed on the carcasses of the cats that we skin. This will give each rat a quarter of a cat. You can see by this that the business is a clean operation—self-supporting and really automatic throughout. The cats will eat the rats and the rats will eat the cats and we will get the skins.

"Eventually it is our hope to cross the cats with snakes, for they will skin themselves twice a year. This would save the labor cost of skinning, as well as give us two skins for one cat.

"Let me know if you or any of your friends are interested. As you can imagine, we are rather choosy whom we want to get into this new skinning operation, but we are reserving several very attractive engraved certificates for you and your good customers."

What's wrong with the whole thing, of course, is that—well, I'm not quite sure. Let's see, it could be—but no, the letter takes care of that. And we all know you can't trust the stock market. Maybe if that fellow who wrote the letter would drop around when I have a checkbook handy . . .

Dead Cat Alert

Forget any weather signs you've been checking, and take my word for it. Spring is definitely here. The Dead Cat Story is making the rounds again.

That's a better bet than daffodils, a surer sign than the calendar itself.

Bud Hughes called, laughing fit to kill. "Here's one you've got to hear," he told me. "It'll break you up. You ready?"

Calling on every resource in the noble journalistic tradition, I tensed myself and waited.

"It happened to a professor from Lambuth College over in Jackson," he said. "I don't have her name, but I got the story from a friend. This professor and a friend of hers drove over here to do some shopping at Raleigh Springs Mall, but they got lost and found themselves in a residential area near the mall. They were driving around when a cat ran out in front of them.

"They ran over it and killed it, but a lady came out from a house and said she saw the whole thing and it wasn't their fault."

I shoved my notepaper out of the way and leaned back. "And?"

"So the lady said she had just one request. To spare the children when they got home, would she take the cat away and dispose of it? So they put it in a shopping bag and put it in the trunk of the car and drove on to the mall, and got out and put the shopping bag on the trunk lid while they looked for a place to dispose of it."

"Yes, yes?" I asked, eager in spite of myself.

"So a woman came along while they were at a distance and they saw her steal the shopping bag and go into a drug store where she ordered something to drink, and then she peeped into the bag, and when she saw the cat she fainted and fell off the stool and hit her head and they had to call an ambulance."

"Yes, well . . ."

"Wait, there's more. The ambulance came to take her away, but as they were leaving, the girl behind the counter ran around and said, 'Wait, this is her shopping bag.' So they put it on top of her on the stretcher, and just think what happened when she came to at the hospital and saw the dead cat again."

In the pause that followed, Hughes spoke again. "You've heard it?"

Well, heard it is one way of putting it. The Dead Cat Story, I told him, has been around for years. I have personally traced it back to the period before World War II, and I'm firmly convinced that Mark Antony interrupted his funeral oration on Julius Caesar to regale the Romans with the story before he whipped them up to that frenzy we have all read about.

The Dead Cat Story has turned up all over the world, in a dozen or so forms. The last time I saw it in print, it was in the Washington Post under an Australian dateline. Years ago I told a Memphis friend about the strange phenomenon and he thought I was exaggerating; a week later, he overheard someone telling it in a New York subway.

Some of the variations are fascinating. There is the Live Wildcat version, much favored by tellers of practical jokes. I have seen at least two versions of the Dead Mother-In-Law Story. The basic elements, though, always remain the same.

And it is always spring when the story rises, like Phoenix from the ashes, to bring a sparkle or something to our days. What there is about this strange narrative that lives in the hearts and minds of humanity is beyond me, but there it is. You may not think much of the tale, but you can count on one thing. It means spring has come. Relax, enjoy and stay on the alert for dead cats.

Supermarket Snake Fails To Check Out

"Either this is another Dead Cat story or it's a really terrible thing," said the lady on the phone. "I thought you ought to know."

I said yes, by all means, please tell me.

"Well," she said, "I'm not going to tell you my name, but this was told me as the absolute truth, and it happened only the other day." And then she told me precisely which supermarket it happened at.

"This woman was looking at the greens—turnip greens, I think— and she felt a little sting. So she drew her hand back, and went on shopping, and then in a few minutes . . ."

"Wait," I said. "A poisonous snake? It bit her and she died?"

"Oh, you heard it too?"

Not lately, I had to explain. The Snake in the Supermarket is indeed nothing more than another Dead Cat story.

But, she said, she heard all sorts of specific details about it. Actually, there were two snakes, and the manager found them when he was called when the customer's hand started swelling, and then somebody called an ambulance, and the poor woman was dead on arrival at the hospital.

And why had there been no warnings from health authorities, no action by officials, no reports in the newspapers?

"They told me it was all hushed up."

People will believe anything, absolutely anything, if you tell them the reason they haven't heard it before is that it was "all hushed up."

The last time we were talking about Dead Cat stories (which I won't go into today), several readers called my attention to a recent article in Psychology Today on other such stories, known to some scholars of contemporary American folklore as "urban legends."

Curiously enough, the article, written by Jan Harold Brunvand, doesn't include the classic Dead Cat story, but the Snake in the Supermarket is there, all right.

Actually, the version Brunvand chose to cite involved a Dallas discount store instead of a supermarket. And the shopper was looking at imported coats, not turnip greens. Otherwise, the details matched.

That was in 1970, and the Dallas Morning News had made exhaustive efforts, and failed, to find any basis for truth in the story. Well, no wonder, It's been making the rounds, in one form or another, for years.

For the sake of prudence, I asked our own news desk if it had had any reports of the snake in the supermarket. Yep.

And were they checked out? Yep.

Any truth to 'em? Nope.

Meanwhile, my original caller had been doing some checking of her own. She called back and told me about it.

"I got to thinking how terrible it would be if that thing had really happened after all," she said. "So I called a friend whose husband is a policeman and asked her to ask him.

"And she did, and he said, 'Yes, I know. Wasn't it awful?' But it turned out he had heard it about an entirely different supermarket in an entirely different time."

So just relax, friends. The Snake in the Supermarket story is a well-documented urban legend, and only a legend. Don't swallow it unless you also swallow Dead Cat stories, and stories about wives who sell their husbands' expensive cars for $5 in intricate revenge plots, and stories about irate husbands who dump loads of cement into strangers' cars in what turn out to be misguided fits of jealousy.

But say, did you hear about that fellow who was found nude in the middle of a busy intersection in a strange city? He and his wife were on a vacation trip, see, and she was driving while he took a nap in the trailer, and she had to stop for a traffic light, and he woke up confused and . . .

Dead Cat Story Growing Whiskers

A new Dead Cat story may be making its way into the folklore of America. Have you heard the one about the woman whose purse was stolen in the rest room?

I got a call about it only this week. The person who told her, my imformant said, got it directly from somebody who heard it on good authority from a friend who knew the victim.

So she had listened and believed—and a couple of days later it turned out that a friend in another part of town had heard the same story from somebody else who had heard it on good authority from a friend who knew a victim who gave different details entirely.

So she told me about it.

Well, actually, she didn't have to tell the whole story, I had already heard it from somebody else who, etc.

What happened, she said, was that this woman was in a rest room and had set her purse down on the floor, and a hand reached under the partition and took it, and by the time she could do anything about it, it was too late.

But the next day she got a telephone call.

"I'm the person who stole you purse yesterday," a voice said, "and my conscience had been hurting me something awful. I'm not willing to bring it back, because I don't want to be arrested. But if you'll go to (address optional), a friend of mine will give it back to you."

Well, the woman wanted her purse back very badly—especially since it contained all her keys and credit cards. So she went to the designated spot and waited.

And waited.

And after an hour or so, she gave up and went home . . .

And discovered that, in her absence, her house had been burglarized.

It is entirely possible that such an event occurred somewhere, at some time, but surely not all over Memphis in the last few weeks. I think we can safely identify it as a Dead Cat story.

That name, incidentally, comes from the old reliable report that has turned up all over the country, and as far away as Australia, about the woman who put a dead cat into a shoebox or some other container and set out to bury it. And along the way it was set down somewhere, and somebody made off with and was later found, stretched out in a dead faint, with the box opened. We have been into such matters before.

But there's another reason the woman who called me wasn't sure how seriously to take the purse-and-rest-room story.

She has heard yet another story, she told me, and somehow it sounds faintly familiar.

In this case, a friend said that a friend had been telling about what happened to a friend whose car was stolen from the driveway one night.

And, would you believe it, the next night the car reappeared in the driveway, along with a note on the front seat.

The car had just been borrowed in an emergency, the contrite note-writer explained, and in an effort to atone for such terrible conduct he (or she) was leaving two tickets to a major out-of-town football (basketball, baseball, whatever) game (concert, whatever), and would the owners please use it in good health?

So, of course, they did. And, of course, when they returned home, they discovered the place had been stripped of valuables, including appliances.

At any rate, it beats dead cats in shoeboxes, or even snakes in supermarkets. There's a profound moral there, you will note. It may not have occurred to you before, but remember: Beware of burglars bringing bounty. If that helps, maybe the stories are worth telling.

Search For Catfish Continues

Our search for the biggest catfish of modern times is picking up steam. Would you believe a monster with a mouth as wide as a man's shoulders, and a weight estimated at 270 pounds?

Now wait. This comes from what sounds like a highly reputable source.

The idea, you may recall, was to establish whether Mark Twain could have been telling the truth when he said he saw a 250-pound Mississippi River catfish—and also to establish whether they grow 'em that big any more.

Now consider the fascinating, even poetic, response of Garner James of Oxford, Miss.

"Forty years ago, with my own eyes," James assured me, "I saw on the gory deck of a shantyboat, moored near the junction of the Big Black with the Mississippi, an overnight trotline catch of catfish, at least one of which was longer than I was (5 feet 10). And it was probably double my weight (then, as now, 135 pounds), since it was much more than double my girth, with a rubbery mouth at least as wide as my shoulders.

"The Commercial Appeal ran a full page of Sunday rotogravure pictures I took on that particular trip, but the catfish were not in the collection. That was because I was then acting director of the Mississippi State Advertising Commission, and the grue on that deck that morning would have confirmed everyone's worst image of the state."

So much for the bare claim. Now for some background.

"As a major contributor to the Viking Press guidebook on Mississippi and as the personal guide to the editor of the National Geographic magazine on a 7-week tour of the state I thought I knew every facet of Mississippi's incredible yet marvelous nexus of phenomena," James said.

"But the strip of bank on the river side of the levees was an altogether different and magical world.

"I was traveling between Vicksburg and Natchez on a U.S. Engineers 'airboat,' a flat-bottomed hull powered by a wood propeller mounted above the low cabin. We could move at 50 knots plus, and jump mudbars or floating logs as readily as any Cypress Gardens stuntman, since the hull at speed drew less than an inch.

"Everything I saw and photographed that day was fantastic, but none more so than the giant fish and their scourge, the shanty-boatman. My friend Eudora Welty later photographed similar 'boat people' on that same Vicksburg-Natchez stretch.

"Recapturing the scene in memory, it seems as primitive and timeless as anything on China's Yangtze. The catfish-killer, bearded and sun-blackened, had a potbellied, driftwood-burning stove in his six-foot cube of a cabin, and nothing else but the pile of rags he slept on.

"He dipped water for coffee straight from the muddy river through an open port on the river side; waste water and waste went out a similar port on the bank side. He drank coffee-laced whisky, and his basic diet was sausage and corn bread made on top of the stove, supplemented no doubt by occasional raids on eggs, chickens, and corn or beans from the other side of the levee.

"He had a gun, which he used to subdue the monster fish when an ax and pole-lashed meathook could not give the coup de grace. The catfish skin was thick and tough enough to make automobile tires."

But what about present-day catfish?

"We have come far in 40 years, but not necessarily in the direction of catfish growth," James observed. "Pesticides washed off the Delta cottonlands have turned their stomachs and stunted their size."

And there are other changes to be regretted. "Characters like that impervious-to-fate shantyboatman are no longer with us: one of the prices we pay for progress. I am sorry that he and Twain never met. Neither would have been surprised by anything coming out of that uniquely strange river."

A perfect report. Well, almost. Doggone it, why didn't he save a picture?

It's All in a Day's Fishing

The secret of successful fishing, the experts will tell you, lies in the bait. Get the right kind of bait and the world, or at least a portion thereof, is yours.

Dave Dick of Vicksburg, Miss., has the right kind of bait.

Dick's story was passed along to me by Jack A. Holsomback of Vicksburg, who was recently named to the League of Imaginative Angling Reporters (LIAR) and wants to share the glory with a fellow townsman.

Sportsmen everywhere will wish to study the details of Dick's adventure, checked and certified as it was by a trusted league member.

When Dick fishes for catfish he whips up his own home concoction for bait. Sometime last year he took an ample supply of it to Old River Lake, baited a trotline, placed his hooks in the water and sat down to wait.

With him he had a weapon known locally as an old mule-ear double-barreled shotgun, which he left loaded on his lap.

Growing drowsy, he tied the loose end of the trotline firmly to his wrist and fell asleep.

He was awakened, Holsomback reported, by two sounds. The first came from "a massive, churning, boiling school of catfish" fighting over his bait. The second was the flapping noise of ducks fighting the fish for the same bait.

Startled, Dick leaped to his feet.

The shotgun fell off his lap and discharged one barrel.

The ducks, by now inextricably tangled in the trotline, took off.

And the line, tied to Dick's wrist, pulled him along. He barely had time to grab his shotgun before he went flying across the lake.

It was a heavy load, including not only Dick and his shotgun but also 50 pounds of hooked catfish, and the ducks tired quickly.

They had barely cleared the lake when they faltered. Dick, shotgun, catfish and ducks all fell into a tall hollow stump filled with honey.

Our hero was pulled relentlessly downward. For a moment, as Holsomback noted, the poor fellow faced a sticky, finny, feathery death.

Then fate intervened. A passing bear saw the honey overflowing from the top of the stump, ambled over and dipped a paw beneath the surface.

Dick jabbed desperately with the shotgun.

The bear grabbed it and drew back, pulling Dick and his assorted companions out of the stump. The shotgun fell to the ground, discharged and hit the bear. And there lay Dick, safe and relatively unharmed.

"Dave swears the story is true," Hoslomback assured me, "and he said he had enough honey, fish, duck and bearmeat to last him all winter."

If anyone doubts the story, I am sure Dick will be glad to show the trotline that did the trick. But thus far he has wisely refrained from giving his bait recipe. After all, some wildlife must be preserved for future generations.

Fish Story Grabs Disbelievers

The provincial ignorance in some areas of this nation—the North and East in particular—is almost beyond belief.

Consider the dilemma of Ed Gamble, a Memphian.

There he was at this meeting in Middleton, Del., he told me, with a lot of intellectual types from all around that part of the country, and he just happened to mention fish-grabbling.

And they wouldn't believe there was such a thing.

He did his best to explain to them about how people catch fish by grabbling or grabbing them with their bare hands, and they simply responded with superior smiles of disbelief. Fish-grabbling indeed.

So would I, he asked, put something in writing that he could send them—something to prove that people indeed can and do catch fish with their bare hands?

Why, of course they do. Anybody with any learnin' at all ought to know a simple thing like that.

The very next person I talked to, in fact, was Mrs. Charlyne Kaminsky, who wanted to tell me something about a woodpecker-on-the-roof situation, so I tried the question on her. Did she know about fish-grabbling?

Lord yes, honey, she said. Why, she knew one old boy was was a real expert at putting his open hand into a catfish's mouth (or letting the catfish grab the open hand) and then balling up his fist and pulling the critter out.

And that's only one way, of course. How about petting or rubbing, where you find a male bass fanning eggs in the shallows and stroke him on the stomach and then pick him up?

We got off into a discussion of technical terms, and that's a confusing field. Different people use different terms, some for the same thing and some for slightly different techniques. But one way or another you can grab, grapple, pet, rub, stroke and I don't know what else to catch fish with your bare hands.

In some areas, mind you, it's illegal, but in others—depending sometimes on the kind of fish—it's not. I called a man at the Tennessee Wildlife Resources Agency in Jackson and he said bare-handed grabbling is legal in this state except in areas 100 yards below dams.

Prudent people will recognize that there is a difference between what's legal and what's wise. The man in Jackson said you weren't going to catch him running his own hands up into some hollow log under the water in hopes of coming out with a catfish. You could come out with a mangled hand instead.

And I talked to a fellow from Middle Tennessee who said why sure, before he got better sense he used to do a lot of grabbling.

What he liked to do was walk along a stream, spot a nice bass or catfish drowsing up under the bank, and slip his hands under it. But he had also reached into dark holes and old logs, and he trembled slightly as he said it.

"You wouldn't believe some of the things I got hold of," he told me. "Why, I have picked up live things that weren't fish at all, and some of them I don't know to this day what they were."

So that ought to take care of Ed Gamble's doubting Thomases about grabbling, and we still have room for Mrs. Kaminsky's woodpecker report.

She knows an old boy over in the Ozarks, she told me, who says he's going to shoot the next tin-roof salesman who shows up in his part of the mountains.

Why? Because he calls his hogs by going outdoors and beating on a pie pan with a spoon, that's why.

"And since some salesman sold some tin roofs within two miles of my house," he told her, "them woodpeckers pecking on the roofs are runnin' all the fat off my hogs."

Let's see what Gamble's friends think about that one.

The Family That Fishes Together

There's nothing like fishing together to unite a couple.

Maybe not in love and mutual admiration, you understand. Maybe in fury and name-calling, boats being as small as they are. But it unites them, that's for sure.

Consider the adventures of a Memphis couple who recently arose at 4 a.m. for a jaunt to Tunica Cutoff. I know what is recorded here is true, because I got it all from the wife, who gave it to me under a pledge of anonymity. And little wonder. Some wives still believe in protecting their husbands from public displays of their own idiocy.

They got to the cutoff about 5 o'clock, she told me, and discovered almost at once that the steering arm on the motor was loose. The husband, as husbands are wont to do, drove off promising to look for help and left her behind to guard the boat.

She got to tinkering with the thing and had it fixed by the time he came back, alone and frustrated.

With no more than a grunt of appreciation for her skill, he told her to help him get started.

She wanted to fly-fish with popping bugs for bream. He wanted to pole-fish for crappie. No doubt feeling generous over her mechanical achievements, he offered a fair compromise: For the first hour of the day they would fly-fish; for the rest of the day they would fish for crappie.

So he promptly settled down in his padded seat in the bow and left her to do what she would.

She found a fine spot for bream, an area filled with brush and debris, and in no time—as happens to all who fish—found her popping bug hung up in the brush. Determined to retrieve it, she began laborously pulling the boat in that direction by dragging on her line.

The husband remained on his throne, ignoring the proceedings.

She drew near the popping bug, stood cautiously, leaned over to recover it—and fell smack into the water, face first. It caused a tremendous splash.

When she rose above the surface, her husband was still fishing placidly from the bow.

She clung precariously to the side of the boat and tried to haul herself in. But her own line, as well as some nearby vines, had become tangled about her legs, and she simply couldn't make it alone.

She was still thrashing hopelessly about, minutes later, when the great man finally turned his head.

"You want me to help you?" he asked absently.

She told him she jolly well did, or words to that effect. Making a great show of the trouble he was going to, he worked his way to the stern, grabbed aholt and pulled. At last she found herself, soaking wet, flopping about in the boat.

In the course of the rescue her flyrod had somehow got broken. Whether her husband was involved in this act she did not say.

But she did say what he did next. He said well, in view of all that had happened, they might as well fish for crappie. Which they did, for the rest of the long day.

But meanwhile, there was the problem of her wet clothes. She took off all that modesty would allow, and spread them out to dry in the sun. Seeking to make a pleasantry about the affair, she referred to a noted Memphis fighter against pornography.

"I hope Larry Parrish doesn't get me," she said.

He turned and looked at her carefully.

"The only thing he'd get you for," he said, "is impersonating a cow." Then he returned to his fishing.

I must say that she told me all this without malice or resentment, but I did manage to get one spark of fire from her.

"How would you describe your husband's appearance?" I asked. She thought it over.

"Oh," she said, "he's just a squatty little old fat fellow."

She even plans to go fishing with him again. It is indeed a remarkable sport.

I'll Bet They Drink Scotch

In a time of constant change, it is not always reassuring to discover that some things remain forever the same.

Fly-fishermen, I discovered the other day, are just as insufferably snobbish as they always were.

That is depressing. You can put up with tennis snobs and jogging snobs and handball snobs and creatures of that ilk, because you realize they are only pathetic slaves to passing fashions and will give up one form of snobbery for another as casually as they would abandon an old pair of shoes.

But fly-fishermen are different. They are often decent enough fellows otherwise, and they do not necessarily sway with every passing breeze. It is only in the matter of fishing that they become—nay, remain—intractable and unbearable.

These morose conclusions stem from a conversation that occurred in the course of a committee meeting of some sort where I happened, by purest accident, to be among those present.

As committees do, this one was wrestling not only with a current question but also with another question someone had brought up about the basic function of the committee itself, which led to talk about missions and criteria and other arcane matters. Inevitably, the group began to fall apart into little conversational subgroups just out of range of the chairman.

A very pleasant member sitting nearby turned to me and asked: "Do you fly-fish?"

Of course you do, the tone said. You look like one of us. I'm only confirming the fact. Pardon me for even asking.

Having been asked that question, in that tone, many times before, I braced myself.

"No," I said modestly, "I'm a spin-caster."

A surge of cold air swept across our end of the table. Another nice-looking fellow nearby turned to stare at me with incredulity mixed with contempt.

"You what?" he demanded. "You can't be serious. You'll have to learn fly-fishing."

I explained that I had learned, had decided I preferred a spinning rod, had even given away my flyrod.

The temperature fell lower. But these were good sports. One of them made a last try.

"You'll have to go fishing with us sometime. You'll see."

I thanked him and pointed out, as politely as possible, that I wouldn't be caught dead fishing with a fly-fisherman, not only because they were snobs but also because anybody who sits in a boat with a fly-fisherman is likely to get a head full of fishhooks.

"In a boat?" cried one of them. "You fish in a boat?"

Realizing that these were samples of those supersnobs of fishing, the waders, I knew I was dealing with the English Country Squire variety, the most extreme of all strains.

"Yes, I fish in a boat," I said, "and I'll bet you drink Scotch."

One of them, sensing a trap, insisted that he didn't. The other admitted it, as well he might. He countered by accusing me of fishing wth battery-operated lures that make noises in the water. After that, the conversation got ugly.

I am a peace-loving man, and if people are fools enough to go around whipping great lengths of line back and forth over their heads, tying their own flies, and stalking the odd trout in the stream behind the manor house, that is all right with me.

But they should have the consideration to do it when nobody else is around, and a sufficient sense of shame to avoid boasting about it in public. In a world wracked with problems of all sorts, and beset with phoniness on all sides, do we really have to put up with the lordly superiority of the fly-fisherman?

Body English

People Will Try Anything . . . Nearly

YOU THINK IT'S a shame and a disgrace that this country can't control its own economy?

Hah. That's nothing.

You can't even control your own body.

No, I don't mean your innards or anything like that. I mean something simple, like making your leg behave the way you tell it to.

An exaggeration or a trick, you say? All right, just listen.

You know what a clockwise movement is, of course—a circular movement in the same direction that's taken by the hands of a clock.

All right, then. Here's your test.

First, get a piece of paper and a pen or pencil.

Then, assume a comfortable position, so you can't complain later that you were too cramped or too stiff or too something else.

Now, start swinging your right leg around in a clockwise movement.

Your right leg, mind you. If you're not sure which is your right, ask somebody.

(If you're left-handed, this doesn't apply to you. We'll get to you later.)

That's right. Nice and smooth. Keep it up a while, so you can get the feel of it. And remember, be sure you're comfortable and have no complaints. It doesn't matter whether you're standing or sitting, just as long as you can keep swinging that leg smoothly.

Now, pick up your pen or pencil.

All right, here comes the challenge. Simply write the figure "6" on the piece of paper while you continue to swing your leg clockwise.

Ah-ha.

Can't do it, can you?

Well, don't consider it a personal weakness. I haven't found anybody yet who could. As your hand goes into the curve of the 6, your leg changes direction so smoothly you wouldn't even notice it if you weren't watching.

If you watch closely, and if you bear down on the concentration, you might be able to prevent a smooth reversal of direction—but the best you're likely to end up with is a jerky diagonal shift of the leg. It won't keep going just the way it was.

Now with left-handers, of course, it's different. I'm not sure how different, because I haven't been able to test enough of them to come up with a clear conclusion.

They have no trouble writing "6" with the left hand while the right leg does clockwise circles. And there may be some indication that, even when they shift to the left leg, they have a little more control over the situation than right-handers. But thus far, the difference doesn't appear to be statistically important.

So there you are. The average normal right-hander simply cannot make his right leg do clockwise circles while his hand writes a "6."

And what possible use is that information?

Not much, I'll admit. It might be helpful for a person who wants to be the life of a party, but who wants to be the life of a party these days?

No, I think its chief function has to be to take out of us any fight that may be left in us. Good night, if we can't even control our own legs, how in the ever-loving, blue-eyed world will we ever do anything about inflation?

Research for Its Own Sake

The other day a reader asked the Sims Laboratory of Unusual Research Problems how you determine whether you're right-eyed or left-eyed.

Today SLURP's experts, as usual, provide even more than was requested: Not just one method, but three.

Plus some notes relating to the relationship between eye dominance and chewing preference. Where else could you get such service?

But first, the eye tests.

Choose an object across the room from you. Now point at it with both eyes open.

All set? Now close your left eye.

If your finger stays on the object you were pointing at, then you're right-eyed. But if your finger jumps over to the left, you're left-eyed.

You can do it in reverse, of course. Close your right eye instead of your left, and if your finger jumps over to the right, you're right-eyed.

(Actually, as one researcher noted, when you point at something with both eyes open you'll see two fingers. But you'll automatically disregard one of them.)

That's one method, and it's recommended by such people as Carol

Gilliland, John Nichols, Judge Willard Dixon and Sgt. J.W. Horton of
the Sheriff's Department, a former firearms instructor.

Does that mean that the dominant eye is stronger than the other?
No, says Horton, not necessarily. But it does tell whether you're
naturally right-eyed or left-eyed. And that's what you wanted to
know, isn't it?

All right, that's one method. The other two are simpler.

Make a funnel with an old newspaper, says Mrs. Maxine Collier,
and then look through it at an object.

You did? All right, which eye did you hold it up to? If you held it to
your right eye, you're right-eyed.

See how simple it is? And some people think an old newspaper is
worthless.

The third test, which Jerry W. Owen says was suggested by his
wife's optometrist, is equally simple:

Hold a finger in front of your face as if it were a gunsight. Now
close one eye and sight along your finger.

That's it. If you left your right eye open, they you're right-eyed. If
you left your left eye open, then you're left-eyed.

If you have given yourself all three tests by now, then you should
have no doubt whether you're left-eyed or right-eyed. In an uncer-
tain world, it is good to know something for sure, isn't it?

But now about tasting, which came up at the same time because
somebody asked which side of your mouth food tastes better in. Is
there an eye connection?

Possibly, And possibly not. One unnamed researcher, who may
have got his information from a fortune cookie, has assured me that
"the taste bud for sweet is on the lower right edge of the tongue,"
but I am inclined to discount that report. Other evidence is more tan-
talizing.

"I am left-eyed," Carol Gilliland reported, "but personally, food
tastes better on the right side."

"I am right-handed, -eyed and -footed," Jerry Owen told me. "My
wife is left-handed, -eyed and -footed. Each chews on the favored
side.

"Two of my daughters are visiting their grandparents, and no information is available from them.

"However, my 9-year-old daughter is at home and conducted the
test. She is left-handed, left-footed and right-eyed, and chews on the
right side.

"We will have an election in Tippah County soon, and the 9-year-
old favors middle-of-the-road candidates.

"Middle-of-the-road is also where everyone in this county drives."

In pure research, one thing always leads to another. You suppose there is any federal grant money available for a study of the political and driving characteristics of right-eyed left-handers?

Some Brain-Teasers Go On Forever

Some brain-teasers go on forever. And cold weather seems to bring them out better than anything else.

So it is that, whenever chill blasts roar around the old homestead and ice defames the landscape, someobdy comes up with the question about the two Indians at the fork in the road.

Everyone has heard it. Almost no one can remember the answer. Fred D., who did remember when a friend put the question to him recently, has passed it along to me—and as a public service for those who forget easily, I'll pass it along to you.

Both question and answer, mind you. This is not, repeat not, a request for sharp readers to provide a solution.

Are you ready?

"You are wandering in the woods," Fred's friend postulated, "and you come to a fork in the road.

"You know inherently that one way leads deeper into the forest and you would possibly die from exposure and starvation if you took it. The second way leads to the nearest town and to freedom and safety.

"There are two Indians at the fork in the road. One of the Indians tells nothing but the truth, and one of them tells nothing but lies.

"You do not know which Indian is which and you have only one question that you are allowed to ask one or the other of the Indians.

"What one question would you ask to find your way to freedom and be assured of your safety?"

Just why the two characters standing at the fork are Indians, no one appears to know. But they always are. Maybe the puzzler was born in the early days of this country, when explorers went so deep into the woods that they were likely to find no one but Indians.

And why one Indian always lies, while the other always tells the truth, is not explained—nor, for that matter, who it is that allows you only one question.

But that is the way it is, and we must face it.

And if you are ready, we will proceed to the answer. If you aren't, and if you give a hoot, you may wish to pause here to see whether you can work the thing out for yourself.

All right, then. Time's up. What question do you ask, and which Indian do you ask it of?

Fred's answer, which is indeed the correct one, as you will find by testing it:

"Pick an Indian, either Indian.

"Ask him the following question: 'If I asked your friend if the left fork was the one leading to town, would he say yes?'

"Positive response means that the right-hand road leads to town.

"Negative response indicates the left-hand road is the route to town."

I keep trying to remember that, but I never do, and it worries me. Some day I may find myself deep in the woods, at a fork in the road, and two Indians may be standing there. And while I'm trying to figure what to say to which one, I'm going to grow a long gray beard and die of starvation.

Phones Don't Like People

Just when it looks as if all the world's major problems are solved, along comes one even tougher than the others.

William A. Glankler is the most recent observer to muddy the waters of mystery. His question is deceptive in its simplicity:

Why do telephone cords twist themselves up?

"I have a straight cord, not the curly type, from the wall to the phone," Glankler told me. "In a month this 20-food cord will have twisted itself up until it is effectively about 3 feet long."

No one will doubt him. And it is all very well to say yes, of course, that happens. But admitting it isn't explaining it. Why do phone cords get twisted?

Glib or timid souls will say it's because people twist them. But do they?

Go check your own telephone technique. Ten-to-one you'll take the receiver off the cradle, hold it to your ear and return it to the cradle without letting go and without changing hands. And you won't rotate it while you use it.

Whatever twist of the wrist you use in removing it will be counteracted by the reverse twist in returning it, right? I think there's a natural law somewhere that says that.

So how come the cord makes complete revolutions during the round trip?

At least Glankler has tried to find a more sophisticated solution.

He has been exploring the coriolis force, that strange tie-in with the Earth's rotation that has been credited by some with affecting the way water runs out of bathtubs in the different hemispheres.

But has anyone reported that telephone cords in the southern hemisphere twist in the opposite direction from their fellow-cords to the north? If so, Glankler hasn't found the evidence.

And if it isn't that, what is it? He has a few wistful questions that indicate how hard he's been looking.

"Is it related to how long one talks on the phone?

"Do women have this problem more than men?

"Do obscene calls affect the degree or speed with which the cord tangles itself up?"

My own opinion is that all these questions miss the mark—that, instead, cord-curling is but another evidence of the baleful attitude of telephones in general.

Let's face it, phones don't like people. They prove it constantly; they never ring when you want them to; only when you don't. They break off important connections in midsentence. They glory in wrong numbers. They wait malevolently until you are in the shower or frying the bacon or watching the climax of a six-hour television spectacular, and then they ring their silly heads off.

So the question isn't motive. The motive is hatred. The question is how they work those cords.

Somehow those fiendish machines have devised a way in which a cord—straight or curly—can be twisted endlessly while you are holding it perfectly still, or even while it simply hangs beside the phone.

It will take a better mind than mine to unravel the mystery. I have all I can handle just unraveling the cord. Perhaps there is a twist expert in the house.

Them As Has Gets

We come now to the old question of how a man's horses could be divided among his sons in compliance with an unusual will.

This thing has kicked around for years, maybe generations, and it's an ideal problem to puzzle over today while you're waiting for the Thanksgiving turkey.

Actually, I've been saving it just for this occasion. The time didn't seem right when Mrs. F.C. and L.N. first brought it up for consideration. (I don't use their full names because they may have long since regretted ever mentioning the matter.)

But you need a good brisk workout before you tackle the groaning board, right? Then get ready.

The man had three sons and a fine stable of horses. His will specified that, at his death, the oldest son was to get half of the horses. The second son was to get one-third of them, and the youngest would receive one-ninth.

In the event of any problems, a wise old neighbor was given full authority to work the matter out.

All right, so when the man died it developed that he had left 17 horses.

Well, you can see what would have happened if the will had been followed exactly: horse-fragments all over the place. Not one of the three son's portions would have come out even.

So the wise old neighbor was called on to settle the matter.

He thought the matter over. Then he sent for his own favorite saddle horse and added it to the old man's stable. That brought the total to 18.

All right," he said to the oldest son, "you are entitled to half the horses. That's 9. Take 'em and go."

Then he turned to the second son.

"Your share is one-third," he said. "That's 6. Help yourself."

And finally it was the turn of the youngest son.

"One-ninth of 18 is 2," said the wise old neighbor. "You take 2."

So the three sons collected their 17 horses, and the neighbor mounted the 18th—his own horse, of course—and rode away.

So everybody was satisfied, and what's wrong with that?

Ah, you say, but something has to be wrong. Maybe with that extra horse thrown in, none of the sons ended up getting his fair share of horseflesh?

But stop a minute. If the division had been made on the basis of 17 horses, none of the boys would have fared as well. Figure it out.

Could Solomon in all his glory have done it any better?

But of course there is something wrong, and I wouldn't want you to miss your dinner worrying about it. So here, for those like me who have to have it spelled out, is the catch.

The father's will was faulty; if you divide an estate into one-half and one-third and one-ninth, you're not disposing of all of it. That man left one-eighteenth of his horses unaccounted for.

Still, the neighbor did the best he could, right? He worked it out so everybody got more than they could have expected to get, so it was fair all around.

Well, not exactly—and here is where one of life's little lessons is illustrated. The eldest son, the one who got the most horses, benefited more than the others, and the youngest son, the one who got the fewest horses, benefitted least.

In short, them as has gets. The little guy is always the one who gets the short end of the stick, even when he doesn't realize it. Now go eat that Thanksgiving turkey.

What's Good for Thistlewaite . . .

Thistlewaite's fatal flaw was a tendency to believe whatever he was told about what was good for him.

He had been that way since childhood. He could still remember the stern injunction his dentist gave him while he was in grade school.

"Brush hard, son! Back and forth, back and forth. No wonder you have so many cavities."

Later in life he would be told that he had so many cavities because he brushed back and forth when he should have brushed up and down. And still later he would be told that he had so many cavities because he brushed up and down when he should have set the brush in one spot, wiggled it, and moved on.

But the thought that he had cavities made Thistlewaite worry about his health in general. To build a strong body, he spent long hours stoking the family furnace, which was insulated with asbestos, and lying in the sun to absorb the solar rays everyone told him were so beneficial.

Even when his head ached, he refused to take aspirin. Everybody knew in those days that, while aspirin might give temporary relief, its long-range effect was calamitous.

Instead, he ate plenty of fruits—cranberries, for example—and spent hours jogging and drinking milk.

As a young man the fear of a heart attack made him give up liquor in all its forms. And when talk of cholesterol buildup frightened him so that his blood pressure shot up alarmingly, he gave up beef, candy and soft drinks.

When sugar-free colas sweetened by cyclamates were introduced, Thistlewaite laid in a six-month supply and began drinking them like crazy.

Meanwhile, he obeyed all the injunctions to get regular chest X-rays in order to be sure he wasn't developing cancer.

Thistlewaite's morale first began to crumble on that day, a number of years ago, when a government agency announced that cranberries were harmful to your health. Even later policy swings in favor of cranberries failed to reassure him.

Then he learned that some dried fruits could cause terrible consequences in his insides because of harmful substances used in their drying.

When cyclamates were banned, Thistlewaite suffered another attack. The shift over to saccharin reassured him, and he was just beginning to recover his aplomb when it was revealed that saccharin could be harmful to his health.

Meanwhile, it had developed that milk could be contaminated by chemicals eaten by cows, that some fish were being taken and sold from polluted streams, and that some poultry fattened chemically could contain health hazards.

Becoming more and more alarmed, Thistlewaite increased his schedule of chest X-rays and began consuming large amounts of Vitamins C and E, both of which someone told him would be of great benefit for whatever ailed him.

Meanwhile, word that the asbestos he had worked around during his youth could cause cancer left his condition even worse.

Then, in one day, he read that sunshine and X-rays could cause cancer, jogging could cause heart attacks, and Vitamins C and E, taken indiscreetly, could produce complex but terrifying results.

His only consolation during this period was in the scientific discoveries that aspirin could actually be of considerable benefit in coronary cases, and that moderate amounts of alcohol might even cut down the incidence of heart attacks.

By now Thistlewaite was so mixed up that he gave up food and exercise entirely and began taking moderate amounts of alcohol at an immoderate rate, popping aspirins hourly, and chewing constantly on the sugarless gum recommended by his latest dentist, who had told him that brushing teeth could be harmful to his gums. (Thistlewaite was not sure he had got that right, on account of his alcohol intake, but it seemed probable.)

That was how matters stood when poor Thistlewaite opened his morning newspaper and read that a dental researcher had determined that the suger substitutes used in sugarless gum could lead to cavities.

They found him later, slumped over his newspaper, a dozen aspirins in one hand, a bottle of bourbon in the other, and hundreds of vitamin pills lying on the floor among his X-rays on a sheet of asbestos insulation. The coroner determined that malnutrition and health warnings had been injurious to Thistlewaite's health.

Mattresses Can Be Dangerous to Your Health

I remember it began in a drug store when I asked for a package of cigarets.

"You'll have to go to the pharmacy counter for that," the clerk said, giving me a suspicious look. "Two aisles over and all the way back."

I walked through vacant aisles and empty shelves toward a vast counter where people waved white pieces of paper and clamored for service. When my turn came, I repeated my order.

"Where's your prescription?" a woman in a white coat asked me. "You know I can't sell cigarets without a prescription."

"Then let me use your phone," I said, remembering a disreputable doctor who owed me a favor. She shook her head.

"You can't get one by phone," she said, "It's against government regulations. He'll just tell you to take two sniffs of snuff and call back in the morning."

"Never mind. Where do I go for a chocolate bar?"

She stamped her foot. "You needn't get smart with me, sir. You know as well as I do that chocolate has been condemned as a dangerous drug. They melted down 21 tons of it in Hershey, Pa., only last week. The Army is transporting it to Montana in sealed tank cars."

"Even Tinker Bells?" A vision of the luscious foil-wrapped goodies swam up from my childhood.

"Especially Tinker Bells. You want to get busted for possession with intent to contribute to the delinquency of a minor?"

"But isn't there anything I can buy in here to munch on?" I pleaded.

"Well, let's see." She brightened. "Jelly-beans are still sold over the counter. No licorice ones, of course."

I said never mind, and walked out.

There was a restaurant nearby. I was shown a table and a waiter came to take my order.

"Give me a nice rare steak and a baked potato."

"You undercover agents make me sick," he snarled. "Look, the Feds checked us out last week. We run a perfectly legal establishment here."

"You what?"

"Ever since the FDA banned high cholesterol foods, we've served nothing but approved substances. Why do you think nobody's eating in here?"

The manager, when I called for him, turned out to be an old school friend. "We have to be careful," he explained, looking about warily. "But I can trust you. Come on, we have a little back room. Wait till you taste . . ."

A siren sounded and spotlights bored into the windows. A voice came over a loudspeaker.

"This is a steak bust. Come out with your mouths open. If you're not out in three minutes, we start throwing in apricot kernels."

My own hoarse cry waked me up.

"What is it?" my wife asked.

"Nothing. Only a bad dream."

"It's your own fault," she scolded sleepily from the floor. "You know the government has determined that mattresses are dangerous to your health. Never mind, let's go get a cookie and a glass of milk. The bootlegger brought them only yesterday."

"Noli Me Tangere!"

One of the best things about some health food stores, it appears, is the invigorating effect they occasionally have on casual customers.

I have heard from such a customer, who is still riding an emotional high brought on by her experience.

She told her story in such dramatic terms that I couldn't help wondering whether she might still be under the influence of some potent food supplement. But who knows? At least if the facts are inflated, you get an accurate picture of the overall experience.

"The other day," she told me, "I set out to purchase some breakfast cereal and, mistakenly thinking myself hearty and happy, entered my local health food store.

"A militant Valkyrie behind the counter sized me up when I walked in, and gave me an agonizing handshake. I cringed as I retrieved my crushed knuckles, and she began her attack.

" 'Aha!' she boomed, beaming. 'Got a touch of the old arthritis, have we?'

"I fought back the urge to say that if I hadn't had it before, I did now.

" 'We must boost the intake of this,' she said, pressing on me an expensive bottle of pills. Common sense said, 'Get out out here while you're still on your feet,' but I resisted, senses reeling, hoping to emerge with at least a tatter of the old self-confident person who had strayed in so unwarily.

" 'I just want some cereal,' I protested, leaning weakly on the counter in an effort to arouse her compassion.

" 'Out of energy, aren't you?' she yo-hoed. 'A bottle of these will perk you up in nothing flat.'

"The sight of the price tag perked me up, all right. It was $36 for 12.

" 'Oh, well,' I said, backing away, 'I guess I'll live out the night anyway.' My motto is always leave them laughing, especially if they're bigger than you are.

" 'You call that living?' she thundered, and reached behind her to grab another jar from the shelf.

"Stung to defensive action, I whipped out my emergency umbrella and pointed its swordtip in her direction, acting out a daydream I once had about aggressive salespeople.

"She advanced anyway. 'Noli me tangere!' I cried, summoning up a phrase from somewhere in my past reading. I wasn't sure what it meant, but it did wonders. She stopped in mid-lope, looking startled.

"My left arm went up in an arty imitation of a fencing position, and I backed out the door. My goodness, I said to myself as I drove briskly home, a little real excitement can do wonders for tired blood.

"I plan to go back at least once a week."

Let it be noted here, before any wounded protests arrive, that I'm sure the lady wasn't describing the typical health food store. I have been in several myself, and they were models of quiet efficiency and low pressure.

Instead, what I think we have here is the ideal example of a zealot in any field, whether it be health food or orthopedic shoes or jogging or political causes or whatever, and also a typical reaction thereto.

That Latin phrase our adventurer used means, very loosely, keep your cotton-pickin' hands off me. A few other mild-mannered victims of aggression may wish to try it for themselves. For the lady in question, it sure beat pills at $36 a dozen.

Put You Left Arm Through The Left Hole

Now and then some truly colossal advance in medical science slips through almost unnoticed. Did you know that, in at least some places, they have three-hole hospital gowns?

Well, they do. Mrs. Ruth Wilson of Covington, Tenn., told me about them, and I have checked out the medical facts, and she's right.

At least she's right about the gowns. She wasn't right, it turns out, in the way she wore one of them.

All this developed when Mrs. Wilson went to the Tipton County Memorial Hospital for a chest X-ray.

For someone like Mrs. Wilson, who is accustomed to the indignities of the open-down-the-back paper gown provided in some medical settings, it was a bewildering experience.

"You won't believe this, but they gave me a gown with three armholes," she told me.

She said it just about blew her mind. There she was, in that little cubbyhold they had put her in, and she had taken off her clothes and picked up the cloth gown they had handed her, and it had three holes in it.

At first she didn't realize they were armholes.

The way it looked, she said, there was a hole on the left for her left arm and a hole on the right for her right arm and a hole in the middle for her head. But the middle hole wasn't big enough for her head. Neither, when she checked, was either of the others.

"I thought, 'Oh, there's something wrong here,' " she said.

She had about decided just to forget the holes and wrap the thing around her when the nurse called and asked if she was ready.

"Well, of course I wasn't ready. I didn't know what to do. Then at the last instant I had the urge to put one arm in two of the holes."

I asked for clarification on that point. She said well, she just put her left arm in the left hole and then shoved her right arm through both of the other holes. Somehow it seemed to work.

"Back in the doctor's office the paper gown was paper because paper is cheaper and I understand why it was split down the back," she said. "But a cloth gown with three holes which opens down the side really has me shook up."

So I called Tipton County Memorial and asked if I could speak to sombody about three-holed hospital gowns, and after an unusually long wait Miss Kerry Overton, the hospital's administrative assistant, came on the phone.

Why yes, she said, they use three-holers. It's for the privacy of the patient.

At first I thought she was putting me on. Since when did a hospital give a hang about the privacy of a patient? But she was serious.

The whole affair is just like a wraparound dress, she explained. You put your left arm through the left hole and your right arm through the center hole, and then you wrap what's left around you and put your left arm through the remaining hole.

You can see what a stunning advance that is. At least you can if you have ever had to wear any of those open-down-the-back outrages. I asked if the gowns were available for men as well as women, and she said of course. And were they something new? Why, no, they've been around for quite a while.

So then I told her how Mrs. Wilson had donned her gown, and she said well actually that wasn't the way to do it, of course. So I called Mrs. Wilson and explained the procedure to her, and she said that was fine but she weighs about 160 pounds and she didn't really think the standard way would have worked for her, but it was a nice thought.

It is indeed. If medical science can solve the problem of the flyaway nightgown, there is no telling what triumphs lie ahead. How long have those things been around? How come the Nobel Prize people didn't do anything to honor their development? And, now that they're here, why doesn't the government outlaw open-backed hospital gowns forever?

Take Two Aspirins

The mysterious misadventures of Bern Keating, Mississippi's answer to Marco Polo, are almost beyond belief.

Keating's work as one of the nation's top travel writers takes him to the countless corners of the Earth. And everywhere he goes, it appears, he stumbles, falls, jumps or is pushed into puns of the most deplorable nature.

It is not the puns, mind you, that have earned his prestige among his fellow members of the Overseas Press Club, the Authors Guild and other great organizations. They know him as an eloquent and intrepid writer, photographer and adventurer in more conventional areas.

Only the readers of this column are blessed, by some special dispensation, with the opportunity to share in his more bizarre experiences.

And now there has been yet another.

Noting recently that months, perhaps years, had passed since we last heard from Keating, I sent an urgent inquiry to his Greenville home. What had happened? Had he been smitten by syntactical symptoms too terrible to report?

The answer, painfully picked out on a typewriter by fingers that must still have been quivering from weakness, came promptly enough.

"Here is the latest medical bulletin on my condition as affected by the serious travel I am forced to commit," he wrote.

"I have just returned from two weeks spent in a lighthouse off the Louisiana coast.

"The wife of the keeper is a delightful Cajun who serves a typical Cajun table of gumbos, jambalayas, red beans and rice, calas rice cakes with molasses for breakfast, that kind of hearty fare.

"With the breakfast rice cakes, for a spicy side dish, she serves about eight inches of andouille, the fiery hot Louisiana style sausage, made from lovingly nurtured swine ritualistically butchered by Grandpere and enchantingly flavored by Grandmere.

"I gorged at all meals shamelessly, but it was at breakfast when she served the andouille that I made my most dazzling display of gluttony.

"Then one morning, Mirabelle caught me popping a handful of pills and learned that I suffer from hypertension.

" 'But you are supposed not to eat the salt, no?'

"I conceded her point.

" '*Mais*, the andouille you have been swilling like a peeg, she is half salt, yes?'

"Shamefacedly, I confessed that the saline content of an andouille was the best part.

"She informed me brusquely that, for my own good, my andouille days were over.

"Next morning, instead of the andouille on my plate, there reposed a pretty little broiled bird fresh gathered from the sea. . ."

And that, as it turned out, was the whole story.

Except, of course, for the conclusion. You may wish to have an aspirin handy for this:

"Because of my malady, I had taken a tern for the wurst."

Clothes Make
The Man

A Hat Is More Than Just A Hat

"YOU NEED A hat," my wife told me.

"I've got a hat."

"But cold weather's coming, and you don't like to wear it."

We were into our annual fall argument. It follows a traditional pattern.

As any truly mature man knows, they don't make hats like they used to. People of discretion, people like me for example, wear them as seldom as possible.

Time was when a man wore a hat he could get his teeth into. Everything was covered and comfortable. The brim stretched out like a mighty oak on all sides to protect him from the elements. It snapped down to make him look sharp.

Alas, no more. In men's hats nowadays, little is big. Unless you want to be a cowboy. Who needs cowboys?

"So get a different style," my wife pursued. "What style do you wear now?"

How would I know? When I grew up, only sheiks and dudes bothered about the names of styles in menswear. I got out my hat and looked inside.

"This," I told her, "is an extra long oval."

She walked away, muttering.

A few days later she was at me again.

"I saw an ad for a hat that would be perfect for you. It's called an Irish country hat. You know, the kind Rex Harrison wears in that commercial."

I turned pale. "You want me to wear a hat Rex Harrison would wear? I'd sooner die."

"Then go look around in a store."

"I've looked around in stores. What do they know? They don't even have pants with full seats. Why should I expect anything from their hats?"

More than pants fueled my resentment. Once I bought a fishing hat in a men's shop. The fish laughed so hard they wouldn't bite.

Late last week she tried again. "I was watching a feature about men's hats on television," she said. "They said more and more men are wearing them again, and there are all sorts of sizes. But don't get the Irish country hat after all."

"Why?"

"Patrick Moynihan wears one too."

I wouldn't have anyway, but that settled it for both of us.

"But I'm sure you can find something," she went on. "How about a fur hat like Senator Muskie wore to Russia?"

"Please!"

"Or a cap? They showed something they called Andy Warhol's working man's cap."

Fortunately, we weren't eating at the time. I almost gave up soup already on account of Warhol.

"Well, I insist that you wear something in this cold weather," she told me. "I know, how about a fedora? They said the Humphrey Bogart fedora is coming back."

Humphrey Bogart? The old snap brim, the old trenchcoat, a kish is just a kish and all that?

I schmiled at her thoughtfully out of the shide of my mouth. "We'll shee, schweetheart," I shaid. "We'll shee."

Follow That Truman!

Signal honors may await the man who refuses to wear a tie, a tale told by a Memphis woman indicates.

This interesting fact has come to light because I noted here recently that I don't wear ties, having long since determined that they are symbols of oppression and torture to which no free man should bow the neck.

("Did you say you never wear a tie?" one reader asked. No, I simply said I don't wear them. Occasional exceptions merely emphasize the rule; in 1979, I believe, there were three exceptions.)

"A year ago," my anonymous informant recalled, "My husband and I were in New Orleans.

"Night drew nigh, and thoughts of French cuisine became overpowering.

"He was on strike against men wearing ties at the time, and had not packed one. He began phoning restaurants in the French Quarter to determine which would allow us to dine, considering his casual appearance.

"Call after call was made, with a 'Yes, M'sieur, we'll be happy to take your reservation,' and then a 'Non, M'sieur, you may not be seated without a tie.'

"I was donning an elegantly tailored outfit, suitable for tied or tieless escort, while listening to one side of these lengthy phone-debates.

"Even cafeterias in the Quarter have a special elan to me, so I was not unduly perturbed whatever happened. My husband, however, has a passion about food and was becoming more and more uptight, even without a tie.

"Finally one of the most elegant, most exclusive, most expensive restaurants of all accepted our reservation even though my husband would appear without cravat and with windbreaker.

"Off we went, both amazed and relieved, our horse-drawn carriage clip-clopping us the few blocks.

"The maitre d' met us with a smile and seated us at a table—in the bar.

"No, we would not be permitted in the dining room, but after all, why should we complain?

"For our table happened to be Truman Capote's table, placed there especially for his dining pleasure, since he also refuses to wear a tie."

Now I grant you that not every man would feel honored to be given Truman Capote's table, but after all, you can't knock success. And it is, anyway you want to look at it, a sort of distinction. No doubt many a wide-eyed tourist stared at our truculent Memphian that night and thought, my, so that's the fellow who writes all those gossipy and highly praised novels and who appears on all the talk shows and who carries a purse.

At least it gave him a night to remember, and a good dinner which he could enjoy without a tie riding up and down on his Adam's apple at every swallow.

All of which has led my informant to offer a word of encouragement to men who hold out for freedom of male necks:

"Continue, gentlemen, to protest this ancient tradition. It may take extra time and energy, and an understanding wife, but it can lead to unusual experiences."

It should be an inspiration to us all. Indeed, it makes me regret the necessity of adding her final report about her husband's reaction to the whole affair:

"On our next trip, he packed a tie."

Maybe he did, but you and I don't have to. If Truman Capote can blaze the path to new freedoms for men, surely the rest of us can follow.

The Neck is First to Go

Vanity is a terrible thing. Everybody knows that, but when you see it turn a man's self-respect into sniveling narcissism, you realize how terrible it really is.

For vanity, great statesmen have become laughingstocks.

For vanity, decent and respectable men caught in the midlife crisis have gone out and bought hairpieces, attended rock concerts, and even abandoned their families.

And now for vanity, a fellow I know has bought his first necktie in 41 years.

Some men must wear ties in order to keep their jobs. I find no fault with them; after all, life is hard and we all have to give up a few freedoms.

But this man faces no such economic need. His job does not require him to wear a tie. There may be subtle pressures, to be sure, but not enough to excuse his act after all these years.

As in all such turnarounds, his decision caused him to feel guilt and shame. Since I have known him for years and respected his contempt of tie-wearing, he at least had the grace to drop me a pathetic little note of apology.

"I woke up this morning gripped by a curious compulsion: Namely, to go out and buy a necktie," wrote this craven friend, whom I will identify only as J.F.

"I cannot say exactly where the compulsion came from. Years ago I had a tie, but it was somehow lost, and I never bought another.

"Since, as you know, my stand on neckties has been both moral and philosophical, it might appear that I am on the verge of violating a sacred trust. Perhaps I am. In any case, the obscenity of the necktie is incontestable.

"I think what I remembered is that I look very good in a necktie. Also, I'm no longer young and my neck is going. As everyone knows, the neck is the first to go.

"And with that, I suppose I have confessed that my philosophical integrity is no match for my vanity.

"So there it is. Since you have long counted me, and appropriately, as a dedicated soldier in the war against cravats (WAC), I thought it only fair to inform you that I now, at least tentatively, move toward the ranks of the turncoats."

I called the old coot—after all, in less than five years he will be as old as I am now—to beg him to reconsider his rash action. Had he really worn a tie already, or was he only trembling on the brink?

Well, he said, he really had bought one. "The one I bought in 1940 cost 50 cents," he said. "Now the damned things cost $8 or $9. But I got one. I've been circling around it ever since."

But didn't he realize that you can't hide a turkey-neck by tucking and folding and pleating it into a buttoned collar, and that a tie won't hide it anyhow?

"I thought maybe I'd wear it loose, like Robert Redford."

Robert Redford indeed. Realizing his case way beyond hope, I bade him a sad farewell and looked again at the last paragraph of his note.

"Should we meet at some future event," he had written, "and should you find it the better part of honor to strike me across the face with your gloves, I shall understand."

With my gloves? Good heavens, the poor old codger really has gone bonkers.

Cuffs for Everybody

The average man, I am convinced, doesn't pay a whole heap of attention to style in the clothes he wears. But he does value comfort, utility and tradition.

There are the dudes, the dapper Dans and the disco dandies, of course. They care plenty about style, and the clothing manufacturers cater to them or even incite them, and the rest of us are expected to go along. Things change before we know it.

There is, for example, the matter of cuffs on trousers.

Several Memphis men, mostly middle-aged or beyond, were having lunch recently when one of them glanced about furtively and said:

"I'm ashamed to ask this, but do you fellows have cuffs on your pants?"

The others looked blank. They weren't really sure.

"I do, on some of 'em, I guess," one finally ventured after glancing under the table. "But why?"

And then the fellow told his story.

He went to a Memphis department store recently, he said, to buy a summer suit. He found what he wanted and left it to be altered.

On the appointed day he returned and tried it on. The fit was satisfactory, and he was about ready to take it away when he noticed something wrong.

"Hey," he said, "these pants don't have any cuffs."

"That's right," said the salesman.

"Why not?"

"We don't put cuffs on pants these days."

Our man was irate. "Well, I want cuffs on my pants," he snapped. "You'll have to take 'em back and put cuffs on them."

"Mister," said the salesman, "In the last five years only two people have asked for cuffs on their pants."

"I don't care. I want cuffs."

So the salesman took the pants back and said all right, he would have cuffs put on them. But he kept looking at his customer strangely.

"Tell me," he said at last, "why do you want cuffs on your pants?"

"Because," said the man, "everybody wants cuffs."

But, he confessed, he felt a little silly as he walked out.

That is a fine example, it seems to me, of the way mature men get pushed around by clothes makers. Unless somebody stands up to the system—and few do—we don't even get cuffs on our pants anymore. Not to mention room to move around in, or comfortable waist lines, or all those other forgotten goodies of the past.

But cuffs are only a symbol. They don't matter. What all this is really leading up to is a complaint about short-sleeved dress shirts.

How come most of them don't have two pockets on them?

Indeed, how come some of them don't have any pockets at all?

If there's anything a decent, hardworking man needs in the summer when he's wearing a short-sleeved dress shirt, it's two pockets to put things in. His coat will be hanging somewhere out of reach. His pants will be too tight for the pockets to be useful. Shucks, he won't even have cuffs to stuff things into.

But try to find a shortsleeved dress shirt with two pockets. Unless you're lucky, you'll wear out two pairs of shoes and a pair of cuffless pants just looking.

And why is that? My own theory is that it's because the dudes don't work hard enough to need two pockets, and the shirt manufacturers can save a few pennies by ignoring the rest of us.

And still people wonder why there's so much unrest among the lower middle class.

What's to wonder about? In a society where you can't easily find two-pocket shirts, let alone pants with cuffs on them, trouble is bound to brew. Mark my words, when the revolution comes, one of the battle cries will be:

"Millions for necessities, but not one cent for one-pocket shirts."

Bottom Line Against Bloomers

The sins committed in the name of fashion are so numerous and so grievous that many people have simply given up. But now and then there comes a time when a person ought to speak out.

There is one matter in particular that I have been brooding over in cowardly silence for some weeks now, and I just can't stand it any longer.

The fact that I am about to begin a week's vacation gives me, I confess, the courage to sound off now, as follows:

Women, please don't let those fashion designers put you back into bloomers.

Oh, I know they call 'em different names now.

They talk about "knickers," and "samurai pants" and "harem pants," and they use all sorts of fancy material.

But when you get right down to it, those knickers and samurai pants and harem pants are nothing more or less than souped-up bloomers, and it's high time somebody pointed it out.

Good night, when even a candidate for Miss America shows up on network television wearing the things—as she did, and you probably saw her—is anybody safe?

Understand, there was nothing really wrong with bloomers at the time they were developed back in the 19th Century.

I have been reading up on the origin of such garments, and it is pretty interesting. Did you know that Amelia Jenks Bloomer, who gets all the credit, didn't invent bloomers in the first place?

History is full of such things. Mrs. Bloomer was a leader in the women's liberation movement about 125 years ago. Another leader, Mrs. Elizabeth Smith Miller, originated the idea of "a style of loose trousers, descending from beneath a short skirt and gathered at the ankle," to allow women more freedom of action.

Mrs. Bloomer endorsed the costume and wore it on the lecture platform, and that's how bloomers were born. By rights, of course, they should have been called millers.

No doubt they were more handsome than the gymnasium-type that was popular in the early part of this century. Terrible looking garments those were, but at least they were useful.

But what can you say about this year's explosion of knickers and samurai pants and harem pants in the nation's fashion centers?

I'll tell you what you can say.

You can say that when a woman comes out wearing them, she looks like she's wearing fancy-dress bloomers.

You can say she looks like Ko-Ko in a bad production of "The Mikado."

You can say her legs resemble Pronto Pups with ruffles.

You can say, "What is this world coming to?"

Why would a woman want her legs to look like Pronto Pups with ruffles?

We all know the answer to that. She wants to be in fashion. At least, that has been the case in the past.

But shouldn't women's fashions be included in women's liberation? If feminism means anything, doesn't it mean release from the baleful influence of outrageous designers? Is it possible that a woman can be enlightened and still look at herself in the mirror and not see what she looks like in today's version of bloomers?

And having said that, I plant to retire discreetly to some remote foxhole for a few days and try to stay out of touch with everybody.

Maybe the world will come to its senses while I'm gone, but I'm sure not betting on it.

Is Turnabout Pantyhose Fair Play?

In these days of less quality for more money, the things some women have to put up with are simply terrible.

I've just been talking to one of them.

She suffers, she told me, from rotating hose.

She did her best to explain the situation for me.

"I put on a new pair of stretch hose last week and sashayed out on some errands," she told me.

"Upon returning home, I happened to look down.

"The heels of the darned hose had worked their way around to the tops of my feet.

"I couldn't figure out which direction they thought we were going, but they looked distinctly odd."

It is hard, at least for a man, to understand the mechanics involved in a thing like that. How can the heels end up on top of the feet?

But she assured me that was what happened.

"This is something that good stretch hose are never supposed to do," she said. "It made me wonder how many places I had been without noticing my hose displacement."

Hose displacement? They actually had a name for the maneuver?

She said no, that was just an expression she had adapted after hearing bureaucrats talk. She was somewhat pleased with the terminology, as she had every right to be, but she was still steaming about the condition.

"The effect was grotesque," she said. "It made me mad as all getout.

"It was a sensation similar to finding your shoes on top of your ears and feeling pretty silly about it.

"All I can conclude from this is that there's no more two-way stretch, just a slow one-way rotation. I suppose if I had walked a bit farther, they would have worked around to my heels again."

And was there no consolation to be found in the situation?

As a matter of fact, she said, there was.

"I'm learning how to time them now," she told me.

"From now on, when my children ask how long I'll be gone, I'll just say something like, 'Oh, I ought to be back home by the time my stocking heels arrive at the top of my feet.' Since they have observed the process themselves, they'll feel secure and won't even have to watch the clock."

I might be inclined to think she was putting me on about the whole affair, except that we have had reports—and evidence—of strange goings-on among women's hosiery products before this.

A few years back, I remember, somebody complained to me about getting a pair of pantyhose that had one foot facing forward and one facing backward.

I treated the complaint with a certain amount of skepticism, and somebody else entirely sent me a pair just like those described. It was amazing. If you could ever have got the things on, you could have walked either direction you wanted without even turning around.

In the case of the backward-forward pantyhose, as I recall, it all turned out to be a matter of error in putting the things together. As far as I know, no trends were set.

So the question now is, are rotating hose the wave of the dismal future, or did our victim just happen to get a faulty pair?

Any help on this matter will be appreciated. If the day is coming when anybody who looks down at a woman's foot is likely to see a heel sitting on top of it, we need to start getting ready for the experience now.

Pocket Lovers, Unite!

Despite all our hopes and the alleged efficiency of a free-market economy, the shirt pocket situation grows steadily worse.

We have been into this situation before and, by golly, we will keep going into it in the future until shirtmakers of the world wake up to the needs of the wearers.

This surly outburst in particular has been provoked by an open letter sent to me by Raymond F. Jones of Olive Branch, Miss.

It is aimed primarily at big stores engaged in Christmas selling, but Jones clearly won't mind if his friends read it and are guided accordingly.

"I wish to advise," he wrote, "that I will never purchase, nor will I accept as a gift, a knitted shirt intended for golf, leisure, or any other purpose that is not equipped with at least one pocket."

There you are. Back there when I first began fighting the good fight for sane shirts, the complaint was that too many shirts had only one pocket.

By now, too many have none at all. Talk about a backward economy.

Surely the shirt manufacturers realize that most men don't carry purses. And surely they realize that, as pants grow ever tighter, space to carry things becomes ever scarcer.

So what do they do about it? Instead of increasing the number of pockets in shirts, they decrease them.

And it has reached the point where even a decent, patient, law-abiding man like Raymond F. Jones (I don't know him, but I'm certain from his letter that his is all those things) is driven to issuing pre-Christmas warnings.

I know we have become accustomed to paying more for less during these inflated times, but there ought to be a limit somewhere.

Knitted sport shirts are all right in their place. But surely a man who dons one should be entitled to find room somewhere to tuck away a few needed items.

Let's say he's going to play golf. Won't he need to carry a pencil and a scorecard in addition to all the other odds and ends he considers essential?

And suppose he wears glasses. Where is he expected to carry the case? In his mouth?

Somewhere in the astonishing increase in the cost of men's shirts in recent years there ought to be a few pennies available for making a couple of pockets. Good night, I for one would even be willing for them to take a bit of material out of the shirttail if they simply can't afford it otherwise.

But instead of two pockets they gave us one. And now they're trying to take that one away. And not only in sport shirts, but in others as well.

Unwary buyers seldom notice the pocket situation until they get home and take the cover off the shirt. By then, most of them assume, it's too late.

So we can expect that, come Christmas, many a man—not including Raymond F. Jones—will find waiting for him under the tree
a beautiful shirt that will be just great until he tries to put something
in a pocket that isn't there.

But it's not too late to let the shirt manufacturers know how we
feel. Matter of fact, this is an ideal time.

Men who abhor pocketless shirts should warn their friends and
families right now, just as Raymond F. Jones has done, that such ob-
jects will not be accepted with gratitude.

People who go shopping for shirts should examine them closely,
even asking questions of salespersons if necessary, to be sure they
are equipped with at least one pocket—and preferably two.

If, as some political observers allege, there is indeed a general
public demand to get back to the basics of life, surely that demand
should include adequate pocket space. Let our motto be: Millions for
shirts, but not one cent without pockets.

Shirtmakers, Have Mercy

The rebellion against the mass-produced uptight look in men's wearing apparel may be spreading.

Remember the fellow who complained here recently that men's pa-
jama arms and legs keep getting shorter? He has been joined by a
victim of what are called tapered shirts.

The newest rebel is Roy Cammack, who describes himself as "the
ultradesirable five-five in height," and he has a shirt proposal.

Change the terminology, he suggests.

Tappered shirts, as any dude can tell you, start out wide at the
shoulders and get narrow at the waist—a shape resembling that of
an average man about as accurately as a high-fashion model
resembles a human being.

But Cammack, not a vengeful person, would not do away with
such shirts. Let them stay on the shelves, he says, but with new
labels reading "Reverse Taper."

As for the alternate?

"True-Taper shirts, gracefully ample in girth, will be stocked in
every store, by law if necessary," he told me.

"The thought, like the shirt I'm wearing, leaves me breathless."

Once that goal is accomplished, he dreams of changing size
designations in general. Instead of Small, Medium, Large and Extra
Large, Cammack would prefer Normal Too Large, Too Small and
Have Mercy!

And going that extra mile, he has extended a generous offer to the clothing people:

"In the self-sacrificing spirit of the true humanitarian, I herewith offer my own body as the prime reference point for the new series of sizes in men's wear. This handsomely tapered frame will inspire an elegance-through-fit heretofore unknown in clothes for men."

Cammack's complaint, as suggested earlier, is neither new nor novel as men continue to groan under the oppressive yoke of the clothing makers.

Not all men have his particular problems regarding height and girth, but hundreds of thousands—nay, millions—fail, for one reason or another, to fit into the tall, bottomless, sylphlike shape on which today's sizes are patterned.

Younger generations may know no better and accordingly believe life is like that. But older men can remember the day when beltlines were not on but above the waist, where the good Lord intended them to be; when there was room to move about in your trousers; even when the shirt with pockets was the rule rather than the exception. Alas, how times have changed.

It is still too early to talk in terms of a full-scale revolution, of course. When they go into clothing stores, men are like sheep. Only now and then does a voice of protest arise. But meanwhile, others by the scores are digging through attics and dusty closets to find and restore clothes that, however they might look, are at least comfortable.

And, from time to time, the occasional rebel speaks out—quietly, so as not to pop off any buttons or burst any seams. And in time, surely, someone will listen.

Collars Deserve Equal Rights

Men who, like me, normally don't keep up with such matters should be warned that yet another clothing outrage has been imported from Europe and is already threatening our comfort, dignity and sense of well being.

Collarless shirts, can you believe it?

I couldn't, until one night a week or so ago when my wife and I were watching a late-night talk show on television. A fellow appeared on camera and began talking, and right away I felt embarrassed for him.

"Look," I said. "His shirt collar must have got turned under. Isn't that awful?"

"That was no accident," my wife said. "That's a collarless shirt."
Aw, shucks, I thought. What does she know?

But the very next day I had a letter from a young fellow who was
telling me how he had just spent a lot of time in Europe shopping for
his fall wardrobe and how he had what he called a "successful recep-
tion" at a place called Studio 54 in New York, and then how he got
home to Memphis and, wearing a Gucci collarless shirt, was turned
down by one of our local night spots on grounds that they wouldn't
serve people in T-shirts.

He thought it was a great joke. It was all Greek to me.

But I have been learning. Studio 54, it appears, is a disco where
you stand outside and the proprietors come to the door from time to
time, choose the customers they are willing to admit, and sneer at
the rest.

It is quite the thing in New York—I even saw it mentioned in
Doonesbury yesterday, which makes it officially in—and it appears
to prove once again that Americans are willing to pay any amount
and go to any lengths if someone will only heap enough indignities
on them.

And Gucci, of course, is some kind of fashion house, in Italy I
think. Until recent years I thought Gucci was an adjective, like
poochy, but one lives and learns.

But back to the collarless shirts. That's what they are, all right,
shirts without collars; just a tiny band around the top that doesn't
even stand up straight but sort of flops around. I have since seen a
number of pictures of men wearing them. All the men, needless to
say, looked like asses.

There once was a day, some of us remember, when a man's collar
was attached to his shirt and could be removed, and when a real slob
was known by the fact that he occasionally went around without a
collar. Now it's becoming the hottest style of the year, and it's sicken-
ing.

It is not simply that I am opposed to change, though constant
change in styles really does get pretty tiresome. It's a matter of
aesthetics.

Collarless shirts make men look miserable.

I believe firmly in equal rights for the sexes, and I know women
have worn the equivalent of collarless shirts for years, and men are
just as good as women. But it is a fact of life that a man's exposed
neck, nine times out of ten, looks worse than the plucked neck of a
chicken. We must face such physiological differences honestly and
make the best of them.

A man needs something to stick up toward his chin, something to
lessen the impact of his Adam's apple, something to shrink into

when the time comes to shrink into something. How do you shrink into a collarless shirt?

No, it simply won't do. This is one time when men should refuse to go along with the dictates of the industry.

"I wear no man's collar" used to be one of the proudest boasts of an independent man, but it sure as shooting didn't mean he didn't wear any collar at all. And if Gucci and Studio 54 have no use for such talk, we're even. I have no use for Gucci and Studio 54. It's high time the men of this country spoke up for their rights.

The Great Coat Uprising

Man may yet hit on a way to get into a small car with a large coat without the whole back end of the garment rising up to persecute him.

The problem was noted here the other day. You wear a long heavy coat because of the cold weather, and what happens? Everything bunches up under you. Misery and bad driving result.

Women appear to have solved the problem, I noted. Maybe they could tell men the secret.

But it's not that easy. Almost immediately I got a call from a woman who said men just don't know how to get into cars—they put one leg in first and then slide over. Of course their coats bunch up under them.

"Women know better," she told me. "They turn their backs to the car, smooth down their coats and sit down. Then they turn around in the seat. Try it."

I did. It didn't work. The trouble, I realized, is that women's coats don't have those slits up the back the way men's coats do. Next case.

A suggestion from J.E.C. seems to make a lot of sense, but on second thought it probably won't work either.

"That back vent may be where the trouble lies," said C. "Get the clothing people to make all long coats with side vents. Then get a firm hold on each side, slide in and voila!"

Fine. But who in our lifetime ever heard of a maker of men's clothes striving to make men comfortable in them? It's the other way around. Disappearing pockets, tight pants—the whole goal is to make us suffer. So why would they move the slits?

But the system put forward by Robert F. Todd sounds like a winner. He gives the credit to the late Congressman Jere Cooper of Tennessee, whom he once saw getting into a car on the town square at Dyersburg.

"As he entered the car from the passenger side," Todd said, "he reached between his legs and grasped both coattails. Pulling them forward through his legs, he then held them in his right hand while using the left to steady himself as he sat down on the seat and swung his legs into the car.

"With a little practice the same technique appears to work equally well from the driver's side of the car if one uses his left hand to hold the coattails."

There it is. The feminine technique, but with the necessary added ingredient—reaching between your legs to grab those plaguey coattails.

And Cooper must have known what he was doing. Todd said the Saturday Evening Post once declared he was the only member of the Congress who could sit through an all-day session and then walk out without a wrinkle in his suit.

I suppose it's worth a try, but one question does bother me.

Could anybody but a congressman do a thing like that in public and not be laughed out of town or arrested?

New Cap Heady Decision

In a world filled with fear, timidity and cowardice, examples of blazing courage are too rare to go unnoticed.

That is the only reason I would consider admitting, with a becoming blush of manly modesty, my own supreme act of daring. It could serve as an example for the faint-hearted everywhere.

I have gone out and bought a cap.

What's more, I wear it.

In public.

The thought still dazzles even me.

For years now, like other prudent men of mature years, I have struggled with hats in an environment grown hostile to hats.

When you wear a hat, it gets knocked off in the new small cars. Winds send it spinning. Young rowdies sneer and snicker behind your back.

But if you are subject to colds in winter, you have to do something to keep your head warm. What is the answer?

The answer is, of course, a cap, a billed cap, the same sort of cap we used to wear when we were kids, the sort you see on youngsters and on the heads of odd older citizens who clearly don't realize how ridiculous they look. I could name you a few of the latter.

But in time a man grows desperate. So recently, talking to a younger man who wears a cap as a matter of course and somehow looks tolerable in it, I borrowed it and tried it on.

Well, it felt snug. It was low enough to fit into any car. I could tell it wouldn't blow off in a high wind. And my wife had been after me for months to buy a cap.

My friend, a fellow named Nick, looked straight at me without laughing. I felt courage well up in me like a mighty current.

"Help me find one," I asked.

And that is how it happened. He took me to a store, tested dozens of caps on me, put them all aside with looks of sick revulsion, and finally handed me a houndstooth beauty.

I donned it. He looked.

"It'll do," he said, or something like that.

It was an understatement. Looking into a mirror, I saw a reflection jaunty without being offensive, confident without being cocky. The word for the overall effect, much as I resisted it, was debonair.

That was only a couple of weeks ago, and already the cap has changed my life.

Getting into cars is a pleasure. High winds hold no terrors. Meeting younger people on the street, I feel less like some felt-domed anachronism than like Ian Carmichael as Lord Peter Wimsey. Confidence flows through my tired arteries, optimism pulses in my veins.

I may get a whole collection of caps. Some day I may even buy a pair of plus fours and a cane. It's a new year and a new world and, by golly, I plan to make a clean break with the old. Clean as a houndstooth cap.

It's Us
Versus Them

Brainwashing Removes The Worry

WHAT IN THE everloving blue-eyed world are commercials on the electronic media doing to our children—and grandchildren?

The question comes, not from me, but from Mrs. Thomas Joe Bailey, who was taken thoroughly aback not long ago when one of her 12 grandchildren called her on the phone.

He wanted to recommend a product for unsightly age spots. Something that, if you put it on, on, would make them fade, fade, fade.

A few days later, he managed to make his point again. She had called to speak to his mother, but Kelly, who is 4, answered the phone.

"Mom," she heard him call, "it's for you. It's Mimi with the age spots."

Just think, she suggested, what kind of future she has in store with a dozen grandchildren listening to the radio and watching television with Mimi-with-the-age-spots in mind.

I have been trying, and it hardly bears thinking about.

Those kids don't know, for example, whether Mimi wears dentures or not. Neither do I, for that matter. But surely that won't stop them from assuring her that loose dentures are no laughing matter, or that a paste adhesive beats powder any day.

The eager little beavers will be prescribing pills for her arthritis, rinses for her hair, methods for dealing with wrinkles, and far, far worse.

We might as well face it: In their eagerness to do good, and spurred on by the electronic examples of their elders, they may well proceed to asking her if she is satisfied with her laxative. After all, dosen't a stranger's voice ask that of a woman on television every day?

As for herself, Mrs. Bailey hasn't dared to speculate where it will all lead. She simply says:

"I get sort of nervous when I answer the phone now."

But it is not only grandmothers who must feel moved to flee from the wrath to come when they watch the evening assortment of commercials.

Truck drivers, by now, must be downright sensitive about their occupation, involving as it presumably does all those visits to some friendly druggist who has just the thing to cure their painful and distinctive problem.

Whole families must have been terrorized into conducting tests on one another to determine whether a stick deodorant is more effective than a roll-on.

And who knows how many thousands of Americans will decide not to take a vacation trip at all this year rather than face all those hazards so dramatically portrayed by Karl Malden? Who wants to be lost in a strange city, racing down crowded streets in search of lost billfolds, purses and credit cards, when you could save all that agony by staying home?

The only cure for all this, as far as I can see, is for us all to take a new look at the concept of brainwashing.

Until now, that has always been considered a terrible thing, usually practiced only by Communists or other evil groups. But maybe, in the right hands, it could be beneficial.

Surely with our advanced technology there must be some way to set a tyke under a machine that would run a rapid brain-scan, identify the danger spots, and prescribe a medicine designed to wash those commercials right out of the brain.

Or maybe it could take the form of a salve. You could put it on, on, on, and sensitivity to commercials would fade, fade, fade.

Shucks, if the thing worked, they could even advertise it on television.

What Television Really Needs

People are always saying what television needs.

You want to know what television really needs? I'll tell you.

It needs a telephone ring that doesn't sound like a telephone ring, that's what.

With all the electronic marvels at the command of all those production geniuses, you would think this simple matter would have occurred to them already. But no. When a telephone rings on a television show, it sounds just like a telephone ringing in the next room.

Don't those guys know anything?

Consider a typical drama on the mighty tube. It will probably be set in a hospital, right? Cardiac arrests are among the biggest attractions right now, some say even bigger than street crime, and no self-respecting network would be without a hospital show featuring a weekly cardiac arrest.

All right, so there you sit watching the drama. The victim is rushed into the hospital, where the chief of surgery is eagerly awaiting him. (On television shows, the chief of surgery is always right there waiting for any victim brought in off the street.) So there's a quick check, a skilled diagnosis, and the cardiac specialist starts pounding the victim on the chest.

And somewhere in the background—off camera, like as not—a telephone rings.

Now that ringing telehone is simply thrown in for the sake of realism, you understand. The idea is to remind you what a busy place a hospital is. It doesn't matter who's on the phone. For all the producer cares, it could be a wrong number. The producer just wants realism.

But what happens in houses all over America?

People rush out of the room to answer the phone.

And by the time they reach it, and find it wasn't ringing, and get back to the set, the victim has already confessed his or her secret— the secret on which all the rest of the script depends—to the brusque head nurse with the heart of gold.

Blooie. One more mighty drama down the hatch.

It's not just in the dramas that ringing phones cause confusion, either. Think of all the commercials people miss because somebody fled from the set to say "Hello, hello—ah, nuts."

And the fund-raising telethons, of course, are worst of all. They have these elaborate setups with tables filled with volunteers all ready to take your call and log your donation, and to get you in the spirit of the thing they arrange to have one or more phones ringing constantly.

So just as you have finally decided you can't wait another minute to call in your contribution, you hear what simply must be you own phone ringing. And by the time you've found you were mistaken, you're so out of sorts you decide not to give anything to anybody.

It's not as if nothing can be done about it. Drama of all sorts is full of artificial conventions which we accept willingly. That has always been the case. If television introduced phone rings that don't sound like everyday phone rings, the public would get the idea right off and be grateful.

But no. They keep ringing those bells, and people keep getting up and leaving the room to see who's on the phone, and plots and sales pitches keep getting lost as a result.

If any mogul wakes up to the obvious and takes corrective steps, fine. If not, what I say is we should quit fooling around with them. From now on, whenever a phone rings on television, irate citizens from coast to coast should go to the kitchen and dish up a bowl of ice cream or something, and then settle down and eat it before they return to the tube. Maybe when the next Nielsen ratings are posted, somebody up there will be sorry.

Speedy Ads Don't Shorten Breaks

Have a feeling that the commercials are coming hotter and faster on television, do you?

Maybe they are.

The Sims Laboratory of Unusual Research Projects hasn't made an exhaustive study of the subject, mind you. And since commercials vary in time and length from station to station, and from one time of day to another, comprehensive tests are hard to make.

Furthermore, regardless of what you may believe, there is no law or federal regulation controlling such matters.

But we have a report here from a SLURP volunteer, and it appears to mesh nicely with a recent news release. Let's examine both.

Our researcher is Mrs. Kenny Sargent, who took tally sheet in hand while she watched a one-hour soap opera not long ago.

At the end of the hour, she told me, she had logged:

27 commercials.

1 newsbreak.

2 service announcements.

11 announcements of future shows.

That adds up to 41 breaks during the hour, if her figures are correct. And, again assuming the accuracy of her measuring devices, the breaks consumed 33 minutes of the hour.

There are those who would say, of course, that the commercials are the best part of a soap opera, but that's another matter. Now for the news release.

This came out nearly three months ago, and I have been examining it off and on ever since with a mixture of fascination and loathing. It begins:

"Speeding up TV commercials so that exactly the same audio and visual material is presented 25 per cent faster made the commercials much more effective, a study by an NYU (New York University) marketing professor revealed today."

The professor cited was one James MacLachlan of the NYU graduate school of business, and the findings were based on experiments using 128 students.

All the students watched a program containing four commercials. Half the students saw the commercials at their normal 30-second speed, while the other half saw the same commercials speeded up to 24 seconds.

And, by golly, two days later the students who saw the speeded-up commercials remembered them more accurately than did those who watched the normal versions. How about that?

MacLachlan said the "time compression" technique used for the study was being tested by commercial advertisers, and added that he expected it would be used on network television "within a couple of months."

More than that amount of time has passed. Are we now receiving time-compression commercials?

It beats me, but the release did appear to explain at least some of that incredibly fast talking you hear on some commercials. It said audio tapes can be speeded up electronically without producing that Donald Duck sound we usually expect. And, of course, the visual portion can be speeded to match the sound track.

So, if you are getting more and faster commercials—SLURP isn't ready yet to conclude that you are—it may be thanks to yet another giant step for humanity in the field of electronics. Will we never cease to be plagued by progress?

And it may be that, in addition to seeing faster commercials, you're remembering them better. And what advertiser can resist a saturation campaign aimed at name recognition?

After all, if you can force 'em to remember your name, they're sure to buy the product, right? That was the philosophy of a major cigaret outfit back in the 1940s. Lucky Strike, of course. Ah yes, you remember it well.

TV in a Depression

Some people blame nuclear science, and all those bomb tests, for the kind of weather we have been having in recent winters.

That, of course, is sheer superstition, based on a dread of the unknown and a conviction that when man meddles with nature something bad is sure to happen. When you examine such an argument, it evaporates. How can anything bad come from bomb tests?

No, the reason is far simpler. And it is strange that no one has recognized it before now.

What is responsible for our terrible winter weather? Television, that's what. Specificially, all those weather reports on television news. Good grief.

It may take you a minute or so to see how it all fits in, but you will. In the meantime, consider the fact that winters were simpler and more tractable in the old days before television forecasters.

We had snows now and then, I grant you, and even an occasional ice storm. But in relentless day-to-day intensity, in the sheer grinding-down effect on human morale, there was no comparison.

From time to time we were assailed by "masses of Canadian air" and that was that. Between times, we returned to normal.

Consider the present. Night after night those people appear on our screens with their charts and their radar and their satellite photos and their bouncing arrows and blinking snowflakes and electronic pointers, and day after day we suffer as never before.

A connection? Of course there's a connection. The pattern is too overwhelming to admit coincidence. And the forecasters are aware of it. I heard one of them this week actually apologize because we hadn't gotten as much snow as he promised.

So these days, instead of occasional masses of Canadian air, we get cold fronts colliding with warm fronts to form stationary fronts. We get inversions. We get highs and lows meeting in mammoth conflicts from which ice emerges.

One cannot overlook the fact, by the way, that while television people offer us highs and lows nightly, they never show so much as one ever-loving medium on their plaguey maps.

They have depressions bringing in sleet, and colliding highs and lows followed by tornados and snow. They bring us agitated air from Texas and Oklahoma, from the Dakotas and Wyoming, from Utah and the Gulf Coast.

Before television weather reports, who ever heard of fronts from the Gulf causing freezing rain in Memphis?

The air waves hear all that guff traveling on them, you can be sure, and react accordingly. It stands to reason. We have been assured, for example, that if you brag enough about plants, they'll grow. It follows that if you predict enough about the weather, it'll snow.

I hold no animosity toward those people, you understand. They're just doing their jobs. They were handed all those maps and charts and dials and photos and told to entertain the public, and they're doing it.

But let their employers give them other and more honest work. They'll sleep better, relieved of their guilt. And the weather will settle down overnight, believe me. It's at least worth a try.

The Real Days Of Our Lives

There are some who scorn that sterling art form, the afternoon soap
opera, alleging that its characters are unbelievable, its plots contrived and its action negligible.

Surely they have not watched for themselves.

A mild disaffection of the innards has given me an opportunity to
catch up on the progress of Days of Our Lives, an epic on which I last
reported three or four years ago. I am glad to say the characters are
still believable, the plots faithful to everyday life, and the pace
breathless. But see for yourself.

For the sake of clarity, let us concentrate on just one character—
Julie, the leading lady and source of inspiration for all Salem, the
typical small town where the story is set.

In my last report, Julie was in despair because rumors said the
child she was carrying was not Bob's. Bob was her husband and, unbeknownst to him, the father, by a youthful indiscretion, of Brooke,
who was vengefully set on marrying David, the son of Julie by yet
another youthful indiscretion.

Let us review only a few of the events that have followed.

At the height of Julie's mental anguish, she and Brooke had a
scene which ended with Julie falling down the stairs, losing her baby
and later divorcing Bob. David, meanwhile, left home, was injured in
an accident and, as so often happens, suffered amnesia.

Julie then married her stepfather and long-time true love, Doug,
whose wife Addie had conveniently died after setting him up in the
supper-club business.

A period of great happiness for these two followed, broken when
David, restored in memory if not discretion, had a friendly encounter with Trish which led to paternity. This was awkward because
Trish, whose stepfather lusted after her in his heart, was the girl
friend of Michael, who was believed to be Julie's Uncle Mickey's son
but was really Julie's Uncle Bill's son because—but let us stick to the
main story line.

At Julie's insistence, David married Trish, who had the baby and
then ran away with it to pursue a singing career, but was cruelly
treated by jewel smugglers and returned home. She and David are
reconciling at the moment.

Other gangsters, meanwhile, had coveted Doug's club, and in fur-
therance of their foul plots one of them carnally attacked Julie, who
was subsequently and unjustly placed on trial for his murder.

After her exoneration, another period of great happiness followed
for Julie and Doug—interrupted only by their concerns for various

amnesiacs, lunacies, kidnappings, shootings, mate-swappings and face-liftings among their nearest and dearest—until Julie was terribly burned in an accident.

In the midst of the resulting skin grafts, she fell under the evil influence of a mad psychiatrist, Laura, who has since been packed off to a sanitarium and written out of the story. Not even Julie's Aunt Marie, who some years ago entered a religious order and became a nun and a nurse because she was in love with her brother Tom, could break the evil spell.

In her resulting desperation, Julie left the hospital and flew to Mexico to get a divorce for Doug's own good, an act which has left him tottering on the brink of alcoholism.

Meanwhile, Julie's evil brother Stephen is carrying on outrageously with the underworld, her cousin Michael is in the clutches of a loan shark, and her ex-husband Bob is about to fall in love with his own unbeknownst natural daughter Brooke, who has had a face-lift and returned as Stephanie.

That, of course, is only a small part of what the critics are missing. I haven't even mentioned Marlena and her identical twin, the drug addict, or Maggie, whose multiple guilt complexes drive her to drink, paralysis and hives, or sweet little what's-her-name, who may die any day of leukemia, or Linda, who has recovered from amnesia and is up to her old tricks again.

But I ask you. If Salem isn't your typical small American town, what is? If these characters are not to be believed, who can be? And if that's not action enough for anybody, what is the world coming to?

Mom Fights Back

Now and then a woman in our midst—and not necessarily a card-carrying feminist crusader, either—just gets so blamed fed up with the whole bloomin' sexist mess that she explodes all over the place.

And it's not necessarily a big issue that whips her to a frenzy. It's one of those piddling things that show how saturated with male chauvinist piggery our culture really is.

Things, in particular, like television commercials.

I have long wondered how any self-respecting wife and mother can watch those things without kicking in the picture tube. And now one of them has come dangerously close to doing exactly that.

She wrote in such white-hot passion that she either forgot or didn't bother to sign her name, but the message is clear. Let those of

us who accept this sort of thing in uncritical silence, even com-
placence, sit back and listen.

"The growing tendency in television advertising to make Mom
look like a dunce (Humiliate the Housewife, I expect it's called on
Madison Avenue) makes me outright mad.

"Is it fun to show what an earnest little dimwit thought her husband wanted with his chicken for dinner?

"(Har, har, she was wrong, it wasn't potatoes, it was dressing!)

"Any housewife I know worth her salt would probably have
dumped the whole dinner in the middle of the kitchen floor at that
point and said: 'How do you like *them* apples?'

"Next there's the husband who rushes home after just having told
his wife the boss is coming to dinner.

"The poor fool of a wife proudly displays a cheesecake she's planning to serve. The boor bays loudly, 'Oh he won't like that—he
doesn't like heavy desserts.'

"The wife then meekly makes gelatin or some such humiliating
thing.

"My dream television commercial has her decorating her
husband's glowering face with the cheesecake, a much more satisfying scene.

"Then comes the nosy kid (or aunt, or travel attendant, or
equivalent spoilsport) who ruins the little woman's whole day by
looking at hubby and crowing, 'Ring around the col-lar!'

"In my dreams, this town-crier ends up being dumped in a large
body of water nearby.

"I'm still awaiting the sassy housewife who, when asked by a
smirking salesman what kind of salad dressing her 'man' would like,
has the guts to reply, 'Whatever we have on hand, I expect. And
anyway, what's it to you?'

"Those will be the days."

Oh, right on. If there were more irruptions like that, it couldn't
help but be a better world. And it's high time we men sounded off in
similar fashion. After all, a lot of us are married, and I for one am
scarcely ready to concede that the woman who took me for better or
for worse became, by that very act, a gibbering idiot.

Especially when she's the one who wrote the letter.

Idiocy is New National Craze

"What this country needs most right now," my old friend Joe told me over a cup of coffee, "is more schools to train unskilled people for high-paying jobs."

"So you're starting a school?"

"It's the least I can do. I'm just completing the curriculum for my all-new ITC Institute for Women. My graduates will earn thousands."

"ITC?"

"Idiots for Television Commercials. There's an unending demand there, and I plan to supply it."

It occurred to me that Joe may be on the right track at last. I asked for details.

"You must have noticed the trend. Day after day, women show up in those commercials doing and saying things so stupid it makes you squirm. Somebody needs to teach them to perform their duties without blushing with shame or blowing their tops. After all, even women have some brains." Joe likes to think of himself as a champion of female rights.

"And how will you teach them?"

"I'm boiling all the commercials down into basic types, and we'll have classes for each. They'll learn to be stupid in specific ways, not just generally."

Hating myself for doing it, I asked for examples.

"All right, take the idiot-woman-in-the-store division. We'll build an entire major out of that one. Ever notice that woman who has a headache and goes into a store where they have headache remedies?"

"I think so."

"That's one. This simple-minded looney is standing in front of two bins of headache-relief products, you'll recall. One is marked, 'LESS THAN MAXIMUM,' and the other is marked, 'MAXIMUM.' She has to ask a man which will give more relief for her headache."

"That shouldn't be hard to learn."

"Of course it is. Actors have their pride, you know. I figure it'll take us at least 13 weeks to persuade our women to look appropriately dumb while they ask a man which bin will give more relief."

"And you'll build a whole major out of that?"

"Not just that one. Think of all the other idiot-in-the-store commercials. There's the woman who has to have a man tell her the product that will clean her kitchen porcelain will also clean her bathroom porcelain. And then there's . . ."

"I get the point. What other majors will you have?"

"I don't want to bore you with the whole list. But think how many commercials involve a man coming to take a product away from a woman for a week, or a month, so the poor fool will learn to appreciate it."

"What do you have to teach for that?"

"The woman must learn to act surprised but docile when this stranger arrives and takes something out of her house. Then she must learn to act pathetically grateful when he brings it back.

"And there's the woman who must register shame when people comment on her husband's dirty shirt collar. We'll have to motivate our students for that—teach them that a woman should know her place, which is washing shirt collars, and stick to it.

"And there are those where a loud-mouthed woman with arthritis tries to pick up a skillet, or a loud-mouthed grandmother claims some food product stole her secret, or a loud-mouthed mother-in-law talks about toothpaste, or a woman with a laxative problem is approached by a complete stranger who tells her to put out her hand. She has to learn to put it out without question."

"And will you hire women with professional acting ability to teach in your school?"

Joe looked at me incredulously. "You never learn, do you? Of course not. That's no way to teach a woman to be submissive and simple-minded. I'll have men with whips. Wish me luck."

If he doesn't make it this time, he never will.

No News is Good News

Todd Dudley, who is 11 years old and knows his own mind, has put up with about all he can take.

He is mad.

He is really mad.

The situation, he figures, has got plumb out of bounds and somebody ought to check into it.

As it happens, I have been nominated for that honor.

Here is Todd's message, written at white heat and with no time for the paragraphing which has been inserted for easier reading.

"I'm very tired of people ruining shows for a crummy bulletin.

"Some people may not care about the Camp David summit talk, but even though we don't care, they show it on every channel.

"I think one station should stop showing bulletins and stand up for their rights.

"It's terrible when a person has been watching a show for three weeks, and then on the last exciting episode, a bulletin comes on and after it's over you don't know what's happened.

"Some kids have a bedtime and would get to watch the show, but then a bulletin comes on and ruins it.

"If you have time I would like you to check into this further and write a report in the paper. I'm not one of those people that would like to just get in the paper, I'm really mad and I bet you'd find out other people are mad too.

"They also infringe on our benefits."

Other people get mad too, there's no question about that. One television newsman commented on it only the other night.

When his network's space drama was interrupted for the report from Camp David, he said, complaining callers lit up the switchboard like a Christmas tree. He said it appeared that people are more interested in wars in outer space than they are in the prospects for peace on this planet.

It was a good point, but not exactly the sort of explanation Todd Dudley had in mind. After all, the Middle East is with us always. How often do we get a chance to see Lorne Greene protect a battlestar that holds the few pitiful remnants of the entire human race? It just ain't the same thing.

So what kind of report can anybody give Todd and other 11-year-olds whose evenings are ruined by reality intruding on fantasy?

Some people would say the point is that they must take an intelligent interest in events that affect their lives. I think it goes deeper than that.

I think the point that Todd and others have to learn has nothing to do with world events at all. It is simply this:

Sooner or later, every good thing in life is interrupted by some crummy bulletin. And we might as well face it.

Philosophers have pointed out that there's no such thing as an uninterrupted lunch either, especially if you're enjoying it.

The phone will bring bad news. A tornado will hit. The house will catch fire. The air conditioner will break down. You'll get fired. The teacher will assign double homework. A tire will blow out. You'll slip on a rug and break your leg.

We have to learn to expect all these crummy things.

Television bulletins are only part of the picture. They are, you might say, the training ground, helping us get used to the fact that nothing ever works out right. Todd isn't going to like this answer, but unless he wants to take on the whole Federal Communications Commission it's the best I can offer.

Let's Crush the 'Hold' Button Tyranny

What this country really needs is some great leader who can get the

"Hold" button off our backs.

You know the button I mean. I't's the one they push immediately after they answer your telephone call at almost any great bureaucracy, either government or business.

You've already been sitting there listening to the ringy-dings until you've wandered off into some sort of daze. Then, suddenly, a voice comes on, emits a sound that may or may not be an identification, and follows instantly with, "Hold, please."

"But . . ." you plead.

In vain. The voice has already gone away for a nice cup of coffee, or a visit with a friend, or perhaps to organize an office pool on how long the latest sucker will hold before hanging up.

One long-suffering victim was telling me the other day how it had been with her lately.

On a recent morning, she said, she had occasion to call three offices supported by the taxpayers of this city and county.

"Each of them answered the phone, identified the agency I had called and then, before I could say a word, added, 'Hold, please,' " she said.

"After I had held for three to five minutes in each case, a voice returned to the line and asked what I was calling about.

"When I explained, I was again told to 'Hold, please,' which I did for another three or four minutes.

"Conservatively, I estimate that I stayed on the phone approximately 25 minutes to get the answers to three questions, none of which required more than a few words in reply. In no case was the question complicated enough to require a reply involving a complete sentence."

Not only that, she said, but later in the week she called a federal agency, where she was put on hold and simply left there.

After 10 minutes she assumed they had forgotten her and hung up to call again.

She couldn't. Her line was dead.

It took a visit to a neighbor and a two-hour wait before her phone was back in operation, and she blames this on whoever pushed that "Hold" button. I'm not at all sure that's possible, but at least it shows how persecuted a person can feel about the whole plaguey setup.

And business outfits are just as frustrating as government agencies, of course. Putting people on "Hold" has become a national pastime.

No doubt there are occasions when it is, in a way, necessary. But, by golly, you can't tell me that a lot of those holds aren't administered to impress the caller, to allow time for a pleasant break or to satisfy some basic sadistic urge.

In today's society, instead of saying, "Let 'em eat cake," our rulers say, "Put 'em on hold." And some people think civilization has advanced. I'd rather eat cake any time.

The anonymous citizen who complained to me confessed that she had grown philosophical about the practice. If she's not calling a relative or friend, she said, she simply waits patiently to be put on hold and makes her plans accordingly.

But it was not always thus.

"There was a time," she said, "when I would have revolted against this injustice. Now that I am almost 50, I have resigned myself to the situation.

"Oh, to be young and revolting again."

Well, somebody ought to be revolting. Otherwise, one of these days the whole country is going to come to a dead stop while, all over the land, people wait on hold. And wait, and wait. You suppose this whole thing could be part of a vast conspiracy?

Diddled to Death by Digital Data

You want to know what's wrong with this country? We're not going to the dogs, we're going to the digits.

Oh, I know that's not a particularly new complaint. But do you realize how far out of hand the plaguey situation has become?

C.M. Ballard knows. He opened an insurance premium notice the other day, took an incredulous look at the number on it and began counting.

It was composed of 35 digits.

You want to put that into perspective? All right, your Zip Code number is 5 digits and headed upward. When you dial a telephone number, you use 7 digits for local calls and 11 for long distance. That doesn't include your credit card number if you have to give it.

There are—or at least there used to be—8 digits in an Army Serial Number. Same number for Social Security.

But 35 digits?

Good heavens, the population of the entire world is expressed in just 10 digits. You doubt that? The World almanac sets the figure at an estimated 4,414,000,000.

Our entire national debt can be stated in 12 digits, leaving out the odd pennies.

Even the credit card in my wallet has only 16 digits, for Pete's sake.

But there Ballard was with a number on his premium notice that began with "34" and was followed by 33 other assorted figures.

"This is higher than I could count," he told me modestly. "So I got help from the dictionary."

And here's how it worked out:

That number on his notice translated into 34 decillion, 110 nonillion, 82 septillion, 256 sextillion, 640 quintillion, 37 quadrillion, 450 trillion, 334 billion, 36 thousand, 682.

("You will notice," Ballard observed, "that I skipped octillion and million, That's because, in each case, there were three zeroes in succession.")

Such numbers weren't practical before computers, of course, and you may well ask what use they are today.

Does the insurance company actually have 34 decillion policies in force?

Let's say it has one policy for every man, woman and child in the world. And let's assume, just to humor the computer, that all those people pay their premiums monthly and that a different number is needed for each monthly payment.

Shucks, you can do that with only 11 digits.

No, what is perfectly clear is that the computers, or their programmers, are deliberately undertaking to make everything so complicated that human beings will become obsolete.

Computers can talk to each other in 35-digit terms without batting a blip. People can't. They have to stop and puzzle things out. They have to insert commas and consult dictionaries and take headache pills. So, out with people; in with computers.

Years ago somebody complained about being nibbled to death by ducks. Ah, for the good old days. Now we're being diddled to death by digital data. Where will it all end?

Take My Money, Please

The ways of high finance are simply beyond the comprehension of mere mortals.

Consider, for example, the case of Mrs. Beverly Nash, who tried in vain recently to open a savings account at two separate banks.

And why couldn't she do it? Well, what it seemed to boil down to was, they didn't trust her enough to take her money.

This story gets a bit complicated in places, but anyone who has been frustrated by a bank lately will surely be able to follow it. First, a bit of background.

Mrs. Nash is in the antiques business. Her husband is a dentist. Mrs. Nash used to work in one of Memphis' largest banks—call it Bank A. The Nashes have been doing business with that bank for 32 years. They have two current loans there plus a safe deposit box and two credit-card accounts.

The other day, after considering all the appeals from banks for persons to open savings accounts, Mrs. Nash decided to open one in Bank B, another of the city's largest. She already has a checking account in Bank C, but she didn't want to get her accounts confused.

All right, you got that? Now, let us proceed.

On the day in question, Mrs. Nash visited Bank B with three checks, totaling about $100. It was around noon, and she waited in a long line to get to the window, where she handed over the checks and said she wanted to open a savings account.

In that case, the teller said, she would have to see one of the vice presidents at one of the desks.

So she got in another line and waited. More than half an hour passed. Then her time came at last. She repeated her statement—that she wanted to open a savings account.

"What do you have to deposit?" the banker asked.

Mrs. Nash displayed her three checks.

The banker looked shocked. "We don't accept checks to open savings accounts."

Mrs. Nash blinked. "Look," she said, "I understand that you have to be careful about checks, but I want to open an account, and I'll be putting money in it on a weekly basis, and I have to start somewhere. Couldn't you take these checks and clear them before you open my account?"

"No," said the banker, "We can't."

"Then, how do I open the account?"

"Well, two of these checks are on Bank A, so you'll have to go there and cash them. The third is on our bank, so when you come back with the money, we'll cash it if you have the proper identification—and after we check to see that there's enough money in that person's account to cover it."

Mrs. Nash said oh, all right, or words to that effect, and went out and got into her car and drove to Bank A and went in.

Again she waited in a teller's line, and again they directed her to a vice president.

By this time she had decided that, since she had made the trip, she might as well open her savings acount in Bank A—the one, you'll recall, where she and her husband have a safe deposit box, two loans and two credit-card accounts.

"We don't accept checks to open savings accounts," said the vice presdient, who finally waited on her.

"But two of these checks are on your bank."

"Sorry. You'll have to cash all the checks first and then bring me the money."

"But don't you see, I don't want any money. I'll give you the endorsed checks, and you can clear them, and then you can open the account."

"It doesn't work that way." And the banker turned to the next would-be customer.

So she gave up in dismay, left the bank and returned to her car.

Then she had an idea.

Two of her three checks were written on Bank A, and the drive-in windows of the bank were open.

Well, by golly, she told herself, she would just go cash those checks and decide what to do next.

So she drove to the window and the little tube came out and she put the two endorsed checks in it.

The teller spoke over the speaking system.

"What kind of identification do you have?"

At this point, Mrs. Nash was beginning to feel sort of put-upon, even though she understood that identification was needed. She decided to do it up brown.

"I said, 'Mastercharge on your bank, Visa on your bank, a driver's license and 17 credit cards,' " she told me. "I sent them all in the tube to the teller.

"She looked at all of them and said that wasn't enough."

By this time, Mrs. Nash said, she had reached "a state of shock and disbelief." Instead of submitting meekly as she had done on the two previous occasions, she demanded that something be done.

The cashier said all right, she would call the manager.

The manager advised her to get out of line and go indoors while they called the check-writers to verify the checks.

Mrs. Nash refused to budge.

So she sat there while they called the writer of the first check, who was at home and asleep. Having been awakened, she said yes, of course she wrote the check.

The writer of the second check was not at home. Mrs. Nash suggested they call her place of business. They called, but she was out.

"Luckily," Mrs. Nash told me, "the people at her place of business knew me and vouched for her check. I got my money."

So the cashier sent the cash out in the tube, along with the Mastercharge card, the Visa card, the driver's license and the 17 other credit cards.

"And I'm afraid when she sent them back I did a nasty thing,"
Mrs. Nash confessed. "I told her I couldn't leave until I checked to
see if they were all there, because if she thought I was dishonest,
then I must assume she might be also."

So she sat right there in line and checked out all the cards, and
finally drove away.

And the savings account she had planned to open?

"I decided," she told me, "to put the money under the mattress."

Ma Bell Has Got Our Number

When you're just out of the hospital and have moved, alone, to a new
city, it is a great comfort to have a telephone and feel that faraway
loved ones can reach you within minutes.

But it's not such a great comfort, Mrs. A. told me, to have a
telehone and discover that those loved ones can't reach you because
the phone company never heard of you.

And it is even less comfort, she added, to call the company on your
own phone and be told, in effect, that you don't exist.

A mixup as splendid as this one needs amplification. Let's try.

Our Mrs. A arrived here recently from another city, found a place
to live, had a phone installed and began work at a new job.

She was especially glad about the phone because her nearest and
dearest relatives were to call her after she got settled. They didn't
have her address and she couldn't reach them because they were
traveling.

But now, she felt, there would be no problem. Hah.

One afternoon last week her new employers told her they needed
her telephone number for their records before she could get her first
paycheck. And would you believe she had forgotten it? Of course you
would.

No matter; she would just call Directory Assistance and get it.

So she called on the office phone. Sorry, said Directory Assistance,
they had no listing in her name.

She called again. Same answer. If she really did have a phone, a
voice suggested, perhaps she had a private listing. No, no, said Mrs.
A. She knew how it was listed because she had done the listing.
Sorry, said the voice.

She got a number to call New Listings, but New Listings was busy.

On her next try she was advised to call her Service Representative, and eagerly checked the book to see how you do that.

To call your Service Representative, you have to know the first 4 digits of your own number.

A sympathetic soul listening to all this suggested that she call the Service Representative of the number she was using. She tried that.

A long and unproductive conversation followed. At last the Service Representative put her in touch with a Mr. X, who said he would look into the matter and call her back. Just to be sure, Mrs. A wrote down Mr. X's name.

A long wait followed. No call from Mr. X.

Her own office was being closed and Mrs. A was frantic. She would need that first paycheck. But perhaps, if she reported her number early the next morning, that problem could be solved?

Perhaps.

She hastened home, read the number on her phone, and called her Service Representative to disuss the listing problem.

The Service Representative couldn't discuss the matter with her because, according to the records, she didn't have a phone listed.

Mrs. A remembered about Mr. X and asked to speak to him. The Service Representative put her on hold and returned with the message that there was no Mr. X working for the phone company.

By now, Mrs. A told me, she was beginning to wonder whether she herself existed, let alone Mr. X. But she perservered. Could she speak to a supervisor?

She got one, told her whole story and was put on hold. At last the supervisor came back with a hearty reassurance: "You are listed, Mrs. B."

Actually, the listing was fairly close to her own name, but different enough to have caused all that trouble. So Mrs. A got it corrected.

But Mr. X appears to have been lost forever. And when I last talked to Mrs. A, she was trying to figure out how to explain all that in three minutes when her worried relatives finally reached her and asked what happened.

Who's Driving That Stolen Car?

Modern police technology is a wonderful thing. In less time than it takes to write a traffic ticket, officers on the scene can check with the computer to determine whether the car has been stolen.

Right? Not in a pig's eye, says Mrs. Mary Ray.

Her own bitter experience began shortly after her husband was stopped last Monday for not having a current inspection sticker. Here, she told me, is what happened after that.

The policemen who stopped him made the routine call to check the car's ownership against the license tag. The reply indicated Ray was driving a car that belonged to somebody else.

To avoid confusion, let's call that somebody else Joe Smith.

Not so, said Ray. The car didn't belong to Joe Smith, it belonged to the Rays.

The officers were reasonable. They noted that Joe Smith's address on their computer report was the same as Ray's address on his driver's license. All right, they said, perhaps there had been a mistake. Better get it straightened out.

So on Tuesday Mrs. Ray called the police department to get it straightened out. They told her she would have to call the country clerk's office.

So she called the county court clerk's office. They said she would have to call the police department.

Mrs. Ray brooded over the matter. On Wednesday she went to the clerk's office, where a woman checked the county computer. It said the car belonged to the Rays.

At that point Mrs. Ray decided the county computer doesn't talk to the city computer.

But what, she asked, should she do? Don't bother, said the woman. If trouble arose, just ask the police to call the county court clerk's office.

Fine. But what if the clerk's office happened to be closed at the time? Mrs. Ray decided to try to get the city computer on the right track.

She went to police headquarters, where various persons told her they didn't know what to do about something like that. At last someone in the traffic violations office said she should return to the county court clerk's office.

She did. No luck. So she went next to Police Director Buddy Chapman's office.

A man there called the county court clerk's office and got a number to call in Nashville. There were conversations back and forth with Nashville, and finally the man in Chapman's office hung up and told her not to worry. She would be hearing from the man in Nashville. He would set matters straight.

As of Friday she still hadn't heard from the man in Nashville. Presumably she and her husband were still driving a car that, according to police records, belonged to Joe Smith.

That in itself leaves Mrs. Ray somewhat uneasy. But there's another little matter as well.

While she was doing all that wandering around, trying to get the ownership matter straight, it occurred to her that they own another car. Might it be a good idea to see who the police records show as owner of it?

She did.

Nope, not the Rays. Nope, not Joe Smith. The second car, according to police records, belongs to somebody else entirely. Fellow named Mc-Something.

Let Them Eat Machines

The lady had the look of a crusader. Not the professional sort, but one of your home-grown, driven-past-the-breaking-point, finally-ready-to-go-out-and-do-battle zealots.

"Banks," she told me, "have just got to quit expecting people to talk like computers."

I asked what she meant by talking like computers.

"I don't know. Beep, beep, poop, blop, yi, gork, zag. Like that."

But what had started all this? Why the fire in those lovely eyes, the tension in those delicate knuckles?

She told me.

"You ever get a new checkbook in the mail?"

I said yes, now and then.

"Then you may have noticed. There's a printed sheet in there saying to be sure and check the account number on the bottom of the new checks with the number on your old checks. And if they aren't the same, call the bank."

"And?"

"Who can read computer numbers? I studied and studied all those marks, and finally I decided they were different."

"So you called the bank."

"Did I ever. Just as sweet and innocent as anything. Bewildered but eager to cooperate. You know."

"And what happened then?"

"Well, this nice lady told me to read off the new numbers to her, if I didn't mind, and I said I'd try.

"And I tried, really I did, but after a letter or so and maybe a figure I ran into computer marks. Nobody but R2D2—you remember the little robot in the movies?—could have read those marks. Dot, dah, creek, ooh, whoosh, blop."

I said, oh, come now, surely she could do better than that. She glared at me triumphantly and took out a blank check.

"Try it for yourself. The best I can make of it, it reads: Exclamation mark without dot, square semicolon, 2 legible digits and half of another one, 3 apostrophes, the middle one heavier than the others— like dot DOOTT dot—and finally three zeroes, an 8, a lot of repetitions, a quotation mark and a square period."

I looked at the check. By golly, she had it right on the nose.

"Go on, go on," I urged. "What happened next?"

"Oh, that's all. I just wanted to tell you about it. Somebody ought to do something. Maybe they can start teaching computer symbols in schools as a foreign language, but what about all us adults? How do they expect us to get the hang of it?"

"I agree. But what happened next with the lady at the bank?"

She put her check away.

"After I got through all that agony she said, 'Honey, just read me the last 4 numbers.' "

I keep warning everybody, but they won't listen. One of these days those machines and the people who preside over them will touch off a revolution the likes of which would make George Washington shiver in his grave.

Was There Life Before Cards?

The day is fast approaching when, unless you have the right cards in your wallet or purse, you will cease to exist.

Don't say I haven't been warning you all these years. Without evidence to the contrary, you won't be a person at all. Only an illusion.

Remember all our little sessions about how many different proofs you must offer to cash a check? Remember the reports on the increasing suspicion and hostility that greet people who try to use cash instead of proving who they are?

And remember the case of the mother who couldn't get her son's Social Security card replaced by showing his birth certificate? That document, it developed, proved his age but not his existence. Something else—a library card, for example—was required by the government for existence.

Ah, yes, and then there was the mother who couldn't get a Social Security card for her son even though she had both his birth certificate and his library card. The card has to be signed, it turned out, and at her library they don't use signed cards.

Now yet another complication has been added to the whole problem, at least in the case of Mrs. C.K. Fisher.

Her trouble wasn't with the government, but with the library. And by now you can see how closely these things fit together.

When she moved last May, she told me, she wanted her new address on her library card. So she went to get it changed.

"But the only way they would make the change for me," she said, "was for me to produce something that had been mailed to me at the new address."

Where there's a will, though, there's a way. Mrs. Fisher discovered that her creditors readily changed her address at her request.

So you can see how it might all work out in a theoretical case.

Let us say you move, and in the course of the move you lose your Social Security card.

The first thing you should do is call somebody you owe money, announce your new address, and ask for a bill.

When it arrives, you are ready to go to the library.There, with a copy of the bill from your creditor and the envelope in which it was mailed, you should be able to get your library card corrected, And, even if it's in a system where your signature is not required, perhaps they will allow you to sign it.

Now! You are ready for the Social Security office. Getting a new card should be a breeze. Your birth certificate will provide proof of age, and your corrected library card will provide proof of identity.

It sounds foolproof, but there is just one weakness. Whatever you do, don't lose your birth certificate, your library card and your Social Security card at the same time. You may never be heard from again.

After this sort of confusion brought on by rising populations, computerization and questionnaires intended to cover all contingencies, Mrs. Tom Craig's experience sounds almost routine.

What happened was, she became the mother of a bouncing baby boy last December, and in time the medical and hospital claims reached the attention of her group insurance company.

And later, the company sent a note.

It was rejecting the claim, it said, until the claimant provided answers to the following questions.

Two of the first three questions were especially intriguing to Mrs. Craig:

Was this a work-related accident?

Was anyone else involved?

Way Back When

Hot Times in the Good Old Days

ONE OF THE more fatuous notions about the so-called good old days is that people then were basically stronger and more adept at coping with problems than they are today.

I bow to no one in my affection for old times, but that idea is pure malarky.

Still, the legend flourishes, and few even question it.

Some do. Only the other day, a young fellow commented to me that he was always hearing how well people got along without air conditioning in the old days.

"How did they manage to keep cool?" he asked.

I was able to answer in two words. They didn't.

Oh, sure, they somehow lived through the long hot summers—those who didn't fall by the wayside, that is. There wasn't any choice. But you've heard that talk of how nobody ever even thought about the heat before we were all spoiled by refrigeration?

Baloney. Absolute baloney.

People thought about the heat, they talked about the heat, they suffered from the heat.

And most of all, they sweated. I mean real sweat, buckets of it, none of this slight discoloration that people worry so much about in television commercials.

(In those times, of course, prim persons deplored the word. The rule was that animals sweated, gentlemen perspired, and ladies glowed. If you want to call that coping with the heat, go ahead.)

Maybe some of the houses were built to withstand heat a little better than some of today's houses, though I doubt that there was enough of that sort of thing to affect most people.

And we did have fans. Fans were great for moving the heat about and even for providing a breeze that might dry off some of the sweat, but don't let anybody tell you they took the place of air conditioning.

Attic fans or variations thereof were fine things, too, especially at night—but not if you suffered from allergies. People suffered a lot more from allergies in the good old days.

If you worked a night shift and had to try to rest by day, life was really tough. You'd toss and turn on a bed so damp with your own perspiration that you couldn't find a dry place to lay your head.

But it was bad enough if you worked in the daytime, even in an office. Giant fans would blow everything off your desk. Perspiration would run down your arms, wilt your color, even drip from your eyebrows. Lay a bare arm on a desk covered with papers, and the papers would stick to your arm.

And you know all that sentimental twaddle about how people were more neighborly in the old days, how they sat out on the front porch and visited?

Well, sure they did. It was too plaguey hot in the house to stay indoors, that's why. You sat out in the dark and fought mosquitoes in hopes of being able to draw a comfortable breath.

Automobile trips were yet another form of good-old-days torture. The sun beat down, the dust poured in from the gravel roads, the sweat ran down the back of the seats, and your clothes stuck to the upholstery. Call that coping?

Of course, people did the best they could with the situation, just as they do today, and now and then a cool breeze would spring up and life would seem wonderful.

But mostly it was just a case of wringing out your handkerchief, wiping your face off again and trying to forget the misery. There were plenty of good old days back then, but there were plenty of hot old days, too. And people didn't cope, they merely endured. Don't let anybody try to tell you different.

How Do You Spell Relief?

If I ever get bit by a snake or a mad dog, I sure hope somebody nearby has a mad stone.

A mad stone, in case you don't know, is a remarkable object, usually said to have been taken from the stomach of a deer, that reportedly will stick to the bitten spot if it's poisonous, and suck out the poison. Mrs. Mary Alice Wofford of Sunflower, Miss., has passed along a remarkable turn-of-the-century memoir that's too fascinating to hold.

Her mother, who is 88 years old, grew up in Choctaw County, Miss., and still remembers the day in about 1902 or 1903 when Cousin Charlie McCafferty's mad stone was used on an uncle's snakebite.

Mrs. Wofford took down her mother's recollections just as she told them to her the other day, and passed them along to me.

Forget about property taxes and gasoline prices and Social Security for a moment and consider this vivid drama from the past.

"I was over at grandmaw's house and my Uncle Bud and Uncle Ceph, lads of about 15 or 16, went seining in the Little By-Wy, which ran through the back of grandpaw's pasture. They were barefoot and a water moccasin bit Uncle Ceph on the bottom of his foot.

"Uncle Bud grabbed Uncle Ceph up in his arms and came totin' him back to the house.

"When grandmaw saw Uncle Ceph's foot, which was all red and swelling fast, she put Uncle Bud astraddle of a barebacked horse and sent him galloping to Cousin Charlie's for the mad stone.

"I remember Grandmaw put a black iron skillet over an open fireplace in the kitchen, filled it with water, but I don't know if she let the water boil or not . . ."

(At about this point, though the narrative doesn't say so, it may be assumed that the mad stone arrived and was dropped into the skillet of water.)

"After awhile she took out the wet mad stone and put it to the fang marks and the stone seemed to sort of suck to Uncle Ceph's foot. Like a leech.

"After awhile, as I watched, it just dropped off.

"Grandmaw put the stone back in the skillet of water and the water turned green as grass. 'Drawing the poison,' she said.

"Then she put the stone back to the bite and again, after awhile, it dropped off and she soaked it again.

"I don't know how long she kept this up. Soaking and draining.

"But finally the swelling was gone and the madstone wouldn't fasten itself to the foot any more.

"Then grandmaw cried and said, 'Thank you God! My boy is going to live.'"

They may not have had penicillin back in those days, but they had their own versions of miracle drugs, all the same. Relief, as you might say, was just a madstone away.

Snipes and Stripes and Wrenches

There were a lot of useless tools in the good old days, but perhaps the most useless of all was the left-handed monkey wrench.

I had forgotten all about it until Mack Stanley brought up the subject the other day.

I suppose that, in today's world, nobody even knows what a left-handed monkey wrench is. Well, that's not surprising. There's no such thing.

But a generation ago, innocent oafs all over the country were constantly being sent for such tools by their sly and chuckling elders.

"The whole town was in on this one," Stanley recalled.

"First, someone sent you up to the Ford garage to borrow the tool.

"When you got there, they said the drug store had borrowed it.

"Old Doc Crawford at the drug store allowed that it was at Dick Cox's little chicken and egg place 'way round on a side street.

"Of course, Dick told you it was back up at the city clerk's office.

"It took some young clucks two hours to catch on."

As for himself, Stanley told me, he was too sophisticated to fall for the gag.

He was so proud of himself at the time that, when somebody sent him for a pair of upside-down pinking shears, he set right off without a question.

But the real thigh-slapper in those sneaky days was the snipe hunt.

My daddy warned me about it, so I never was suckered myself. But I did take part once in a snipe hunt arranged for somebody else's benefit.

By now, the details of the thing are sort of faint. But the general outline is clear enough. A whole gang of kids—or adults—began talking up the plans for a snipe hunt, and somebody was sure to ask innocently what a snipe was.

Explanations varied, I'm sure, but the general idea was that the snipe was a creature that was good to eat but hard to catch, and everybody had to work hard on the job.

As it turned out, the innocent victim was taken out into the middle of the woods and left with a flashlight and instructions to stay put, flashing the light, until the others drove the snipe to his spot. The others would be out beating the bushes to head it in that direction. At least that's the way I remember it.

What happened, of course, was that the poor slob was taken out there and left, while everybody else went back to town and whooped it up about what a great joke they had played.

Sooner or later the victim would show up, wondering what had happened to everybody. Wow, talk about fun.

While I escaped that pitfall, I do have a faint memory of being sent to the pressroom of the first newspaper I worked at, with an assignment to ask for some striped ink.

When an editor with a mean tone in his voice—if that's not redundant—yells at you to do a thing like that, on the double, you do it first and wonder why later. No wonder reporters used to be considered bitter and cynical.

Well, we've come a long way since those unenlightened days.

There's nothing very funny about such stunts, after all, when you stop to think about them. Surely nobody sends trusting souls on fools' errands any more.

Or, come to think about it, do they?

Remember When?

Recent talk about various noble pursuits of a past generation of kids set Don Morris to reminiscing.

Remember back when you made your own scooter or wagon and decorated it with bottle-cap reflectors? Remember marbles and mumblepeg and Red Rover?

Well, yeah, sure.

Then he hit on a real memory winner.

"Remember when Cokes were a mere 5 cents?" Morris asked.

"Dad always took us driving each evening after supper, and he always stopped at our favorite store where we each got a Coke and a jawbreaker.

"There were four of us children. We would always have a contest to see which one of us could make his Coke last the longest.

"The same three of us would always lose to my kid brother, who would sit there and sip his so blamed slow we couldn't stand the suspense, let alone the pressure.

"To top this off, he would make us watch him sipping till the trip was over, gloating over the fact he had won."

With me and my brother it was hot chocolate at breakfast on cold mornings.

We would sit there eyeing each other, smelling that luscious aroma and dawdling till the chocolate skimmed over and our parents lost their patience.

"Hurry up. You'll be late for school."

So each one of us would obediently take the smallest possible swallow and try to make the oatmeal last a little longer as a cover-up.

It was on one such morning that I learned—or to be precise, was invited to learn—a great truth about life. That was when I was maybe 7 years old, and the memory has come back to haunt me many a time. Why didn't I learn?

The skim had formed on both our cups like dirty ice on a pond in winter, and our father was looking at his watch impatiently.

My brother checked the chocolate level in my cup and dawdled with his napkin.

I checked the level in his cup and fiddled with my spoon.

And my father reached into his pocket, got out a nickel and laid it on the table.

"All right," he said, his voice edged with exasperation. "Let's see which one of you can finish first."

No bass ever leapt for a lure with more enthusiasm. I had grabbed up that cup, thrown back my head and tossed off the remaining chocolate before the echoes of the coin striking the table had died away.

My brother hadn't budged.

It was a moment of glory. He was two years older, but I had won out. I turned expectantly to my father.

"Well, now," he said, putting the nickel back in his pocket, "that's the way to do it."

And that, in effect, was the end of it. I had to sit there and watch my brother gloating over his final sips of chocolate while my father explained reasonably that he hadn't promised to give anybody the nickel, he had merely expressed an interest in seeing who finished first.

It was small thing, but it was an early signal of the way our lives would go. My brother hadn't been slow on the uptake; he just had an instinctive distrust of any promise that wasn't spelled out, preferably in writing. He grew up to be a lawyer, of course. And the gullible kid brother grew up to be a newspaper reporter.

I can't blame my father for that. He tried to show me the ways of the world. But at least I can sympathize with Don Morris about his smart-aleck brother. No matter what you read in fairy stories, it's always the crafty ones who win in the end.

A Knight in Distress

We are always hearing tales about how, in times past, knights rescued damsels in distress.

This is the story of how damsels rescued a knight in distress, and left him marked for life. If you cannot endure raw agony, stop here.

But if you stay until the bitter end, and if the drama recalls an incident that scalded your own psyche forever, feel free to share it. Sometimes, talking about such things helps.

I learned about the tragedy during the course of an informal lunch, where the talk had somehow turned to the tortures endured by youngsters who are called upon to perform on stages before audiences of their peers.

One fellow had told, brokenly, of the night he appeared on a high school stage with his saxophone and an accompanist, to deliver a solo entitled "I Love a Little Cottage." All went well, he said, until he had made his way successfully through the final repeat. Then he discovered he couldn't remember how to stop.

He tootled through that repeat half a dozen times and then, in mid-note, stopped and walked off the stage, his musical career wrecked forever. Today he can scarcely endure the sight of a saxophone.

In the silence that followed, a hollow voice sounded.

"Once," it said, "I was a knight in King Arthur's court . . ."

At the time, the speaker said, he was a lad of perhaps 11 years. His school had decided to produce a play about the Knights of the Round Table, and he had been chosen to be one of the knights. To this day, thanks to the gentle memory blocks that make our sufferings tolerable, he cannot remember the name of the play or even the knight he was to represent.

But at the time, he was filled with excitement. It was to be his first appearance on the stage—and furthermore, he was to construct his own costume.

He lived in a ranch-style house (the significance of that will appear later) and for weeks the house echoed with his preparations.

All by himself, he constructed a suit of cardboard armor, painted it silver, and built a splendid shield to go with it.

"My family was proud of me," he said softly. "it was a beautiful job. I put it on and marched about for them. I could hardly wait."

The night came. The family piled into the car, along with the suit of armor, and drove off to the school.

Our hero entered, went to a designated classroom, garbed himself in shining armor, and prepared to go on stage.

There's another memory block here. He is not sure now whether the auditorium was the gymnasium; it may have been. At any rate, the stage was at one end of the room, and could be reached only from the front.

He had known that all along, of course. Undaunted, even proud, he entered from the rear of the crowded auditorium and strode down the aisle toward the stage. Mercifully, he can't remember whether his visor was up or down.

But his armor gleamed and glittered in the lights, and the unicorn on his shield flashed in the envious eyes of his schoolmates. This was glory.

Down the aisle he marched, turning as he approached the stage, waving his shield gracefully as he reached the steps that led up to it.

The steps that led up to it.

Aye, there's the rub.

"I hadn't thought about the steps," he confessed. "I had built that whole suit of armor without thinking about steps. There was simply no way I could walk up the steps in my armor."

So there he stood, while the admiring murmurs turned to silence and the silence turned, ever so slowly, into raucous laughter. And he was still there when two teachers approached, gently picked him up between them, carried him onto the stage, and set him down where he was supposed to stand.

"After that I don't remember anything." he said, "except that I never moved and I never was able to speak a line. The other actors had to get along without me. The teachers had carried me up! I just stood there."

Later, he was bundled up and taken home. And in time he even learned to face his schoolmates again.

But his acting days were over. He grew up to be an economist. Who knows what secrets lurk in the hearts of men?

Warning: Corn Silk Bad For Your Health

As you have no doubt surmised from recent news, something drastic may have to be done about the great corn crops in this country. But first, a word to you old geezers who sneaked out behind the barn 30, 40 or 50 years ago and smoked cigarets made of corn silk.

Aha!

Thought you got away with it, didn't you?

Well, you didn't. At last your sins have caught up with you. The Food and Drug Administration has determined that corn silk may be dangerous to your health.

You doubt it? Then ask yourself this: Do you feel as healthy and vigorous now as you did then?

Those things take time. No doubt the evil fumes are working away inside you right this minute. If you're not sorry already, you will be in another 30 or 40 years.

The big picture, of course, is even more unsettling. If corn silk may be dangerous to your health—either in cigarets or, as it turns out, as a food additive—then emphatic action is indicated.

One step would be to recall all corn now on the market in order to remove any silk sticking out of the ears.

No doubt the corn lobby will protest if that is tried. Instead, the FDA might settle for warning labels, similar to those on cigaret packages, attached to every ear of corn in the nation.

In time, of course, they'll just have to figure out a way to grow corn without silk.

But I can't help feeling viciously triumphant at the thought of all those fellows who smoked corn silk back in the days when I didn't.

We all knew our elders didn't approve of it, and that should have been enough for us. But there are always some people who will go right ahead and do what they know is wrong.

I knew a few corn silk smokers—big, blustering bullies, most of them, who would brag during recess about their exploits and poke fun at others who hadn't followed their lead.

Oh, they must be worried now. As far as I know, the government hasn't set its laboratory rats to smoking corn silk, but that step is bound to come. And somewhere down the road we'll see the results, and they'll be awful. Results with laboratory rats are always awful.

I think it is safe to say that nobody over 50 today who smoked corn silk as a child is entitled to feel safe for the rest of his life. Remember, it can take a long time for those evil effects to show.

But for those of us who didn't indulge, there are no such fears. At last we have come into our own.

And why were we so good and obedient? I don't know about the others, but in my case factors were of supreme importance.

1. My father had a big razor strop and used it freely, even when he wasn't preparing to shave.

2. There wasn't an ear of corn anywhere near where I lived.

So I never smoked corn silk. Cross vine, yes, but it hadn't even occurred to our parents to warn us against smoking cross vine, and there was plenty of that around.

And until the FDA gets around to cross vine, I can feel smug and secure. After all these years, the adage has been proven true again. Virtue, like cross vine, is its own reward.

BVD Must Stand for Something

The wonders of progress never cease. Who of mature years among us could have dreamed we would live to see the day of comic-book underwear for kiddies?

But it's true. Now Dick and Jane may be fitted out in styles of underwear bearing such names as Superman, Shazam, Wonder Woman, Hulk and the like, all appropriately adorned and all offered under a trademark that would make a gopher gulp.

Underoos, they're called. "Underwear that's fun to wear." May the saints preserve us all.

I know the question marks me as hopelessly old and out of date, but I have to ask it anyway. Who ever said underwear should be fun to wear, especially for kids?

There was a time when underwear was just what it said and no more: Something you wore under your other clothes. You didn't think of it in terms of "fun," for heaven's sake. You wore it or you got a good spanking.

Those were the days of BVDs, one-piece affairs that buttoned up the front and could bind and pinch like crazy as you grew larger. I never knew what BVD stood for—the schoolyard wisdom was that it meant Born Very Dumb—but even then, I suddenly realize, the slogan-writers were busy at their trade.

"Next to myself, I like BVDs best," the character in the advertisements said. Well, that was bad enough, but even he didn't come right out and claim the things were fun.

As for fancy designs or illustration on them, nobody would have dreamed of such a thing. They were cloth; that was all that mattered for underwear. Shazam Underoos? A kid would have been laughed off the playground.

Winter was another matter, of course. We wore long-handles, similar to BVDs in that they were one-piece deals and they, too, buttoned up the front.

There were only two kinds, too large and too small. When you first got them, still stiff and smelling department-storish, they were so tight you could hardly bend over. No wonder discipline was easier to maintain in schoolrooms in those days. A roomful of boys wearing long-handles is not likely to be a group trouble spot. Everybody is too busy scratching.

But as the garments grew older and lost their shape, the problem changed. Those tight cuffs at the ankles began to sag. You had to bunch them up to pull your stockings (that's right, black-ribbed stockings) up around them, and then they would come unbunched and pooch out. And they showed through your shirt at the wrists.

As spring approached and you shifted from stockings to socks and begged for a return to BVDs, the gathering of the long-handles under the sock-tops became more and more precarious. Socks just couldn't hold the plaguey things in place.

But while there may have been many complaints related to our underwear, none of us ever dreamed of questioning the institution itself. Man was made to wear underwear, and to suffer. We all knew that. Fun to wear? Ridiculous. Cute pictures and designs? Unthinkable.

I do not believe in torture for its own sake, mind you. If underwear can be made less uncomfortable, fine. And that has been accomplished, at least to a degree. But how are children ever to be taught what a really hard, cruel, rotten world this is if they're conned into believing that wearing underwear is fun?

This is, of course, a minority report. Nothing must be allowed to stand in the way of progress. But even progress can go too far, and I think it is time for us older citizens to make one thing perfectly clear.

If some firm, spurred equally by the success of Underoos and Billy Beer, decides to try the whole thing on adults, some of us will rise up and rebel. By dingies, I will submit to a heap of modern-day indignities, but durned if I'll ever willingly wear a pair of Billy Briefs.

Kids Like Frenzied Sharks

Back in the good old days, kids behaved themselves in school and never got into trouble, right? None of the disorder and senseless misbehavior you find today. By George, teachers enforced discipline in those days.

It's a lovely thought. It almost seems a shame to spoil it.

But just so we don't get too plaguey insufferable about the old days, let us look back to a scene in a Memphis school one spring day just over 40 years ago.

I got this report from Mrs. Lou Young, who got it directly from one of the participants. It might be worth noting that the culprit in question grew up to be, as far as I know, a reasonably respectable member of Memphis society. At least he's a professional man, if that proves anything.

He was in the 10th grade at the time, Mrs. Young told me. Just down the street from the school was a mom-and-pop candy store where the kids went every morning before school to squander their lunch money on candy.

"One of the favorite confections," she said, "was a round, hollow sugar ball, filled with flavored sugar syrup."

Nonviolent innocence out of the past, huh? Yeah.

"On the day in question, the students were suffering through a compulsory study hall, overseen by an elderly teacher.

"She was drowsing over a book at her desk. It was a glorious warm, sunny day. Silence reigned over all, which is an intolerable situation for the young."

So after a while one of the boys decided he had had all he could stand. He reached into his bag of goodies, pulled out a candy ball, and lobbed it across the room at a friend.

"His friend got out his own treasure sack and replied in kind. Unfortunately, he missed his target and the candy hit the wall, shattering and then dripping its liquid sugar syrup down the wall."

And that shocked all the well-disciplined kids into frightened silence, right?

Wrong. All over the room, students looked at the mess, tasted blood (or the sugar-syrup equivalent thereof), reached into their own candy sacks, and followed suit.

"The teacher dozed on, blissfully unaware of what was taking place. Candy balls filled the air, hitting the walls, ceiling, floor, desks, students, dripping the sticky syrup over all."

As our young outlaw, now a dentist, put it when he recalled the scene for Mrs. Young: "They were like sharks in a feeding frenzy. Just went insane."

The girls in the room began to scream as the goo covered their hair, clothes and faces. The teacher awoke to pandemonium, took one look around, and fled for the principal.

"When he got to the room and surveyed the wreckage, he was speechless. By this time the combantants had run out of ammunition, and slowly began to realize the enormity of what they had done."

The first verdict of authority was that the entire class would be expelled. Happily, this was modified.

"Instead, the boys spent the next three weeks after school washing down the entire room, from top to bottom, to remove the now-hardened sugar syrup. Then they re-painted every inch of it."

And the teacher who had dozed through the moments before the frenzy broke out retired at the end of the year. Well, maybe she had planned to anyhow.

The whole episode is, of course, a deplorable blot on the proud history of Memphis, though it is still remembered warmly by some of the rascals involved. But it possibly might serve as some slight consolation to today's teachers. Some of the members of that very class, no doubt, are among those who wonder most vocally why discipline isn't what it was when they were kids.

How To Score Big at Mumble Peg

Now that we've had an advance taste of spring, small boys all over the country must be getting in condition for their first games of mumble peg.

Yeah, sure. Especially if they're in their declining years and have long, long memories.

I had forgotten all about mumble peg, also known as mumblety-peg or mumble-de-peg, until Frank Coyle brought it up. He said he'd never seen a girl play mumble peg.

Shucks, I haven't seen a boy play it either in more than a generation. But back in the days when pocket knives were used primarily for pleasure rather than mayhem, mumble peg was a top sport on all the best playgrounds.

My recollection of the rules is hazy by now, as is that of various grizzled veterans of the game I have consulted. But basically, the idea was this.

You got a small peg, maybe a little bigger around than a pencil and only a few inches long, with a sharpened end. Then you drove it a little way into the ground, and play began.

The object was to toss or flip your pocket knife in various ways so the blade—or blades—would stick in the ground.

Sometimes you opened the long blade out straight and the short blade at a 90-degree angle, balanced the tip of the short blade on the ground, and flipped the handle upward with your finger. If the knife landed with either blade stuck in the ground and none of the handle touching, you were a winner.

There were as many variations as imagination provided.

One oldtimer recalls flipping his knife off each finger and thumb in succession. Whenever it fell flat, you lost your turn and had to start over. When it stuck up 10 times in a row, you won.

Another veteran remembers the cross-arms caper. You put your left hand on your right shoulder, thrust your right hand between your body and your left arm, and flipped the knife.

Others remember flipping from the knee, or the ear, or from flat on the palm with an inside loop.

And the peg was the penalty device.

Every time your knife stuck in the ground, if I'm right, you got one blow on the peg with your knife handle. Down, down went the peg as the experts did their tricks.

Then somebody's knife would land flat and it was penalty time. The loser had to put his face down to the ground, get the end of the peg between his teeth, and pull it out. Hence, "mumble," which means among other things to chew or bite as if with toothless gums.

Many's the mumblin' mouthful of dirt we losers consumed.

It doesn't have anything to do with the energy crisis or the latest act of terrorism, but it does seem worth recording.

Knives were used for more sinister purposes in those days too, mind you. But not always. It's good to remember that, once upon a time, losing a contest with a knife could mean no more than a mouthful of dirt. And they do say history repeats itself. We can only hope.

Mule Ride to Gunnison

I tell you, little kids were great mule riders in Mississippi in the good old days.

Remember the recent account of a lad who spent a summer trying to ride a mule from Ruleville to Drew? He never made it, because the mule always balked at a spot where a cotton gin's blowpipe crossed the road. But he did a heap of riding.

That reminded Memphis' Max Millstead of the memorable ride he took on a mule named Kate back in the early spring of 1917.

This one should go in the record books. Little Max was 12 at the time, and he rode that mule from Blue Mountain to Gunnison.

How long a trip? Four days and three nights, as Millstead recalls it now. Nobody but him and old Kate. The distance, by his estimate: 120 miles.

It happened because young Max's grandfather moved from Blue Mountain to Gunnison and needed somebody to move Kate for him. The job fell to Max, who lived at Blue Mountain with his mother.

"So one morning," he told me, "my mother fixed me a big lunch and, having no saddle, I put some blankets on Kate and slung a rope over her with loops in each end for stirrups."

The roads were all dirt, and none of them were marked. Max had to ask the way constantly, but people always gave him the right directions. The only unfriendly experience of the trip came just before dark the first day.

"I stopped at a house and asked to stay all night. They asked where I was from, and when I told them, they closed the door, saying I was from flu country." That was the year of the great influenza epidemic, but Blue Mountain was hardly its center. Besides, Max had traveled only about 20 or 25 miles.

Still, he shrugged his shoulders and rode on till he came to a churchyard, where he spread his blankets, ate part of what remained of his lunch, and settled down for the night.

He was wakened by a dog sniffing at his lunch bag and set off on his second day. Within a few hours, it turned cold and began to rain—freezing rain.

Max rode on until about dark, and this time he was in luck. A kind lady at a house where he stopped took him in, had Kate put in the barn and fed, dried Max's clothes in front of a big fireplace and fed him. "I will never forget those biscuits," Millstead told me. His face and hands were swollen from the cold, but fire, friendship and food brought him around in no time.

On the third morning, the rain had quit and the weather was warmer. He lit out again, made good time and spent the night at a logging camp where he was treated well.

"Next day, I pushed old Kate, as I had been doing all along, covering a lot of ground," he said. "I rode from sunup until almost dark, as I had every day. I don't see how Kate went as far every day as she did."

Late in the afternoon, he came to a railroad, saw the Gunnison water tank in the distance, and abandoned the dirt road for the railroad. A little more effort and he had made it: A boy of 12, traveling alone on an elderly mule, with blankets for a saddle and a rope for stirrups, on unmarked dirt roads, across most of the width of Mississippi, in bad weather, during a flu epidemic.

After that, all that remained was to visit with his grandpa a while and return home—without Kate.

Well, sir, that took a bit of doing, too. To make the trip by train, you had to go first to Memphis, then to New Albany and finally to Blue Mountain, via three different railroads. Here's how young Max did it.

"My grandpa gave me enough money, he thought, to buy train tickets back, plus some to eat on.

"In those days you couldn't buy a through ticket over three different railroads. So I bought a ticket to Memphis.

"The Central Station at Memphis was the biggest thing I had ever seen. Three levels. Lower level was the ticket office, second level the main waiting room, third level a smaller waiting room and gate to the trains.

"I went to the third level, as I had to lay over a couple of hours. No one was in this waiting room at this time, so I lay down on the bench. As I almost fell asleep, I decided I had better hold my money in my hand."

At that time, he had all of $5 left for the remainder of the trip.

"I went to sleep and all of a sudden waked up. Not knowing how long I had been asleep, I rushed down to the lower level to buy my ticket to New Albany. When I got to the ticket window I had no money."

So there he was, penniless and scared to death in a big city and imagining all sorts of terrible things that could happen to him.

"This was worse than all that ride with old Kate," he recalled. "I wasn't afraid of the country, just dogs and Memphis."

"I rushed back to the third level, and there was my money in the seat where I had been. The good Lord really took care of me that time.

"I grabbed that money like I was stealing it and went back and bought my ticket. In the meantime all the excitement had made me hungry.

"I bought something to eat and, not knowing how much my ticket would cost from New Albany to Blue Mountain, I spent too much."

So when he got off the train at New Albany, there he was with a problem again: Not enough cash to pay for his ride to Blue Mountain.

But that was no problem for a now-seasoned traveler. It was "only about 10 miles" to Blue Mountain, so he set out walking.

"I walked to Cotton Plant and bought my ticket the last five or six miles," he concluded triumphantly. That boy knew how to come home in style.

All that is more than 60 years in the past now, but Millstead told me he can remember it as if it were yesterday. And indeed, who could forget such an adventure?

And sometimes, thinking back on it, he gets to musing.

"I wonder," he told me, "why kids even 15 and 16 years old have to be led across the street by a policeman."

That may sound unreasonable to some people. But not to anybody who rode a mule from Blue Mountain to Gunnison and then went home the way Max Millstead did.

Age Of Autos

Traffic Violators Alive and Well

THERE'S GOOD NEWS, and there's bad news.

First the bad:

Citizens who fail to pay their traffic tickets in Memphis must continue to live in fear of execution.

Now the good:

The execution won't necessarily be fatal.

I tried to clear up this matter several years ago, but it didn't stick, so let's have a go at it again. Because people keep getting nervous.

There is, for example, the case of James E. Farris, a new resident who got an overtime parking ticket recently.

"For my minor crime of parking two minutes longer than I should have, I received a citation in the amount of $2," he told me.

Well, that was just the beginning. Then he read what was on the ticket under the heading, "TO THE OWNER OF THE ABOVE DE-SCRIBED VEHICLE."

It said if he hadn't paid that $2 within 15 days, a summons would be issued providing for a court appearance.

Furthermore, failure to appear, or conviction, would result in a judgment at least double the amount originally levied, along with $20 court costs.

Then came the grim assertion that set Farris' teeth on edge:

"Execution will follow."

Somewhat nettled by the business, Farris got in touch with me to complain. He understood, he said, that our police commissioner was noted for some very stern ideas about dealing with criminals—but execution for failure to pay a $2 ticket?

He couldn't help wondering what they would do to you if you committed an offense of a more serious nature.

That wording has been on traffic tickets for some years now, and every few months I hear from somebody who feels it might be just a trifle severe to get wasted, as it were, for overparking.

Way back there, I undertook to explain that the execution referred to wasn't really a killing, but a bit of jargon meaning that action would be taken. In fact, as I recall, some young fellow in the city attorney's office confessed at the time that he had put the words in as an exercise in legal levity.

But with new people arriving in town and getting confused

regularly, I called Mrs. Joyce McMackin, City Court clerk, to learn how matters stood and whether any changes were planned.

She is the one who orders new printings when supplies of the tickets run out, and it happened that she was just about to order some more at the time I called.

So what about the execution threat? Would it remain on the form?

Well, she said, it had been there since before her time, but she would do some checking on it.

And had any indignant or fearful citizens ever complained to her about it?

Nobody, she said, except one friend who called her shortly after she took office and asked if the ticket meant she would kill him if he didn't pay up. Since he was a friend, she said yep, that's just what it meant. She wouldn't have said that to a stranger, she assured me.

Later, after she had had time to check the whole matter out, we talked it over again. And the execution bit will stay when the new forms are printed.

She talked to the city attorney's office about it, she said, and also to the administrative judge of City Court, and everybody agreed it was perfectly legitimate. To a lawyer, "execution" in that sense simply refers to a judicial writ empowering an officer to carry out a judgment.

So there you are, fellow motorists. Violate a traffic ordinance and fail to pay up, and you won't be executed—but the court's judgment will. You have to take reassurance where you can find it these days.

Don't Make Me Say 'I Told You So'

Unlike some pious hypocrites, I am always happy to come right out and say, "I told you so."

And it was no surprise whatever to me when the Insurance Institute for Highway Safety estimated this week that right-turn-on-red laws have boosted collisions at intersections by 20 percent a year.

Of course they did. Any fool could have predicted something of the sort before the laws were even passed. I predicted it.

Back there when Memphians first began talking about the idea, I said it was stupid.

You let motorists turn right on red and you're going to have more crashes, I pointed out.

That's roughly equivalent to saying that if you stand in the rain you'll get wet, but it was too deep for some observers.

And what chance, I asked, would that endangered species, the pedestrian, have if cars were allowed to turn right on red lights? Good night, it was almost an impossibility already.

But no. If knocking off a few pedestrians would save a pint or two of gasoline, then the Federal Highway Administration, which seems to have been behind the plan, figured it was worth it. And it estimated the increase in accidents would be "relatively insignificant."

And Tennessee joined in the noble program for gas conservation through greater automotive and pedestrian destruction.

I can't help recalling that, when right-on-red turns were first denounced in this space, certain wisenheimers assured me I was a simple-minded nut.

Wasn't I in favor of saving gas and speeding up traffic? Did I have any proof that cars and people would get smashed as a result of the new plan?

Well, sure I'm in favor of saving gas. The best way to do that is to drive less and at more moderate speeds, not to go around knocking off pedestrians.

As for speeding up traffic, no. I'm not in favor of speeding up traffic. It's fast enough already.

And as for proof the new plan wouldn't work, how are you going to prove that kind of negative except by common sense?

But now the figures from the study are in—and note it's not a government study, but one by an insurance outfit which has a vested interest in accurate traffic-safety figures.

And, according to them, right-on-red laws mean about 20,000 more collisions a year, 1,400 of them involving the poor disappearing pedestrian.

So what did the study recommend? Why, outlawing right turns at red lights, of course. Back to square one.

Whether that good advice will be followed is something else again. A nation obsessesd with what is called getting government off our backs may well decide that it's fed up with all traffic regulations of any kind. Already the enemies of the 55-miles-per-hour speed limit are howling for the right of free men to drive as fast as they jolly well please.

Cry havoc and let loose the dogs of war, or whatever the poet said. In short, let the person behind the wheel decide for himself or herself how and when to open the gates of eternity, regardless of who else might be involved.

So pedestrians who are already too frightened to cross some intersections in Memphis, even when they have the light, should not take too much comfort from this week's report. Nothing at all may come of it.

The only consolation in the whole situation may be that, pretty soon, so few people will be able to afford cars that the problem will solve itself. I hope I never have to say "I told you so" on that too.

Do It Yourself and Save

Ever think how much money you can save by changing the oil in your car all by yourself?

A friend and associate of Jack H. Cosby Jr. got to thinking about that, and moved from thought to action. The results exceeded his wildest expectations.

I got the details from Cosby, who agreed he could probably give a more dispassionate account than his friend, a modest fellow we will call Harold.

Somebody showed Harold how easy it all was, so he got himself a ramp to elevate the front end of his car and bought the necessary oil and a new oil filter.

He ran the front end of the car onto the ramp in his carport, crawled underneath with pan and wrench, unscrewed the oil plug and watched the dirty oil drain into the pan. Beautiful.

Next he began unscrewing the old filter.

It came off easy as pie. Along with it came some hot oil, which landed on Harold. He jerked back, knocking over the pan of dirty oil. It ran all over the carport and driveway.

But such things happen. Harold put the old filter in a plastic garbage sack off to the side and cleaned up the mess. Then he put in the new filter and began pouring in the new oil.

His wife had been admiring his work from a distance. As he finished pouring in the second quart, she spoke.

"Harold, I don't believe all that oil should be running out the bottom like that."

Well, it was simple. Harold had forgotten to replace the oil plug. Those things happen. He cleaned up the mess, replaced the plug, poured in fresh oil. The job was done.

All that remained was to put things away. Harold dumped all the junk in the garbage bag and picked it up.

Everything fell out. The heat of the old filter had eaten a hole in the sack. Oil began spreading on the concrete again.

Harold set the sack in the grass, put all the junk back in it and cleaned up the concrete a second time.

Then he reached for the sack again, forgetting the hole was still in it. This time everything landed on his lawn, the oil forming a dirty slick.

Harold decided to wash it down with gasoline.

When the gas didn't work, he decided to burn it off. He lit a match and tossed it into the grass.

Cosby, who told me the whole story, was eloquent about how high the smoke and flames billowed. House-high, he said. When stomping wouldn't put out the fire, Harold ran for the garden hose, turned it on and came charging back.

And that resulted in the final problem of the day. The hose ran out before Harold did. He sat down very hard.

Still, it all worked out just fine in the end. He got the fire out and cleaned up everything, and now his car has fresh oil and a new filter and nobody was paid to do it. At this point, Cosby said, Harold has only one question.

Anybody want to buy a ramp?

Nozzle Styles Pump SLURP Study

The time has come, Jay Daneman believes, for the Sims Laboratory of Unusual Research Projects (SLURP) to make a study of a neglected area of gasoline consumption.

"With the majority of people now filling their own gas tanks at self-service pumps," he told me, "SLURP should survey the different methods used for pumping gas."

It sounds like an idea whose time has come. And Daneman has started the ball rolling with two classifications of his own.

First there is what he calls the One-Handed Fender-Leaner.

You have no doubt observed this species. Its habitat is usually limited to cars whose tanks open on the side.

The OHFL grasps the pump in one hand (which one, presumably, depends on whether the subject is left-handed or right-handed), inserts the nozzle into the tank, and squeezes, meanwhile leaning on the fender in a casual way. This is what might be called the offhand approach.

The other type observed by Daneman is what he calls the Two-Handed Bumper-Squatter.

In this case, in all probability, the tank opens on the rear of the car. The THBS, clearly an uneasy and anxious sort, grasps the pump tightly in both hands and, with elbows close to sides, squats gradually until pump and tank meet.

One is tempted to speculate that the THBS pumps gas in occasional nervous bursts instead of in a continuous flow, but adequate research has not been done on this point.

In preliminary work of a follow-up nature, SLURP has been able to make tentative identification of a couple of other species.

There is, for example, the Meter-Watching Side-Pumper.

This species is characterized by its awkward stance, occasioned by the fact that, while the hand is busy pumping gas in one direction, the eye is busy following the breathless progress of the cost meter in another. Often the pumping arm is flung across the body as if to protect the owner from the horrible upward progress of the meter.

In at least one case, SLURP was lucky enough to interview a rare specimen, the Alternating Climate-Activated Hand-Protector.

During cold weather, our study indicated, the ACAHP pumps gas with one gloved hand and keeps the other hand in its pocket. During warm weather—the pump itself, as many observers have noted, being cooler than the surrounding air—the ACAHP pumps two-handed in order to cool both hands simultaneously.

Thus far, our studies have not taken us deep enough for adequate reports on such subspecies as the All-Thumbs Cap-Fumbler, the One-Handed Wallet-Clutcher, and the Pump-and-Palaver Extrovert.

Clearly, much work needs to be done on the whole subject. But, with Daneman's help, SLURP believes we are off to a splendid start.

Our only fear is that, just about the time the study is completed, the use of even self-service gas will have become so expensive that cars will be abandoned and all our work will have been for nothing.

Perhaps it is not too early for someone to go to work to save all these relatively new but already endangered species before it is too late.

City Sticker Gums Up Works

As we get deeper into the year, more and more motorists are wrestling with the problem of installing new city stickers on their windshields. It is hoped that the following tips will help you on the job.

Getting your sticker in the first place is, of course, another matter entirely. Let us assume that you have passed this barrier, found a free afternoon, and decided to go out in the driveway and change stickers.

At this point, you would do well to consult our handy checklist of items that will speed up your work.

You will find the following equipment useful:

1 brown bag from the supermarkets.

1 scraper equipped with a razor blade, preferably one less than 15 years old.

1 first aid kit.
1 whisk broom.
1 ball-peen hammer.
1 small anvil or other heavy flat surface.
2 large pairs of pliers.
1 copy of Roget's Thesaurus.

Take your equipment and the new sticker, with all the material attached thereto, to the scene of the coming struggle. Caution: Do not attempt to remove the sticker from the other material inside the house. It may blow away.

Arrange the heavier tools on the hood of the car where you can reach out for them without too much trouble. Don't try to take them all into the car with you. If you do, you'll sit on them or lose them.

Step one: Seize the scraper in your left hand and attack the old sticker, which is affixed to the inside of your windshield on the right side, about where the glass curves in most cars.

Eventually, of course, you will find removal of the old sticker is impossible. But good sportsmanship requires that you make the effort. Give it an honest try; you'll feel better later.

After you have skinned three knuckles, or after the razor blade has broken and cut off the end of your thumb, pause in your work and get out the first aid kit. You are allowed 10 minutes for repairs. During this time, consult Roget for appropriate expletives. End of Step one.

Step two: Consider alternate ways to proceed. Now is the time for persons who have completely blown their tops to reach for the hammer, smash the windshield, and go buy another one. Caution: Be sure to decide before you remove the new sticker from its envelope.

If you can control yourself, put away the hammer and determine to give up on the old sticker, leave the remains, and put the new sticker above them.

Step three: Take out the new sticker and attached material, which you will find all done up in staples and plastic.

This package cannot be penetrated by the unaided human hand. If you doubt it and have the time, break a fingernail trying and then reach for the anvil and the pliers. Using them, you can remove the staples in only a few minutes. Opening the little plastic bag will take longer. Courage! You can do it.

Finally, pull out the new sticker, peel off the transparent cover, affix the sticker to the windshield above the tattered remains of the old sticker, take a deep breath, use the whisk broom to collect the 4,389 bits of paper, old sticker, backing, bent staples and the like from the inside of the car, place all fragments in the brown bag, and retire to your house.

Follow these instructions to the letter and your troubles should be only minimal. Total physical and emotional recovery should take not more than two days. If pain persists, see your doctor.

Chaos Doesn't Always Triumph

Some days don't waste any time, they're bad from the word go. And Mrs. Liz Baker sensed that trouble lay ahead when the whole family overslept.

"With four children to get ready and feed, you can imagine the confusion even an average morning can be," she told me.

But somehow she got them all ready: Sarabeth, who is 9 and goes to a private school, the twins Chris and Rhea Lynn, who are going-on-4, and the baby Mitch.

And then there was the mad scramble into the car—the one her husband never has any trouble with—for the carpool.

They got away from home late.

But they made their two stops and picked up their other little passengers, and all was well until a wail went up as they arrived at school.

The flag was being taken in.

"That means you're late!"

She comforted the young scholars and rushed them out of the car. As they disappeared inside the door she drew a sigh of relief. Then she and Chris and Rhea Lynn and Mitch headed for home. . .

Where an interesting sight awaited her when she opened the front door.

There on the mantel was Sarabeths's little red lunchbox. Forgotten.

So off they went again to the school, Mrs. Baker and Chris and Rhea Lynn and Mitch, and they made the trip without mishap.

On the way back, her three passengers grew mutinous. They demanded doughnuts.

"After the morning we'd just encountered," the long-suffering mother told me, "I thought it would be a treat."

So they stopped at a doughnut shop and piled out, all four of them, and went in for doughnuts.

And that was when Mrs. Baker discovered she had come off without any cash.

And a minute later was when she discovered the woman in the doughnut shop wouldn't take a check.

Not only wouldn't take it, but was pretty blamed outraged just to have been asked.

So back they went to the car on the lot, Mrs. Baker carrying one child and dragging two others, and everybody very cross about the whole thing.

And that was when Mrs. Baker discovered the car—the car that always starts for her husband—wouldn't start.

She tried and tried. And the children did their best by complaining. But nothing worked. So back they went into the doughnut shop to use the phone.

And that was when she discovered the woman in the doughnut shop was even more outraged that anyone would wish to use the shop's phone in an emergency.

"That phone," she snapped, "is to be used only for business."

So chaos always triumphs, right? Wrong. As she stood there desperate and forlorn a low voice said, "Honey, where do you live? Maybe I can help."

And would you believe it, it was a kindly construction worker who had a pickup truck outside, and he took all four of them with him into his cab, and he drove them every foot of the way home, leaving the car behind where Mrs. Baker's husband later started it with no trouble.

And not only that, but the kindly construction worker handed the children a sack just bursting with glazed doughnuts when he let them out, and everything went wonderfully the rest of the day, so you see life is pretty good after all.

But if I were you, I wouldn't count on it. My own surveys show that surly doughnut women outnumber kindly construction workers 100 to 1.

White-Knuckled Seat-Grabber

The occasional vagrant hint of spring in the swirling breezes has set some Memphis husbands thinking of their spouses in terms of our feathered friends.

At least, that is the impression conveyed by a message I have received from a reader who prefers the sly pseudonym of Papa Bird. (After all, it doesn't take a wise old owl to know when to remain anonymous.)

The message is filled with chauvinistic affronts, of course, but I pass it along in the interests of ornithological research.

"Since you seem to have a sincere appreciation of nature's various marvels," my informant begins, "I have a few field reports to throw your way concerning the anguished body-language of my wife, the front-seat back-seat driver.

"You must understand that this good woman never utters a sound while I'm driving, other than the odd stifled scream.

"Her gestures, however, would make a buzzard weep."

From there, our critic goes on to specifics in which it is difficult to imagine some slight hint of resentment is not lacking.

"On some occasions, she closely resembles the white-knuckled seat-grabber . . ."

These are times, I take it, when the odd stifled scream does not suffice and the poor woman opts for upholstered security, seeking comfort from her agony in the rich textures and rounded corners on which she perches. Meanwhile, one can easily imagine Papa Bird leering at her out of the corner of one eye while he appraises his life-and-death chances with the other.

"During narrow squeaks, which admittedly any driver has during a session of Memphis Roulette," our embattled driver continues, "she is the terror-stricken window-holder.

"I think this posture is supposed to restore balance after one of my swerves, but she never enlightens me. Indeed, she doesn't utter a mumblin' word. She merely hangs on, breathing somewhat asthmatically."

But this clearly terrified victim has other bird improvisations up her sleeve, or perhaps under her wing, if the report is to be believed.

"I once glanced casually over her way during a traffic maneuver at which I have achieved consummate skill," my informant continues, "and discovered there a perfect specimen of the female throat-clutcher.

"And after a close race on the expressway one day, during which I just managed to beat out a car that was trying to enter, we both had to pry her shoes out of the floorboard.

"It was one of her finest performances as the wild-eyed brake-stomper."

A question naturally arises. Why, in view of such mute but agile agony, do the couple not reverse places?

Our family critic had an answer for that:

"I would be glad to let the dear woman do the driving, but she hates the way I do the yellow-bellied whooping crane. And that's only when we're parallel parking."

Lady Driver Takes Scenic Route

You never know when danger will strike. Or where, for that matter.

Consider the case of Mrs. Lenoir Black and the others in her golfing foursome at Colonial Country Club.

Mrs. Black remembers the occasion as if it were only yesterday, though actually it was a week and a half ago. The Colonial Ladies Golf Association was having its annual "spring scramble" to initiate the new season, and some 60 women were on the course, dashing around in about 30 golf carts and banging golf balls in all directions.

Well, sir, Mrs. Black's foursome holed out on No. 1 (I think that's the right expression for it) and headed for the No. 2 tee.

And when they topped the hill in their two little carts, you won't believe what they saw.

A big red Buick was whipping around the No. 2 green and heading right at them. Fast.

Thinking back on it later, Mrs. Black marveled at the situation.

"That car would have had to go at least a mile on a 4-foot cart path, winding around lakes and up and down hills and around sharp turns to get there," she told me.

I asked what she and her fellow golfers did when they saw it.

She said what did I think they did? They got their carts off the cart path, quick. A golf cart is no match for a Buick of whatever color in a head-on collision.

So then what happened?

The car roared up to where they stood, or maybe crouched, and came to a halt.

Two little gray-haired ladies were in it, barely visible above the door.

One of them leaned her head out and asked politely:

"How do you get to the expressway?"

It is not every day that somebody in a red Buick pulls up near the No. 2 tee of Colonial or any other golf course and asks directions. But one of Mrs. Black's associates was equal to the occasion.

Either that, or she was too jolted to stop and think.

"Why," she said, "you just go down this golf path and turn right at . . ."

Then the eerie quality of the whole situation began to dawn on the golfers.

"Where are you going?" one of them asked the driver.

"To the eye doctor's," she said reasonably.

There was a pause while everyone thought that over.

Then one of the golfers asked another question.

"How did you get on a golf course?"

"Are we on a golf course?" one of them asked.

"I told you we weren't on the right road," the other muttered bitterly. "There's not even any lines."

From there on, the situation began to get a mite confused.

One of the little ladies said something about a bridge being out. The other kept saying she had told her there weren't even any lines. It was never established precisely which bridge was the proximate cause of the confusion. In fact, it was never established precisely how, whatever bridge was out, the ladies had ended up swinging around the No. 2 green and bearing down on the No. 2 tee.

But later, Mrs. Black told me, she tried to figure the whole thing out. And the best she could work it, those little ladies had probably driven across or in the vicinity of the 10th hole, the 18th, the 17th and the 16th before they found themselves at the No. 2 green. No wonder there weren't any lines.

Eventually they were pointed in the general direction of the pro shop, and reached its vicinity, where somebody got into the car with them and drove them off the golf course, and the spring scramble continued without any casualties having been suffered by the 60 women and 30 golf carts. Nobody is sure how it all worked out safely.

For that matter, nobody knows yet whether the little ladies ever got to the eye doctor's. But at least everybody is hoping they did.

Help Wanted

Somewhere in Memphis at this very moment a woman may be driving around in circles, growing more and more frantic as time passes —lost in a parking garage.

This is only a theory, and it is probably wrong. They do say lightning never strikes twice in the same place. Still, the possibility is enough to haunt my dreams.

Because I actually talked to her. She told me how she got lost in a downtown garage and how she eventually escaped. And she promised she would be back in touch to review the details.

And since then . . . silence. Do you blame me for worrying?

She had driven downtown to pay a bill, she said, and she went into this garage and was given a ticket and obeyed the sign that said she should go right until she found a place to park.

So she did, and somehow she found her way out of the garage on foot and paid her bill and tended to whatever other errands she had.

And then she returned, and somehow found the right floor, and there was her car, and all was well.

It was when she began driving, she said, that the trouble started.

She circled round and round, looking for the exit, weaving around all those tight corners, and at last she saw something familiar ahead.

No, it wasn't the exit. It was the space where she had originally parked.

She tried again, taking different turns, going up and down ramps, beginning to feel a trifle claustrophobic.

And then . . . and then . . .

Back to her same parking space again.

She hit on a plan. What if she deliberately took only the ramps leading upward? Eventually she would reach the top level.

Then, she reasoned, she could make her way safely down, taking only the ramps that led downward.

That didn't work either.

At this point I began losing some of the details of the story. I couldn't keep up. Somewhere along the way, as I remember, she grew desperate enough to drive against the arrows. I think that's how she finally got out.

But I'm not sure. I asked if she would go over it again, and she promised to get back in touch. But she was nervous about it. She was worried that the story would damage her professionally.

Why? Because she's a geography teacher, that's why. What would the kids say if it turned out their geography teacher got lost in a parking garage?

Still, she promised to give me the details again, and I've been waiting ever since. It's been a week or so now, and this vision keeps rising before me.

She has decided that no parking garage is going to lick her. So she has cooly, and with conspicuous bravery above and beyond the call of duty, returned to the scene and set out to solve the riddle. And she had been driving around and around ever since, growing weaker and weaker, more and more desperate.

I keep telling myself that's nonsense, and I really believe it. Otherwise, it would be my duty to go look for her. And I wouldn't dare; I get lost in parking garages more regularly than geography teachers do.

But if you don't, and if you're in one and see a haggard driver going around in circles, holler at her. Ask if she's a geography teacher. If she nods, tell her to follow you. We all need all the help we can get these days.

Dog Day Afternoon Revisited

Winter weather brings out the worst in everything, including cars, heating systems and the cruel japes of fate.

Consider the experience of a Memphis man during one of last week's bitterest days.

After a cold and busy morning elsewhere, he arrived at his office about noon and discovered the central misheating system was on the blink again. The room temperature was about that of a cold-storage locker.

Undaunted, he got out an old plug-in-the-wall heater, set it to work and called his wife to see if all was well at home.

It wasn't. She was ill and had promised to remain indoors, but she had ventured out to the supermarket to save him a trip later—and a tire on her car had gone flat on the supermarket parking lot.

The family service station had been able to give her a ride home with her groceries, she said, but for a variety of weather-connected reasons they were unable to change the tire at the time.

So after he got home he would have to drive to the station, ride in the repair truck to the scene and drive her car back to the station when the tire was changed. That, of course, would leave him with two cars, but they could work that out somehow.

"Don't worry," he said. "I'll handle it. Who has your keys?" They have duplicate sets of keys to both cars.

"The station."

"All right. Try to forget it."

He settled down to work and turned on a desk radio to cheer himself up.

It wouldn't play.

The cleaning women, he decided, must have dislodged the plug from the socket. He got up and painfully moved a four-drawer file cabinet to see.

Nope. It was still plugged in.

About then he noticed the room was getting colder.

Sure enough, the heater was dead. It had overloaded the circuit and knocked out all his wall sockets. But never mind, he knew where the circuit box was.

He went there. It was locked.

Locating someone with the key took only an hour or so, most of which he spent walking up and down an empty corridor to stay warm.

He would have typed up some work instead, but his electric typewriter was out too.

Eventually the man came, the heater and typewriter were restored to life and he shivered through the afternoon.

When he drove home, his wife met him at the door.

"Good news," she said. "The station got the car off the parking lot and changed the tire. All we have to do is go get it."

Thankfully, they plunged out into the cruel cold together to drive to the station. And sure enough, her car was ready and waiting.

"You take it and drive on home," he told her. "I'll go in and sign the ticket."

"What about my keys? They're inside the station."

"Never mind. You take mine and I'll use yours."

So she drove away in her car and he shivered into the station, where they handed him the ticket and his wife's key ring . . .

From which she had prudently removed all keys except those for her car.

I Stalk the Expressways

Well, good buddy, I was in the front rank of cars stopped for a traffic light at one of Memphis' busiest intersections, and I was in the right lane, headed north. Ten-four?

So the light turned and I moved forward, and looked smack into the cab of a west-bound 18-wheeler.

He hadn't made his light. But he had gotten about a yard into my lane before he stopped.

Traffic along there is fierce, blood-thirsty and vengeful. Stray an inch or two over your line and you're wasted. I came to a full halt and considered my options:

(a) Try to change lanes? Out of the question in rush traffic.

(b) Cheat a little on the center lane? Edge around him, thereby crossing the lane line for a moment? Last resort only. Too many trophy-hungry motorists.

(c) Wait for the light to change? Useless. He would still move before I did, and if he moved it would be a signal for all east-west traffic to move. I would be surrounded, pulverized, ingested.

(d) Persuade him to back up? The car behind him, perhaps, in expectations of such a move, had left plenty of space.

Hopefully, I opted for (d).

I peered skyward toward where the king of the road sat behind his mighty wheel. He ignored me.

I tapped the horn, a timid tentative tap, a sorry-to-bother-you tap, a shy question mark of a tap.

He looked down, a sleepy lion examining an ant on the veldt.
My eyes pleaded. His merely bored.
I motioned, a gentle pushing motion, a would-you-mind-awfully-old-chap motion, an I'll always-be-grateful motion.
And he sneered. He sneered!
All my life I have read abut people sneering. I have seen actors sneer according to both Broadway and Hollywood standards. I have followed the descriptions of great writers. I thought I knew what a sneer was.
His was like nothing the actors had performed or the writers had described. Nobody had taught him. He knew.
He accomplished it without the lift of an eyebrow, the curl of a lip. It was a sneer born deep in the recesses of his skull and propelled casually outward between unblinking eyelids. It told me I wasn't worth the eyebrow bit, the lip language. It told me I had been examined and discarded and forgotten.
And that was it.
The righteous rush of adrenalin was sufficient for me to forget cars, caution and calamity. I twisted the steering wheel leftward, gunned the engine and shot perilously past, burning rubber. Before sanity returned, it helped.
But since then, I have been preparing. Anyone, when sufficiently aroused, can become relentless—a motorized stalker of the streets and expressways, an implacable messenger of retribution.
Someday my time will come. There will be other intersections, other lights. At one of them I will see that face again. And when I do, I'll be ready.
I'll sneer right back. After that, he may never be able to drive a trailer again.

Mad Driver At 11 O'Clock

Where, Mrs. Beverly Siegrist demanded yesterday, does being a courteous driver stop and being a sucker begin?
To ask that question in Memphis, some would say, is like standing in the middle of Times Square and asking where New York City is.
But she didn't mean in what city. She meant at what point. Observe.
"I am referring specifically," she went on, "to those motorists who speed down the third lane (the one that says 'Lane Ends—Must Turn Right') and when they get to the end where they 'must turn right'

they expect us poor slobs who have been moving at 15 mph, bumper to bumper for the last eight miles to let them in our lane."

Sound familiar? It should. There are only two ways you could have failed to have the same experience yourself: (1) You don't drive or (2) You're one of the linebuckers yourself.

Mrs. Siegrist hasn't waited for an answer to her question. She has acted.

"It got so bad the other morning I couldn't control myself," she confessed.

"I rolled down my window, shook my fist at the offender and yelled:

" 'May your life be full of left turns and yield signs.' "

No doubt the offender pulled in ahead of her while she was rolling the window back up, but at least she found some comfort in the gesture.

Which is more than most of us find, and the frustration isn't limited to "Left Lane Ends."

Who among that tiny sane minority of us has not been cut in on at an expressway entrance?

It's rush hour. We get into the right lane along with all the other suckers to take our turn at entering the expressway.

The lane on our left, ostensibly for drivers who don't plan to enter the expressway, is almost clear.

The minutes pass like hours. At last we reach the entry ramp.

Whoosh!

The whoosh is from the grinning jackass who came speeding up in the left lane, found a space no bigger than a breadbox in front of us, and whipped into it.

So where does being a courteous driver stop, as Mrs. Siegrist asked?

I have a dream.

One of these days I'm going to have a car with retractable machine guns mounted on both sides toward the front.

They'll be aimed low, to shoot out the tires and rake the soft underbellies of opposing cars, wiping out oil pans, steering assemblies, mufflers, floorboards.

One feint, just one cottonpickin' feint, by a smart-off driver and click.

Up come the flaps.

Out slide the gun barrels.

RAT-A-TAT-TAT!

Then, Mrs. Siegrist, you'll have your answer. Even Job, let us remember, lost his patience at last.

Drivers, Let's Run Over Today's Lesson

All over town, little girls and boys are learning to say their ABCs, to be polite to their friends, to raise their hands if they wish to speak, to brush their teeth and all those good things.

It is only fitting that drivers of the same achievement levels—that is to say, the typical drivers you will encounter on any given day—be given a little course of their own.

All right, students. Everybody join in. This is the way we drive our cars, drive our cars, drive our cars.

1. Drivers who back out of driveways onto busy streets are likely to get their little fenders busted. If they don't, they should. Right?

2. Drivers who come head first out of driveways, shoot across two lanes of traffic and turn left on the far side of the street shouldn't be surprised it they get their little heads knocked off.

3. Drivers who race down a busy street changing lanes seven times a minute suffer from something we call hyperactivity. We should feel sorry for them and try to help them. The best help would be a year in the hoosegow, but don't count on it.

4. Drivers who plan to turn should not wait until the last moment to set their turn lights blinking. Their little friends behind them will be proud to know their plans in advance.

5. If you are driving in the right lane on the expressway and see a car preparing to enter, what should you do? No, no, stepping on the gas and trying to head it off at the ramp is not the answer. We'll try that one again tomorrow.

6. If, on the other hand, you are the driver on the ramp, should you pull out 18 inches in front of a speeding car and shift slowly into second gear? No? Good, somebody's learning.

7. In parking lots, we should all try to place our cars between the lines. Many of our playmates don't understand that. They think they're supposed to straddle the lines. That is a different game, called Somebody Murder the Bum.

8. If you plan to turn left at a busy corner, you should get all the way into the intersection and wait for your chance. If you don't, you'll never make it, and the car behind you will never make it, and the driver behind you will gnash his little teeth. That is good for dentists but bad for drivers.

9. If you plan to turn right on a red light, you should come to a full stop first. That is dangerous, because the car behind you may smash your rear end, but you should try. The full stop gives pedestrians time to get out into the street where you have a better chance to hit them.

10. Finally, what happens to good drivers? They grow up and suffer from heartburn and hypertension. And what happens to bad drivers? Right. They grow up and move to Memphis. This is the way we grind our gears, grind our gears, grind our gears. Now, does anybody want to go wash up?

Discovering the Turn Lane

The car was moving west on Winchester, in fairly heavy traffic, when the driver decided to make a left turn in the middle of the block.

Nothing could have been simpler. Immediately to her left was a turn lane marked off with yellow lines and adorned with turn arrows. It was empty and inviting.

Did she use it?

Of course not. She came to a full halt in the traffic lane, left-turn light blinking bravely, and sat there while traffic piled up behind her.

Eastbound traffic was light, but she was a cautious driver.

She sat there a long time. At last, when the closest approaching car was a full block away, she made her turn.

Her face was serene, her hair unruffled. But there is no way to estimate how many drivers trapped behind her ground the edges off their teeth, suffered heartburn, or were beastly to their spouses later as a result.

Even as nature abhors a vacuum, so do three of every five Memphis drivers abhor a turn lane.

It is, they are convinced, a hazard to be crossed, not a haven to enter, some evil trick of the traffic engineers, designed to produce chaos.

So they ignore it, and produce chaos of their own.

It's one of the ironies of progress. We can get a man on the moon, but we can't get a driver into a turn lane. Except at right angles.

You and I know that. It's all those nuts we have to share the streets with who don't. So, for our own safety, it's up to us to educate them.

Let us try one more time. Clip this and mail it to a dimwitted neighbor, or post it on the office bulletin board:

1. A turn lane is a lane provided by the government, at a cost of millions of dollars, for cars to enter before they make turns so they will not impede the flow of traffic. Turn lanes are especially marked and have little turn arrows in them.

2. You do not cut across turn lanes. You ease into them. All the way in. You do not simply get your hood in the turn lane and leave your

tail light blinking in the other lane. Where your hood is, there let your tail light be also.

3. You do not use turn lanes, as some arrant oafs are wont to do, to pass cars on the left. Granted, it seems a shame to waste them. But now and then someone actually uses them in the way they were intended.

If we can ever get that little lesson across, then we can move on to other matters like the proper technique for entering expressways. But we must take one thing at a time.

And the way things are right now, when the day finally arrives that the whole world runs out of gasoline, you know where we'll all be. We'll be sitting and fretting behind a left-turner who refuses to enter a turn lane.

When the motors all die, we will no doubt get out of our cars, march forward like a mighty army, and tear that car and its driver into little pieces. And it will be a consolation of a sort. But it won't be worth the long walk home.

Long Live the L.O.L.

No one, it seems to me, has paid proper tribute to the magnificent contribution of the Little Old Lady to American folklore.

With or without tennis shoes, in fact or in fiction, she has relieved our frustrations, acted out our fantasies, given smart-alecks their comeuppance, and eased our throbbing resentments in a thousand ways.

You think I'm leading up to something? You're right.

A former Memphian now living in Fort Lauderdale, Fla., Marilyn Snyder, has just passed along an item from The Miami Herald in which the Little Old Lady appears at her impeccable best.

In this case, she is identified not as LOL but as "an elderly but truly elegant woman," but the principle is the same.

Here, according to the newspaper, is what happened.

It was during a shopping rush at a crowded mall in Fort Lauderdale. Our heroine was about to guide her Rolls-Royce into one of the few parking spaces available.

"Out of nowhere," the story said, "two young men in a sports car zipped into the space ahead of her."

Sets your blood boiling, right? Not out of sympathy for the Little Old Lady, though of course there's an element of that, but mostly because you can remember the same sort of thing happening to you.

And, of course, that wasn't enough. As they got out and began walking toward the mall, one of them looked back at her and shouted:

"That's what happens when you're young and fast."

But don't grind your teeth to points. In tales of this sort, you can always count on the Little Old Lady to rout our common enemies and mete out fitting retribution with a fine flair.

As the two young scoundrels departed, the story continued, they suddenly heard noises behind them:

BAM. BAM. CRUNCH. CRUNCH.

They turned in time to see the elderly, elegant woman repeatedly smashing her Rolls into their sports car.

And when whe saw they were looking, she called out a message of her own:

"That's what you can do when you're old and rich."

Though the story is billed as absolute fact, there are some—and I am one of them—who will doubt it.

But the point is that it doesn't matter. Once again, the LOL has brought glory and triumph to every put-upon driver in the nation. That, rather than the paltry question of truth, is what counts.

And it was essential that the angel of vengeance be, indeed, a Little Old Lady. Where would the grandeur of the gesture have been if she had been a burly truck driver?

No. For justice to prevail, for the delicious juices of victory to flood our veins, our deliverer must be old and frail.

And that Little Old Lady, or one like her, had been around for a long, long time. My heart still sings at the memory of a little story that delighted Memphians more than 30 years ago.

In this case, the offender was a driver of a mammoth sedan who, with brazen indifference to the rights of others, halted his car across the crosswalk at an intersection while he waited for the light to change.

By happy chance, a Little Old Lady had been about to walk across the street.

And when she saw the car, she neither flinched nor turned aside.

She marched straight up to it, opened one of the rear doors, crawled in, opened the other door, and emerged triumphantly—leaving both doors wide open behind her.

Presidents and potentates thrive and are forgotten. Generals fade away. Causes come and go. But the Little Old Lady, bless her unconquerable spirit, lasts forever. If she did not, it would be necessary to invent her.

Beware Speeding Stop Signs

Where do all those lists of "actual" quotes come from, anyway?
Nobody ever seems to know for sure, but they're all around us.

There's one assortment of "actual excerpts" from citizens' letters
to the government that has been making the rounds, with occasional
updating, since World War I. There are "actual boners" by
schoolchildren, "actual letters" to welfare agencies, and so on. And
there's never any way to pin them down.

So when a reader sent me a collection of "actual descriptions on
traffic forms" taken from the Arizona Safety Association News, I
thought hey, we've hit paydirt at last. Great list of quotes, and a
reliable source to cite.

Just to be sure, though, I called the Arizona Safety Association
and asked Dudley Young, the executive vice president, about it.

No, he said, the quotations didn't come from any known source in
Arizona. He had picked them up from another publication. But he
felt that if they made people think about safety, they were certainly
worth using.

Well, heck, why not?

Here, then, is today's safety lecture, courtesy of some unknown
collector who surely wouldn't have invented any of these actual excerpts from accident reports. Remember to think thoughts about
traffic safety as you read them.

"Coming home, I drove into the wrong house and collided with a
tree I don't have."

"I collided with a stationary truck coming the other way."

"A pedestrian hit me and went under my car."

"The guy was all over the road. I had to swerve a number of times
before I hit him."

"I pulled away from the side of the road, glanced at my mother-in-
law, and headed over the embankment."

"In my attempt to kill a fly, I drove into a telephone pole."

"I had been shopping for plants all day and was on my way home.
As I reached the intersection, a hedge sprang up, obscuring my vision. I did not see the other car."

"I had been driving for 40 years when I fell asleep at the wheel and
had an accident."

"As I approached the intersection, a sign suddenly appeared in a
place where no stop sign had ever appeared before."

"To avoid hitting the bumper of the car in front, I struck the
pedestrian."

"My car was legally parked as it backed into the other vehicle."

"An invisible car came out of nowhere, struck my vehicle, and vanished."

"I told the police that I was not injured, but on removing my hat I found I had a fractured skull."

"The pedestrian had no idea which direction to run, so I ran over him."

"The indirect cause of this accident was a little guy in a small car with a big mouth."

"I was thrown from my car as it left the road. I was later found in a ditch by some stray cows."

"The telephone pole was approaching. I was attempting to swerve out of the way when it struck my front end."

"I was unable to stop in time and the car crashed into the other vehicle. The driver and passenger then left immediately for vacation with injuries."

"I was on my way to the doctor with rear end trouble when my universal joint gave way, causing me to have an accident."

Think on those quotes, then, and resolve to drive more safely. And if you can't be safe, try at least to come up with some completely original explanations on your accident report. Somewhere, someone may be making a new list.

People In High Places

Fast Tax Break Beats Zone Defense

NOW THAT MEMPHIS is in a new decade and firmly determined to solve its racial problems, Don Duckworth has what could be a whale of an idea.

His answer: Neighborhood basketball.

Look at the basketball teams around the country. See all those great black players? Hear the crowds cheering for them?

That, says Duckworth, is something we can build on.

"My proposal," he told me, "calls for dividing the city into, say, 16 population neighborhoods as equal as possible.

"Each will be allowed sufficient time to develop a basketball team composed of its residents . . ."

(The key word there, alert readers will note, is "residents." You gotta live in the neighborhood to play on the team. Beginning to get the idea?)

". . . and a schedule will be played, eventually determining the champion, the runner-up and the standings of all teams."

And now comes the payoff.

"Awards will be in the form of exemptions from property taxes for the neighborhood that has the winning team. And for the others, the higher a neighborhoods's team finishes, the lower the taxes will be.

"Other incentives will be such things as more garbage pickups, better bus service, bigger libraries, more street lights and the like. Those awards will be made for winning consecutive championships, for being the best sports, and for being the most improved team or showing the most spirit.

"This will provide a bottom-line approach so well used by our banks and businessmen, and will encourage residents to attract neighbors proficient in the game of basketball.

"Under this plan, most Memphians would welcome topnotch players of whatever race, creed or color as neighbors, knowing that such neighbors can minimize their taxes and enhance their city services."

The concept is so brilliant as to be breathtaking. Observers have noted for years that racial prejudice can survive almost anything but economic self-interest. Imagine a neighborhood that wouldn't give up bigotry in return for lower taxes and better serivces!

And beyond that, there's the thrill of sports competition to make the color line disappear. Duckworth went into that, too.

"Among the many benefits derived from this plan," he noted, "would be more community involvement by our citizens attending games, pep rallies and cheerleading contests . . . the excitement of hiring and firing coaches . . . the fun of yelling at the referees and voting for all-star teams.

"Memphians will get to know one another better.

"In a few years busing will not be necessary. A homogenous community will exist with desirable demographics."

And there is the outside world to consider:

"Our national image will receive a very favorable press. Racial problems will be non-existent. Industry and commerce will be more easily attracted to a city that is working together and whose people are more interested in rebounds, assists, free throws and turnovers than in the color of a resident's skin or how fat he or she is or the pedigree of someone's great-great-grandfather."

It could be only an ideal dream but you never know. Citizens groups in alert neighborhoods would do well to start scouting high school basketball teams, just in case. If we can't clear up prejudice any other way, maybe tax-exempt basketball can do the job.

Caucus Call of the Pot-Bellied Legislator

Bumper sticker observed on a Memphis street by an alert colleague: "DANGER: LEGISLATURE IN SESSION."

But let us turn from the perils of politics to the wonders of natural science. Can it be, A. J. Counce wonders, that birds in these parts have Southern accents?

The question arose after a friend told him a duck call record he bought in Illinois is no good for hunting Arkansas ducks.

That set Counce wondering about other birds.

When he lived in Missouri, he assured me, male cardinals could be counted on to chirp, "Pretty, pretty." Females went "Cherk, cherk."

"But here in Memphis I hear a different, more romantic call from the male," he said. "It goes 'Pretty, pretty,' and 'Oh yeah, oh yeah,' and 'Come here, come here,' and 'Sweet, sweet, too, too.' "

Furthermore, he insisted, he had heard Memphis woodpeckers say "Peanut, peanut" and "Hull, hull."

It doesn't pay to ignore such matters. After all, one never knows. So I've been checking around, and it develops that there is at least a mite of substance in Counce's findings.

Consider ducks. Henry Reynolds, our outdoors editor, says they quack the same in Tennessee or Arkansas as they do elsewhere—assuming, of course, that they're the same kind of ducks. But it is true, he said, that duck calls good in one area won't work in another.

At Reelfoot Lake and in the Louisiana swamplands, for example, you want a high-pitched call. In woodlands, the call should be more mellow. But that doesn't reflect on a duck's dialect. It's for carrying purposes. As far as ducks are concerned, difference in accents belong to the calls.

As for other birds, a leading authority in our midst said no, birds don't chirp with different accents. At least not in the usual way.

If a bird says "Tire" in Iowa, for example, it doesn't say "Tar" in Tennessee. If it chirps "Cuba, Cuba, war, war" in this part of the country, it doesn't chirp "Cuber, Cuber, wawr, wawr," up East.

On the other hand, he said, there are individual variations and what you might even call local dialects in some birds' songs. The song of the common yellowthroat in Memphis sounds different from the song of the same bird in Middle Tennessee.

And mockingbirds mock different birds in different parts of the country.

As for that bit about Memphis woodpeckers saying peanut and hull, my man was baffled. Perhaps, we agreed, it has something to do with President Carter.

All in all, it's at least enough to put us on our guard, which brings us back to the bumper sticker noted above. If you're in Nashville in the next few weeks and hear what you think is a yellowbellied sapsucker, look closely. What you're really hearing may be the caucus call of the potbellied legislator.

Justice Not Only Blind but Deaf

My old friend Joe was waiting for me when I got to the office yesterday. I tried to head him off.

"Whatever you're selling, I don't want any," I warned him.

"You mean you're against justice and profits? You don't want to get rich protecting your fellow man?"

"Oh, all right. What is it?"

"I'm launching the Alice in Wonderland Correspondence Law School to train lawyers to handle cases in City Court."

"And what do you expect me to do about it?"

"Enroll, of course. You can make a fortune defending innocent people. Did you read this story about the guy Judge Robert Love threw in jail because he didn't have a lawyer?"

"Yes," I said, "and I'm confused, Everybody agreed it was a case of mistaken identity, didn't they?"

"Right."

"The police arrested a man on a charge of driving while intoxicated, and he showed them a stolen driver's license? And they booked him, photographed him, and took his fingerprints and let him out on bail, and when he failed to show up for trial they went after the owner of the license?"

"Right again."

"So the innocent guy went down and explained it to the police, who agreed he wasn't the man they arrested and didn't even look like him, so they took him to the prosecutor's office?"

Joe grew impatient. "Yes, yes, of course. But he still had to appear in court, and when he kept insisting on explaining the mix-up himself the judge tossed him into the cooler until he got a lawyer."

"I simply can't understand it," I said. "I don't see why he had to go to court in the first place. But even if he did, doesn't the Constitution guarantee every person a right to defend himself? And isn't a defendant considered innocent until proven guilty?"

"That shows how the lay brain works," Joe snorted. "You're talking about the Constitution of the United States. I'm talking about City Court in Memphis. Can't you see the difference?"

"So what will your correspondence school do?"

"To practice law, you have to pass the bar examinations, so we'll take care of that. A tort, tort here, a tort, tort there, here a tort, there a . . ."

"Get to the point. Lawyers have to specialize these days."

"Exactly. Our graduates will specialize in stating the obvious to City Court judges and prosecutors. Like you think today's Wednesday, right?"

"Of course it is."

"Hah. Try telling that to Judge Love without a lawyer."

"And what can your graduates expect to make?"

"Well, the guy who got thrown in jail said he didn't hire a lawyer because it would have cost him $500. I checked with a lawyer, and he said that's about standard for a DWI defense. Our lawyers will take only mistaken identity cases and charge only $250 each. Man, they can mop up."

"You think there are that many cases of that sort?"

"There must be. The judge and the city prosecutors agreed they had no responsibility to act on the clear facts in this case without a lawyer representing the defendant. Can't you see that leaves the door wide open?

"Come on, you'd better sign up. I can have you defending innocent people for a profit within a few months. Under our court setup here, you can make a fortune."

"I'll think about it," I promised him. "It does look promising. Gee, I always knew that justice was blind, but . . ."

"Exactly. But in Memphis it's deaf too, unless you hire a lawyer."

Prisoners Aren't What They Used to Be

FROM: Office of the Director

TO: All Personnel (Copies to be posted on all precinct bulletin boards)

SUBJECT: Prisoners, Escape of from department vans

INTRODUCTION.

1. This office recognizes that mistakes will happen, even in the best-run departments.

2. It is further understood that everybody is human.

3. Still and all, fellows, certain events which occured Friday night last do tend, fairly or unfairly, to make us look less than our best.

BRIEF SUMMARY.

1. In view of the fact that some personnel may be unaware of the events hereintofore cited, the following summary, based on preliminary findings, is provided.

2. Four prisoners arrested on gaming charges escaped custody under what can only be described as unusual circumstances.

a. Referenced escape was made from a police van.

b. Referenced van was backed up to a rear door at headquarters at the time.

c. Referenced prisoners walked, ran or hobbled from custody in full view of police officers in the parking lot.

d. Any or all of said prisoners may have been armed with dice, playing cards or other similar dangerous weapons.

e. One prisoner escaped on crutches.

3. This office takes some comfort from the fact that the man on crutches was recaptured about an hour later. Good work, gang.

4. Still and all, gee whiz.

PROPOSED ACTION.

1. As stated in the public news media, this office is conducting an investigation to determine exactly what happened.

2. Somebody's in trouble.

3. Harsh as it may sound, even an officer going off duty will be held responsible if it is established that he stood idly by and watched an escaping prisoner walk, run or hobble from custody.

INTERIM RECOMMENDATIONS.

1. While the exact circumstances surrounding this daring break have not been fully established, it is considered advisable to recommend the following procedures for use whenever prisoners are being unloaded at headquarters.

a. Van doors should not be left open and unattended if hardened gamblers or other dangerous types remain unshackled inside.

b. Van drivers should equip themselves with old-fashioned dinner bells, firecrackers or other noise-makers, which they can sound in the event they lose contact with officers in charge.

c. When prisoners are waiting to be brought into the detention center, any personnel within the vicinity are urged either to assist or at least to watch intently and be prepared to holler, "There he goes!"

CONCLUSIONS.

1. Never trust a prisoner to escort himself into the detention center unassisted. Some of those fellows can't be relied on worth shucks.

2. Even an off-duty officer should be willing to pitch in when crises arise right there on the plaguey parking lot.

3. If we mess up like this on gaming arrests, how and when will we ever find time and personnel to get around to violations of equal importance, such as assault, arson, muggings, shootings and like that?

Bring Back Mark Twain

We can only be sadly grateful, for his own sake, that Mark Twain wasn't alive to read the terrible revelations unearthed in this newspaper by Terry Keeter.

Revelation No. 1: At the International Frog Jumping Championship in Calaveras County, Calif., a sport and locale made famous by Twain himself, they rent frogs from a scientific supply house to do the jumping.

Think of it. Rented frogs from supply houses, jumping where once jumped the celebrated Dan'l Webster, ketched by Jim Smiley and lovingly trained to respond to the cry, "Flies, Dan'l, flies!" Rented frogs where Smiley was outfrogged by a mysterious stranger who loaded poor Dan'l with quail shot before the contest.

Now the jumpers come from a scientific supply house. Chosen, no doubt, by computers. And arrogant, no doubt, unlike Dan'l, who was modest and straightfo'ard, for all he was so gifted.

But revelation No. 2, being closer home, is even worse.

In Memphis, a city Twain singled out for singular praise and affection, a frog jumping contest is scheduled on the mall. And the first entry—indeed, the only entry as of the time Keeter wrote—is a ringer, an African bullfrog borrowed from the Memphis zoo.

A strange situation. As Smiley said of his frog after he paid off the bet, it 'pears to look mighty baggy, somehow.

Forget Calaveras County. Consider the reputation and good name of Memphis, a city known to some citizens as a suburb of nearby Bullfrog Corners. A shortage of croakers here? The idea is insupportable.

When the mysterious stranger needed a frog to set alongside Dan'l, Smiley didn't recommend a zoo or a supply house. He just went out to the swamp and slopped around in the mud and ketched one and fetched it in.

The years have been kind to Memphis bullfrogs. But has time perhaps produced lesser men than Jim Smiley?

At this late date, the question is moot. What remains, it appears, is for the sponsors to consider some kind of alternative. And it just happens that one was suggested by a Memphian only yesterday.

"If they can't find enough frogs," she asked me as we were eating breakfast, "why don't they use politicians?"

At first I wasn't clear how it would work. But by golly, the thing has possibilities.

What the contest sponsor would do, as I get it, would be to round up a whole bunch of local officeholders—not all of them, mind you, only those who wait to be told what to think—and line them up at the starting line.

Then, when the whistle blows, the people who do their thinking for them would holler, "Frog!"

And they'll jump. Nobody can doubt that. They night not be able to match Dan'l on being modest and straightfor'ard, but they'll outjump any frog Twain ever laid eyes on. It's worth a try.

Asteroids Versus Mississippi Mud

There's something reassuring, even inspiring, about the nuttiness of Memphis city officials. You can rely on them to do the most outlandish thing possible in almost any given situation.

Who else, for example, could have come up with the idea of an electronic space-age video-game arcade smack in the middle of a
Mississippi River museum building?

And who else could have thought of calling it the "Paddlewheel
Arcade," in honor of the Mark Twain era?

Who else indeed but our own city leaders, who are rounding off the
sharp edges of the $60-million Mud Island development, a project in-
tended to bring tourists from all over the world to celebrate the
history and tradition of a mighty river.

Remember back when we were first hearing about this heady
dream?

We had something special here, and we needed to cash in on it.
Right? The Father of Waters rolling right past our doorstep, and the
whole world thirsting to learn the lore of the river.

So what we would do, see, would be to build a monument to the
river, a place where people could get a good look at it and see how
the whole system worked and learn about its history. And, by golly,
that would be a tourist attraction worth talking about.

But now they're getting a little worried about the total take, so
they'll fix up a 1,100-square-foot room in the museum to resemble a
riverboat gambling saloon, and they'll have carpeting and wainscot-
ted walls and murals of the river, and brass lighting fans and all that.

And what will be featured in this quaint old Paddlewheel Arcade?

Why, 40 to 60 coin-operated space games.

Deluxe Space Invaders. Asteroids Deluxe. Lunar Rescue. Monte
Carlo. "Every new model machine that's on the market," says the
amusement-arcade operator who will run the thing and split the profits with the city.

What family in America wouldn't drive a few hundred miles to let
the kids feed quarters to space machines they couldn't find
anywhere else except maybe in every mall and movie lobby and shopping center in the country?

I think it's a great idea. Oh, they might improve matters a bit by
changing the names of the games. Instead of Asteroids Deluxe, how
about The Great River Race, with one asteroid named Spaceship
Natchez and another the Robert E. Lee? That'll give the kiddies
historic insights they wouldn't get anywhere else.

But on the whole, I like it for the sense of continuity it gives our
community. Remember the totem pole in Confederate Park?

That was years ago, back when E.H. Crump was running things.
He gave the city a totem pole he bought on a trip out to the Pacific
Northwest, and it was duly installed in Confederate Park, subtitled
"A Tribute to the Old South."

Of course totem poles were never made by Southern Indians, let alone Old South Confederate Indians, but there it was. And there it stayed until it was finally laughed off the lot. The last I heard it was somewhere out in a corner of the fairgrounds, more or less hidden by the shrubbery.

If they would just clean it up and install it on the prow of the 1870s riverboat reproduction they're planning for Mud Island, I don't know what more we could ask for.

Unless they have another meeting and decide to serve authentic Mississippi River lobsters in the restaurant. Just wait till they think of that.

Mud Island in the Space Age

I am in receipt of the following letter from Ned C. Stancliff, general manager of Mud Island:

"As a reader of your daily column, I compliment you on your refreshing approach to various topics. However, in reading your editorial approach to our retail space, I find you forgot to deal in facts.

"The retail space is not located 'smack in the middle of the museum building,' nor are we 'fixin' up a room in the museum to resemble a riverboat gambling saloon.' Maybe you need to misstate facts to help get your point across. Regardless, I just wanted you to know the facts regarding our retail space.

"I certainly look forward to your columns and your interesting viewpoint, but I will remember not to take your point of view as fact.

"Thank you for your time."

Now that is an ideal example of how to call a fellow a liar without ever failing to be a gentleman yourself. I had said some un-complimentary things about putting space machines on Mud Island, which I understood was intended as a sort of Mississippi River theme park, and he didn't like what I said.

And I want to say right now that Stancliff himself quoted me right.

Well, almost right. I didn't say "fixin' to." I almost never say "fix-in' to." But I did use the phrase "they'll fix up . . ." so there's no point in quibbling over that.

Stancliff's objection, the best I could gather, was that I said Mud Island officials plan to install 40 to 60 coin-operated space games "smack in the middle" of a river museum building, and that the room was going to be fixed up to resemble a riverboat gambling saloon.

He didn't dispute the space games, so I suppose we can take that as correct. The trouble was with that smack-in-the-middle-of-a-museum-building bit, and with the gambling saloon decorations.

And he may have objected because I didn't call space for the electronic machines "retail space." I wasn't quite clear about that.

But I wanted to correct any grave errors on my part right away, so I called Stancliff yesterday morning immediately after reading his letter. He was out of town, not expected back until today or tomorrow. I asked to speak to someone else in authority.

First I had a pleasant chat with Mrs. Cindy Erlich, director of marketing division, and she explained the museum problem.

That arcade won't be smack in the midle of the museum building. It'll just be in the same building with the museum. The building is called the River Center building, and it will have 100,000 square feet, and 25,000 of those square feet will be museum. Other footage will include the room where the space machines will be.

I'm not sure how to describe that room, because Stancliff didn't like the statement that it was being fixed up to resemble a riverboat gambling saloon, and I don't want to compound the error.

Mrs. Erlich said actually it is themed to a paddlewheeler riverboat but not necessarily a gambling saloon. She said it was more like a grand salon.

I asked about the difference between a grand salon and a gambling saloon in a riverboat, and she referred me to Michael Sievers, museum director.

He said, well, actually the room had a riverboat theme, with elements of a grand salon. He said the old riverboats didn't have gambling saloons.

I asked where people went to gamble on those boats, and he said to the grand salon.

So I want to apologize publicly to Ned Stancliff.

The space-game arcade isn't smack in the middle of the museum building, it's in the same building the museum is in. And the room won't resemble a gambling saloon, it will have some elements of a grand salon.

I can see where that makes a lot of difference, and I surely am sorry about it. Being a country boy, I never was sure about the difference between saloons and salons, and when a museum is in a building I tend to think of the building as a museum building. But that is clearly wrong.

I do want to say, though, that I feel more than ever that I don't need to misstate facts to help get my point across. Space games in a sort of grand salon in the same building with a river museum? Gol-ly.

Staying Awake on Election Day

Sensitive souls in our community must have breathed great sighs of relief at word that the rhetoric in the campaign for mayor has cooled along with the weather.

Indeed, the account in this newspaper said, four candidates who appeared at the same meeting made "none of the charges and countercharges that marked earlier appearances."

Thank goodness for that. Flesh and blood pressure, it is generally agreed, can stand only so much. But to some aging observers, the invective level had sounded pretty low already, at least compared with former days.

It is true, I suppose, that feelings must have run riot recently when one candidate said he was "somewhat saddened" to know that someone had written that another candidate said he was an idiot.

Strong words indeed. The other candidate, it should be noted, promptly responded that he didn't think his opponent was an idiot, and that all he had said was that "some idiot" had made a suggestion he disagreed with. Thus a soft answer turneth away wrath.

But, for all its drama, the whole affair shows how far we have advanced on the long and somewhat boring road to political responsibility. Not many years ago even the use of a word like "idiot" would have been considered a sign of a limited vocabulary or a deprived imagination.

Can anyone believe, for example, that the late E.H. Crump would have been content with referring to an unnamed person as "some idiot"?

Never. Not the man who once said of a political enemy that he was "the sort of man who would milk his neighbor's cow through a hole in the fence."

Such talk did not encourage study of what are known as the relevant issues, of course. And it is certainly better to have issue-oriented appeals, where a candidate assures us that he is in favor of increased services along with lower taxes, or more benefits with fewer costs, or even the completion of Interstate 40 without environmental damages or infringement on Midtown neighborhoods. Those are things you can hang onto.

It is only from a distance that the old days look good, but those politicians of the past did have a flair that puts today's image-makers to shame.

Remember when the late Gordon Browning, first a Crump ally but later a foe, brought a motorcade into town with the sound truck blaring that fine old song, "I Want to Meet the Bully of the Town"?

Nobody ever dozed off in the middle of a campaign like that.

And it wasn't only in Memphis, of course. When Harold Ickes, that noted curmudgeon of the Franklin Roosevelt days, wanted to comment on an opponent of FDR, he didn't talk vaguely of some idiot. He merely said he saw where Tom Dewey had tossed his diaper into the ring.

Sometimes, it is true, those old campaigners abandoned plain talk in favor of fancier words. But even then the approach was direct.

Back in the 1940s a candidate for the U.S. Senate in another state went about the rural areas asking his listeners if they were aware that his opponent "is known all over Washington as a shameless extrovert." Not only that, he continued darkly, but "this man is reliably reported to practice nepotism with his sister-in-law, and he has a sister who was once a thespian in wicked New York." And to top it all, he concluded, it was an established fact that the fellow, before his marriage, practiced celibacy.

We can only give thanks that such affronts to an informed electorate are behind us, and that today we are given clear-cut unvarnished outlines of political plans, principles and images in order to make our choices. Now all we have to worry about is staying awake on election day.

Bet You a Quart of Strawberries

One of the proudest traditions of a free nation is that, in America, justice is blind.

And it's more than simply a pious claim. It's true, and you can prove it for yourself any time you wish. Take an example. Better still, take two.

My own faith in the awesome blindness of justice was reinforced last week by examples on opposite sides of this great continent—the cases of one David Begelman in California and one Jacqueline Datcher in a Maryland suburb of our nation's capital.

The news item about Begelman, a former president of Columbia Pictures, where he made $400,000 a year, told of his sentencing for stealing $40,000 from his own studio.

He had done it by forging endorsements on checks.

Why would a man who is already making $400,000 a year want to steal $40,000 more? Well, it's puzzling. Even the judge, Thomas Murphy of Burbank, Calif., was puzzled. He said Begelman's actions smacked of a "death wish." He said the affair was "bizarre, as bizarre conduct as you'll find anywhere."

And, having thought it all over, he fined Begelman $5,000 and put him on three years' probation.

Think of it. And some cynics clain that a $400,000-a-year man with what smacks of a death wish cannot find justice in America if he is guilty of $40,000 worth of bizarre conduct.

The item about Miss Datcher said she had been convicted, by a jury of her peers, on a charge of petty shoplifting—specifically, eating two strawberries at a Maryland supermarket near Washington.

Miss Datcher said she didn't eat any strawberries. A store detective testified he saw her lift her hand to her mouth.

The corpus delicti, or whatever a lawyer might call the merchandise involved, was, of course, unavailable for submission as evidence. But the assistant state's attorney, a man named Courtois, apparently scored a telling blow with a statement that will live in the annals of strangled syntax if not in the history of law.

"Obviously strawberries in a chewed condition is depriving someone of the value of his strawberries," he was quoted. "Strawberries in a swallowed state even more so."

The jury (six men, six women) found the defendant guilty. Sentencing has been set for later, and Miss Datcher had more than a month to wonder whether she'll get the maximum penalty: a $500 fine and 18 months in prison.

Time alone will tell whether bizarre conduct and death wishes are considered extenuating circumstances in a petty shoplifting case. Presumably Miss Datcher doesn't make $400,000 a year, but she has, by her own account, spent $300 in legal defense already. That ought to be bizarre enough to help a little.

Surely we cannot tolerate strawberry-munching in supermarkets. That strikes at the heart of a free-enterprise system. And for all we know, the judge may follow the Begelman precedent, fine Miss Datcher one-eighth of the value of two strawberries and let her off with a warning.

But it is heartening to know our legal system is so flexible, so capable of adjusting to circumstances, that it is possible to get probation and a $5,000 fine for stealing $40,000, but also possible to get 18 months and a $500 fine for eating two strawberries.

There may be weirder worlds than ours in the universe, but I'll bet you a quart of berries none are in our particular galaxy.

Next Year, There Won't Be Any Money Left

All year long there has been a stream of off-again, on-again pronouncements from Washington about Social Security.

The system will go broke by 6:30 p.m. next Tuesday.

The system's in no trouble at all. Sound as a dollar.

By next year there won't be any money left to pay retirement benefits.

Nothing to worry about. Just a temporary shortfall.

Cost of living adjustments must be eliminated. Cost of living adjustments will continue. Cost of living adjustments will be delayed.

It has taken me a while to figure it out, but I think I've finally hit on the reason for all this.

Somebody in Washington has decided the best way to get millions of people off the Social Security rolls is to scare them to death.

Many old people have frail constitutions and delicate health. They worry a lot.

What better way to handle them, then, than to keep them in an agony of apprehension about the future until their puny old hearts just can't stand it any longer?

The technique, of course, is to keep 'em off balance. It's a variation of the good-guy, bad-guy routine said to be used in some police interrogations.

First you tell them everything is fine. Then you tell them the whole system is about to collapse. Then you say no, that was a mistake, everything's fine. Then you say well, actually, disaster really does lie ahead, but if we just cut enough benefits we might be able to drag it out a few years longer.

A few months of that, and the victims should either keel over or begin begging for lower benefits.

It's an ingenious approach, but I'm not entirely sure it will work.

Some older people seem to get healthier when they get good and mad. Their juices start running more briskly. Their eyes light up. They get up out of their rocking chairs and go looking for a fight.

And a lot of them seem to be getting awfully sore about everything that's been said since they were promised that Social Security and Medicare wouldn't be bothered by anybody.

One of the things that might make some of them want to fight is a statement the other day by Social Security Commissioner John Svahn.

"There is a myth that has grown up in America," said Svahn with evident disapproval, "that Social Security is a program for maintaining everyone at a middle-class level in their retirement years."

Well, you don't say. Have people really been believing something like that?

And does than mean that the 35 million people now getting benefits from old age and disability funds are living at a sinful middle-class level and expect to continue their lavish life-styles in spite of all an alarmed government can do to get them to quit wasting money?

Anybody who had found a way to maintain a middle-class level on nothing but a Social Security pension ought to write a book about it. The book would be an overnight best-seller, and the author could go off Social Security entirely and live a life of real middle-class security.

But meanwhile, the Senate Finance Subcommittee on Social Security has begun holding hearings on what to do about Social Security and Medicare, and the House Ways and Means Committee already is drafting legislation.

And it might be well for them to keep one thing in mind.

A lot of those old people who are on Social Security, or about to go on it, might just be ornery enough not to die of fright after all. They may have made up their stubborn old minds to live a little longer than they planned.

Long enough, for example, to vote in one more election.

Jogging All the Way to the Bank

You have to hand it to the members of the United States Senate. Those fellows show style above and beyond the ordinary definition of the word.

Five of them, as you may have read, put on sweatshirts the other day and jogged back and forth in front of the Capitol.

What for? Well, as The Associated Press put it, they wanted "to dramatize what they said was the economic belt-tightening of the new fiscal year."

It must have been a stirring sight. As all that money for domestic programs was drying up, our sturdy lawmakers were out there sweating in the morning breeze to show that, just like former welfare recipients, they too can face the music.

Well, almost.

This is the same Senate, you will recall, that only last week voted itself what amounted to a combination tax break and pay hike for the new fiscal year.

On the one hand, it voted to remove the limit on tax deductions its members can take for their living expenses in Washingon.

The limit had been $3,000 a year. Now the sky's the limit. How's that for economic belt-tightening in the new fiscal year?

On the other hand, it also voted to remove the limit on what members can earn from making speeches when they aren't working for the salaries we pay them.

The limit had been a paltry $25,000 a year. Now the sky's the limit. And how's that, buddy, for some more economic belt-tightening in the new fiscal year?

So now, organizations with axes to grind may hire our senators as often as they wish, for as much pay as they wish, to make remarks at the end of lavish dinners, and everybody will be happy, and economic belts will be tightened all along the speaker's table.

There may be a little belching as a result, but you can't have everything.

Ah, but even that's not the limit of the Senate's style.

Just to show they really and truly mean it about belt-tightening, the members of the upper chamber acted the same day on the minimum Social Security benefit matter.

You remembr that. Earlier, Congress eliminated the $122 minimum of Social Security pensions for nearly three million people, and President Reagan signed the law, and then a bit of an uproar broke out.

A lot of bleeding-heart liberals and welfare chiselers and others of their ilk began complaining that some elderly and infirm people now living in luxury on $122 a month might have some problems on less. People began having second thoughts on the matter.

President Reagan himself, if I understood him correctly in his recent address to the nation, said it had been all a misunderstanding. They didn't really mean to eliminate that $122 minimum. They just wanted to be sure it wasn't misused.

So the House went to work and passed a bill restoring the minimum.

And what do you think the Senate also did on that same day, after having voted itself a tax break and a public-speaking bonanza, and after some of its members had got out and jogged to dramatize the economic belt-tightening?

They indefinitely postponed action on the bill to restore the $122 minimum, that's what.

Now that the jogging-in-front-of-the-Capitol precedent has been set, no doubt it will become an institution of sorts.

Every time they make another budget cut in the days ahead, senators will put on their sweatshirts—each of which, conceivably, may now be listed as a Washington living expense—and get out for a morning jog to dramatize the economic belt-tightening.

But I have an idea they won't just jog in front of the Capitol.

After the photographers are through snapping them, they'll probably jog right on down to the nearest bank to deposit their latest checks for speaking engagements. That's what I call style.

Congress Hard Hit by Inflation

Every day we learn some shameful new fact about the way the underprivileged are treated in this country.

Now it develops that we don't even provide child care centers for what must be the hardest-working and most underpaid of all American workers—the members of Congress.

What are we thinking of? How can they go about their duties if they have to worry about what's happening to their children?

But at last something is going to be done about it, maybe. Rep. Ed Jones of Tennessee is chairman of a House subcommittee that's looking into the matter. The encouraging word was in this newspaper the other day.

Subject to congressional approval, it appears, a center will be set up in rented church space near the Capitol for the children of House and Senate members, as well as the children of their employes.

And strange as it appears, some citizens are already casting jaundiced eyes at the whole plan.

One of my wife's eyes, for example, is jaundiced. That's the one she cast on the story.

"Now we're going to pay for babysitters for congressmen," she announced, showing me the story.

I said aw, gee, surely she was wrong. Didn't the story say the center would be self-supporting?

"I noticed that," she said. "I also noticed that one of the sponsors said something about 'initial financial support' being needed. Where do you think that's coming from? And besides, the center is to be managed by a congressional committee. Who pays when a congressional committee manages something?"

"Well, shucks," I said. "I saw that, too, but I thought that meant the members of Congress would dig into their own pockets for the initial financial support. The management too."

She looked at me out of her other eye, the one that isn't jaundiced.

"You're so sweet and innocent you'll believe anything," she said. "You'll even believe a member of Congress will spend his own money."

So I went back and read the story again. It said a lot about how a child care center would "ease the burdens of families of staffers and congressional employees." Could it be that the congressmen aren't really concerned about their own kids, but only the kids of their starvation-wages employees?

No, it couldn't be that. Because the story said the center would also be for the use of House and Senate members.

And after wrestling with my earnest desire to think nothing but good of a member of Congress, I had to agree that "initial financial support" sure sounded like use of additional tax money.

What it gets down to, then, is that we simply must face the facts, bite the bullet and pay up.

Surely we wouldn't claim that members of Congress must be penalized for having children. Well, all right, then. The only way not to penalize them is to provide initial financial support and management costs for babysitting.

After all, what group deserves a lift more in these inflated times?

I tried to explain all this to my wife, but she wouldn't buy it. She seemed to think that even the remote possibility of tax dollars for Congressional babysitters was in the same class as 60 percent pay raises for that other deprived group, the members of the Memphis City Council.

But that's the sort of thinking that progressive statesmen have to put up with all the time. Taxpayer are ornery. Personally, I look forward to the day when no senator's child must go untended simply because the people of America are too stingy to foot the bill.

Comfort Caucus Combats Sweaty Decorum

In the chaotic swirls of inactivity that have shaken the nation's capital this summer, one significant event was allowed to go almost unnoticed and unsung.

In its own way the event was unique. It showed what great minds can achieve when they are sufficiently aroused.

Given an energy-connected challenge worthy of its mettle, the House of Representatives actually acted swiftly and with dispatch. Let no one call that body indecisive and ineffective again.

In less than the twinkling of an eye, the House considered and rejected a proposal that its male members "may dispense with coats and/or ties so ling as suitable, dignified, tasteful and appropriate clothes are worn."

Lest the historic event be forgotten, let us review the happenings of that fateful day.

At least in theory, thermostats at the Capitol have been dialed up to 78 degrees. Some members of the lower chamber found themselves hot and uncomfortable as they went about their wearisome duties.

Onto the floor walked Rep. Jim Mattox (D-Texas), wearing a short-sleeved shirt. He had donned it for a purpose: He intended to deliver a speech saying that, since it was so hot in there, members could set an example of how to cope with the energy crisis.

John Lengel of The Associated Press was able to report later at least one sentence of what Mattox had intended to say:

"Let us shed our coats and ties, roll up our sleeves and let the American people know we're serious about solving the country's energy problems."

Heresy? You bet.

The member from Texas never got an opportunity to offer his proposal. Speaker Thomas P. O'Neill Jr., that great champion of decency and dedication in government, took one look at Mattox' sleeves and ordered him to leave the chamber.

"The gentleman," he declared, "knows he is embarrassing the chair—me."

Mattox didn't leave, but he didn't deliver his speech either. O'Neill wouldn't recognize him.

And later in the day, when Rep. Morris Udall (D-Ariz.) offered a resolution on behalf of what he called the "comfort caucus," permitting dignified but coatless garb for the men, it was instantly tabled by a 3-to-1 margin. As one outraged member commented:

"I think we have a few shreds of decorum left in this place and we ought not to drop them."

Even thus, when sufficiently inspired, can our elected representatives respond to the moral equivalent of war. They may not be able to agree on any plan to help the country, but they can guard their shreds and doze in sweaty majesty.

One might argue that the whole occurrence was a sort of charade—that actually the members aren't in the chamber long enough between vacations and junkets to care what the temperature is. Right now, for example, they are preparing to take off all of August. And they're only recently back from the Memorial Day vacation, which followed the Easter vacation, which . . .but why go into that?

The real point, as I see it, is that the House has assured its dignity, and Speaker O'Neill had been protected from embarrassment, and reasonable men have once again been discriminated against in the matter of summer clothing.

It may not add up to statesmanship, but it's a start. Nero fiddled around in much the same way while Rome burned.

We, the Landlords . . .

People are always talking about how mean landlords are, but there's another side of the picture that doesn't get much attention.

I know. In my own small way, I'm a sort of landlord myself.

It doesn't really amount to much. I have a financial interest in a great big house up northeast of here, and let me tell you, you wouldn't believe how picky tenants can be.

Matter of fact, I've been paying for my equity in that house for all my adult life, and the only financial rewards I've received so far are occasional tax benefits. That means I don't have to pay taxes on what I pay for maintenance and upkeep of the place.

The way I figure it, that house has been a losing proposition for me from the first, but here lately it's got downright troublesome.

We moved in a new pair of tenants last January, a couple of real nice-looking people named Ron and Nancy, and they seemed just right. Did a lot of talk about austere living, cutting expenses, relying on individuals to lift themselves by their own bootstraps, saving money, cutting back on frills—all those things that delight a landlord's heart.

But they were scarcely in the place before they began complaining that it wasn't fixed up right. Needed refurbishing, they said. Everything rundown and dreary looking.

Well, we might have worked out some deal to reduce the rent, but the trouble was they weren't paying any. So we told them we had a modest fund set aside for that sort of thing, and they were welcome to use it.

Nope, they said. They needed a lot more than that. Some friends of theirs would just go out and ask the public to give them money for it.

It can give a landlord a bad name if tenants start appealing to the public to help them fix up their houses, but that's what happened. So those friends got busy, and in no time at all they had raised more than $822,000 to take care of repairs and refurbishings.

Well, that hurt. It wasn't only the embarrassment, it was the fact that the people who gave the $822,000 got tax deductions for doing it. But we landlords gritted our teeth and tried to make the most of it.

Then, the next thing we knew, some other group had chipped in a few thousand more to fix up what they called a cosmetology room for Nancy, because our house didn't have what she needed in cosmetology rooms. More bad marks for stingy landlords. You see how it goes?

We thought that would all die down and maybe we could work at restoring landlords' reputations as good-hearted, generous people, but darned if another problem hasn't arisen.

Nancy has what they call a social secretary—they live as well as they can, considering the hard times—and she was in the newspapers yesterday complaining that the house has what she called "a terrible tablecloth crisis."

Why, once, Muffie said—Muffie's her name—she saw "a little rip in a beautiful linen overlay" and had to sew it up right quick before Nancy's luncheon guests arrived. And another time, she said, "one set of tablecloths, to my complete and utter horror, went out to the dry cleaners and shrunk."

And Muffie went on to say they only had six changes of cloths to choose from. I tell you, it sounded pitiful.

Somebody asked if they couldn't buy a few new tablecoths from what was left of that $822,000, but Muffie said no, they didn't have the money. There's only about $100,000 left, and it's already earmarked for other redecorating plans.

So I suppose we landlords will be held up to ridicule again, and there'll be another welfare campaign to buy tablecloths for those unfortunate tenants at the White House.

And here we landlords sit, stuck with a very bad public relations problem and no way to get out ot it. Ron and Nancy have a four-year lease.

It looks like three more years of complaints, complaints, complaints, and more appeals for public assistance. I can't help feeling a little bitter about it. But, then, what can you expect from people who live in public housing and don't have but six changes of tablecoths?

Nancy Keeps Her Head

My old friend Joe is usually full of optimism and good spirits, but his brow was dark and his eyes flashed when he accosted me.

"You ought to be ashamed of your profession," he snapped. "All of you are just alike. You love to destroy people's reputations, don't you?"

"What in the world are you talking about? Who's determined to destroy whom?"

"The Washington press corps is out to get Nancy Reagan. Oh, don't look innocent. Nancy herself said just the other day that the press makes her sound terrible. And now they've done it again."

"Done what?"

"Made her sound terrible, just like she said."

"How did they do that?"

"They showed her talking to a reporter on television."

"Now wait a minute," I protested. "You mean that NBC News interview, don't you? I saw that. I thought she was treated with great respect."

"Yeah, but that Chris Wallace who interviewed her asked questions."

"What's wrong with that?"

"She answered them, that's what. You can't tell me somebody didn't plan that."

"And what did she say that has you so upset?'

"You heard it. She said she and her husband have tightened their belts and are making sacrifices just like everybody else because of inflation."

"So?"

"That made her sound ridiculous and you know it. She also said she didn't think that holiday trip to California was something to be denied the President. Good night, I heard one estimate that the trip cost the government $62,000, just for that one weekend."

"Oh, come on. I don't think the press has made a big deal of that trip."

"Maybe not, but the same day she was saying that, some pathetic little 70-year-old woman was telling Democratic senators she couldn't make it with her $306-a-month Social Security check if the administration closed her hometown's health center. Don't you see? The whole idea was to make people figure how many years' worth of Social Security payments went into that weekend trip."

"And that's all of your complaint?"

"Not on your life. Wallace asked how the Reagans were tightening their belts and she said they're not making any money in Washington."

"Well?"

"Everybody knows the President makes $200,000 a year, with a free house and utilities and a personal physician thrown in along with all those free trips and those other things. How tight is a $200,000 belt?"

"And?"

"And she said they're not spending as much money as they were. Of course they aren't, with the government picking up their bills."

"Is that all?"

"That's only the beginning. She said, and I quote, 'We're doing the things that all people are doing now with inflation. You're just pulling in. You have to. We're selling our home in Pacific Palisades, which we dearly love.' Well, of course people know they'll still have a ranch near Santa Barbara and they'll make a killing if they sell that Palisades place for the $1.9-million asking price."

"And you blame the network for showing her saying those things on television?"

"I do. They had to know how it would sound to people who're barely making ends meet. It was a plot, I tell you. But I want to give Nancy credit for keeping her head. There's one thing I'll bet they were just praying she would say, but she didn't."

"What's that?"

" 'Let 'em eat jelly beans.' "

Kissing Leonid Brezhnev

After considerable thought, I have at last had to give up my own portion of the dream that any American can grow up to be president.

Others, yes. It's still a great dream. But not I.

I could never kiss Leonid Brezhnev.

That has nothing to do with politics. Even if Brezhnev were the greatest friend the free world ever had, I still couldn't kiss him.

And it's nothing personal against the man himself. I suppose if you have to go around kissing men, he's as good as any.

I don't hold anythng against Jimmy Carter, mind you, for embracing Brezhnev and kissing him on both cheeks after the two of them signed the SALT 2 treaty. Hugging, embracing and kissing have become a part of world diplomacy. I say we're lucky to have a president who can kiss without flinching.

It's just that many men of my generation could never manage it. We have been marked for life by early taboos.

We were taught from childhood that it is unseemly for one man to kiss another, regardless of the circumstances.

I realize now how foolish that was, but there you are. It was a different world in those days. Men or boys kissed women or girls. Women or girls kissed men, boys, girls and women. But there was something forbidden abut one male kissing another male.

Today it's common. Diplomats do it. Celebrities do it. Athletes do it. Rodeo stars even kiss their horses, which I assume is about the same thing. And the world is probably better for it.

But that is today. And times have changed.

The last time I can remember kissing a man was in my earliest school days, back when it was a rule that you always kissed your parents goodby.

One morning when my father let me out of the car at school, I leaned over to give him the expected peck on the cheek, and he drew back in embarrassment. Then he mumbled something. I don't remember the words, but the message was clear. I had become too old for that kind of foolishness.

It left me with a strange feeling. I knew he wasn't blaming me for anything, but I also knew I had almost done somethimg terrible. I wondered whether to shake hands, but settled just for jumping out of the car and running.

We never said anything else to each other about it.

Later I was to learn that you showed friendship or affection for other males by whacking them on the back or beating them about the arms or punching them in the ribs or, except when your father left you at school, shaking hands.

Kissing was for female relatives, and they were the ones who did the kissing. All you did was try to endure it.

Still later, of course, I discovered that kissing could be a rather pleasant experience when it was indulged in with an appropriate member of the opposite sex.

But even that was different from today's kissing. That was romantic kissing. Social kissing, where married couples go around kissing each other's spouses in public as a matter of course, was improper. And random kissing, where everybody kisses everybody else regardless of sex, was unthinkable.

In today's world, when as small a thing as a touchdown can touch off an orgy of mass masculine osculation, the old-fashioned attitude seems a little preposterous. But there you are. Times have changed, and I haven't kept up.

So I think it is only fair to announce now, long before the primaries, that I will not run if nominated nor serve if elected. I am simply not cut out to be a kissin' president.

Shucks, when you get right down to it, I'm not even sure I could kiss Margaret Thatcher.

Critters

Your Typical Woolly Bear

Would-be woolly bear researchers throughout the Mid-South have been champing at the bit as mid-September approaches.

How long, they keep demanding, before the Sims Laboratory of Unusual Research Projects (SLURP) launches its annual woolly bear survey to determine the nature and severity of the winter ahead?

Goaded by such pressures, SLURP has acted at last. Today we offer the ground rules for volunteer researchers in the project.

Certain major changes have been made, in accord with latest scientific findings. You can't simply drift along in research of this sort; you have to be on your toes every minute to keep up with a woolly bear. The following information is essential for proper presentation of all WB reports.

Reports should state the area in which the sighting of the WB (or WBs as the case may be) occurred. That helps make our forecast more accurate. The weather can be a lot colder in Raleigh, for example, that it is in Whitehaven. And a WB in Covington, Tenn., may bear an entirely different and more woolly message than does one in Jackson, Miss.

Ignore the direction in which the critter is traveling. SLURP has worked along directional lines in the past, but we have decided it's just not worth it. Accumulated evidence indicates that, when it comes to knowing where they are going and why, woolly bears are just as confused as everybody else.

Numbers of WBs observed may still be of significance. If possible, make a bear-by-bear count; if not, estimate the size of the herd to the best of your ability. But do not scorn the evidence of strays. They may know something the others don't know.

Now for the major innovation, representing the very latest in conceptualized thrusts related to quantitative analysis of involuntary woolly bear prognostications: Distribution of colors.

Your typical woolly bear, unless it has gone hogwild from fear, excitement or pride at the prospect of the winter ahead, will be found to be divided into three general color masses.

Each end of the creature will be covered with black bristles. A center, or near-center, portion will be reddish, orange or what have you. Latest academic findings suggest the spatial relationships among these segments is significant.

The theory is that the 13 segments of a well-constructed WB represent, roughly, the weeks of winter. Black bristles, cold weather. Reddish bristles, milder weather.

Therefore:

Count the segments and identify the colors of each. Or, if you are unable to count segments or feel that such counting constitutes an invasion of WB privacy, measure them. Do not use metric measurements. Metric reports will be ignored.

In reporting the color count, proceed from stem to stern, fore to aft, front to rear. For example: 5 segments black, 4 segments reddish, 4 segments black. That would mean, of course, that according to that particular WB's estimate, the first five weeks of winter will be severe, the next four weeks mild, and so on.

Finally, do not—repeat, not—send the woolly bear itself. If you do, all your credentials will be canceled, a special malediction will be invoked in your behalf, and your name and address will be given to a firm that writes vicious anonymous letters on request. SLURP has had just about enough of such nonsense. Let us proceed scientifically and with decorum.

Forget the Arms Race

While all the brass hats in Washington are worrying about Russia getting ahead of us in the arms race, the Soviets are about to blindside us on another front entirely.

They're planning to pass a law to regulate dogs, something that has never worked in this country.

Think of the implications. Think of how Third World nations will react. If the first effective control of dogs comes from behind the Iron Curtain, what can anybody expect of the Free World?

But there you are. Recent news dispatches report that the Russians plan to end dog-coddling in the Soviet Union sometime around the first of next year.

It's high time for somebody to do it, but why does it have to be the Communists?

Still, you can't help admiring what they plan to do. Consider some aspects of the proposed new order.

Dogs will be banned from "gardens, parks, squares, boulevards, embankments, beaches and other places set aside for relaxation and public use."

Residents of apartment buildings adjacent to public facilities like kindergartens, medical clinics and recreation areas will not be allowed to own dogs.

In cities, special areas will be created for the walking of dogs. Owners—get this, now—will be required to bring their own shovels and pails.

Stiff taxes also will be levied on city dog owners, but part of the reason for that wouldn't apply in America. In Russia, it develops, dogs get free medical care, including X-rays, hospitalization and house calls by veterinarians.

No wonder their domestic economy has been faltering so badly. Even in America nobody ever thought of that.

But, now that the dog problem has come to the attention of party leaders, the whole situation is going to be straightened out.

Articles have appeared in the Russian press, pointing out that dogs create messes in courtyards, elevators, parks, stairways and sidewalks. Readers have complained about being bitten. Pravda, the Communist Party daily newspaper, has estimated that about 180,000 to 190,000 Soviet citizens are bitten by dogs each year.

That's remarkable in itself; Soviet dogs must be unusually restrained. I would guess that in America the figure is closer to a million.

Even in Russia, it develops, dog lovers insist on snapping back at any move to exert reasonable control over, their pets.

One reader had the gall to tell Pravda, "Dogs never bite anyone for nothing."

I would call that a typical example of misguided Communist thinking, except that you can hear the same thing said any day in America —despite the fact that thousands of us can testify from experience that there's not a word of truth in it.

So with the new year, Russia appears to be ready to usher in a new era of freedom from the tyranny of dogs and their owners—while in the Free World we go on being victims.

Right here in Memphis, for example, how many owners have you seen carrying their own shovels and pails when they take their dogs for walks in front of other people's property?

I bow to no man in my love for America, but I wish Russia the best of luck in its noble experiment. If the only way we can learn dog control in this country is by seeing it work first in Russia, then so be it. Forget the arms race for a while and get started on the dog-control race.

Masked Marauders of Memphis

Almost any night, Mr. and Mrs. Maurice Stanley of Memphis might look up and see a masked face peering in at them through a bedroom window.

They don't scream or call the police. They just go for the dogfood and feed the raccoon.

But usually that look in the window isn't necessary, because the feeding has already been done.

After the come-to-supper bell had been rung.

And sometimes, by golly, in the Stanley bedroom itself.

In a city populated by thousands of raccoons—and by perhaps hundreds of families that put out food for the varmints—the Stanleys may have set some kind of record.

There's a wooded acre out behind their house and for years now, coons have been coming up to be fed, usually six or eight of them, every night the Stanleys are at home. It could be that theirs is the biggest boarding house for raccoons in town.

All this began back around 1974, when the Stanleys happened to see a coon walking across their patio about dusk one evening.

They hustled up some food for it and the rest, as they say, is history.

By now, a typical evening goes something like this.

About 5:30 or 6, Mrs. Stanley goes and gets the dry dogfood—she buys 25 pounds of it every two or three weeks—and rings the bell.

Food is scattered on the patio, just outside the bedroom window, and the Stanleys settle down indoors to watch.

And the coons come, two or three at a time, sometimes fighting among themselves, to grab up the food in their paws and take off.

Occasionally, on their way to or from the food, they'll stop off for a quick dip in the fountain-pool on the patio.

That goes on for a couple of hours. Every night. Spring, summer, autumn, winter.

Sometimes the coons get impatient and come before the bell is rung. Sometimes, for added entertainment, the Stanleys, open the big floor-length windows in the bedroom, spread out a paper on the floor, and entertain indoors. The coons come right on in and make themselves at home.

But on other occasions, if time is passing and the bell hasn't rung, some of the critters will come up to the windows, rise up on their hind legs, and peer impatiently through the glass.

It's quite a sight to see a raccoon looking in through your bedroom window, but the Stanleys are used to it.

Somebody had told me the coons rang a bell when they were hungry, but Mrs. Stanley said that isn't quite the way it is. Actually, she said, a little bell rings occasionally while they're eating.

That's because there's a little flexible hacksaw blade in the yard, rigged up with a tiny bell on it, and from time to time dogfood is taped on it. When a coon grabs the food, the bell rings.

Well, coons are pretty smart. Give them enough time and enough hacksaw blades, and it wouldn't surprise me if they learned to play Chopsticks.

The way Mrs. Stanley has figured it out, the babies are born around March and April, and by the end of June they're big enough to be brought along.

They come in litters of up to four, with their mothers, and they're quite wild. They usually hide in the shrubbery. It takes them about a year to get up the nerve to join the grownups in the bedroom.

Word about the Stanleys' interesting setup has gotten out, and when guests come they're usually eager to see the coons. If it's after regular eating hours, Mrs. Stanley simply rings the bell and serves a late snack.

It might be worth noting, by the way, that there's no foolishness about trying to pet, fondle, or hand-feed the animals. Those little varmints look cute, but they can bite.

Aside from that precaution, though, everything is as friendly and frisky as you could like. And what about spending a couple of hours every night just watching raccoons eat?

"It beats watching television," says Mrs. Stanley.

Would A Peppy Woodpecker Peck?

After all these years, somebody has finally come up with what sounds like a solid solution to the annual woodpecker problem.

You know the problem I mean. Every spring, woodpeckers develop this infuriating habit of banging on houses all over town and rousing the sleeping residents therein.

The victims holler for help, but nobody knows what to tell them. Rubber snakes on the roof? Forget 'em. Noises calculated to scare away the peckerwoods? You should live so long. Strips of metal? Save your time.

But now Nell Wade of Moscow, Tenn., has reported on a relatively simple method by which she woodpecker-proofed her own roof— and it could work for you.

"I lived through a whole spring and summer of rat-a-tat-tat outside my bedroom window every morning, usually about 6 o'clock, the first year after we built our house," she told me.

"I tried everything.

"I threw bricks and anything else I could get my hands on.

"I'd sneak around the corner and fire off a pistol or shotgun, trying to scare the pests away. The only thing I'd scare was myself.

"My husband even nailed pieces of sheet metal over each new hole they made, hoping they would break their beaks, but they would just start another hole."

Then, she said, some kindly person—she doesn't remember who—told her what to do.

"In desperation, we did it.

"We poured a can of ground cayenne pepper into some sorghum molasses and painted the mixture over each hole.

"And that was it. They never bothered us again."

Mrs. Wade isn't sure about how the word got around. Do woodpeckers have some way of telling other woodpeckers, "Wow, that's hot"? Do little heat waves rise from the pepper-and-sorghum mixture and warn the birds away?

All she knows is that the treatment worked.

"I see lots of woodpeckers having at it in the trees around the house," she told me, "but they leave my house alone."

She's glad to pass this word along, she said, "but I don't want to hear from all those bird lovers out there about my cruelty to our fine feathered friends."

Because she figures that she loves birds as much as the next person. She feeds them in the winter. She won't even keep a cat because she knows what cats do to birds.

But there are limits, by golly.

"And if I ever again hear what sounds like a concrete drill outside my window, you can bet your bottom dollar I'll get out the paint brush and apply another coat of cayenne and molasses."

And good luck to her. A temporary dose of hot-throat strikes me as pretty mild medicine for an overactive woodpecker—especially one that operates at 6 o'clock in the morning. Good night, people have killed for less. The affected birds probably just flew away, sneezed a few times, drank plenty of nice cool water, and joined Roof-Blasters Anonymous.

So remember that when spring comes. It may work for you. Millions for pepper, but not one cent for rat-a-tat-tat.

Smile At The Birdie

Wonders never cease. We have shared reports of ducks down chimneys in the past, but prepare now for something truly sensational.

Would you believe a starling in a toilet bowl?

Trust me. I'll never lie to you. Besides, I've consulted authorities.

The adventure of the flushed starling occurred at the home of Mrs. G.B. of Huntingdon, Tenn. Those are real initials for a real person. Mrs. B. and I have discussed the matter at some length.

A while back, she told me, she had occasion to flush a toilet in her home. Hearing noises above and beyond the usual gurgles, she glanced down.

There in the bowl, just above the water line, was a starling, wet, stunned and resentful. It glared at her.

She and the starling were alone in the house. Put yourself in her place. How would you feel?

Mrs. B. was frightened but plucky. As she put it later, "I kept telling myself, 'Don't panic. Think of some way to get him out of the bowl and out of the house.' "

She remembered that her husband, a fisherman, had a dip net in the garage. It was a time for action. She closed all the doors, rushed out for the net, returned, spread it over the bowl and, "with words and gestures," urged the bird to fly upward.

At last it did. She flipped the net over, dashed outdoors with it and released her captive.

The starling shook itself and flew away.

But looky, I said, was she sure the starling hadn't been in the house already? Absolutely, she said. Then could someone have been playing pranks on her? No way.

And anyhow, she said, the same thing has happened to a neighbor down the street, except that it was a squirrel instead of a starling.

It sounded convincing, but I knew there would be skeptics. I consulted a friend who said yes, he thought it might be possible. But he's in the lighting business.

So I called a contractor, William "Buddy" Mills, and he waffled. Well, he said, maybe. No, he went on, he just didn't see how it could happen. On the other hand, he concluded, if it could happen Pete Edmiston would know. Pete Edmiston is in the plumbing business.

And Edmiston said yes, it could indeed happen. There is this vent pipe that goes up to the roof, see? And a bird, or a squirrel, or a rat, could tumble down the vent pipe and then, in its efforts to escape, get into the pipe from the toilet bowl and work its way through.

But how, I asked? Would it hold its breath and swim upstream? He didn't explain it in those same terms, but it amounted to the same thing. And he said that, in cases he knew of, it didn't happen while the toilet was being flushed. But still, if the bird was en route at the time, it could happen.

So there you are. There is no hiding place down here. Don't say you haven't been warned. Some day, somewhere, just when you least expect it . . .

A Bird In the Hand . . . ?

There may be such a thing, Mrs. Doris Hamilton is beginning to believe, as carrying aid to dependent robins too far.

Look what's happened to Bowser.

That rascal flies around the neighborhood, but she won't leave home.

When the weather's bad, she comes and hollers at the bathroom window to be let in out of the rain.

When she's hungry, she demands to be fed. Ad she doesn't just want food thrown out to her; she opens her beak and waits for somebody to pop it in.

And when she's lonely, by golly, she just comes indoors to visit.

Where, Mrs. Hamilton asked me yesterday, will it all end?

It's easy enough to say where it all began.

About a month ago, in April, Mrs. Hamilton's daughter Kim came home from school with a small bird she had picked up along the way.

It wasn't a baby, but it didn't look fully grown. And it appeared to have been pretty badly mauled by something. Feathers were missing from its tail and around its neck. It loked like a female robin, generally beat up and miserable.

Well, Mrs. Hamilton said, they had to do something. So her husband called the zoo for feeding instructions and they went to work.

They fixed up a box in the game room for the bird to sleep in. They fed it hard-boiled egg mashed up with warm milk, using an eyedropper. They began adding soft-boiled meat, as directed.

The bird thrived, and soon began to be called Bowser because, like a current singing star, her mouth was always open.

And life has become hectic for the Hamiltons.

After a week or so in the indoors box, Bowser could stand and run around. They took her outdoors and installed her in a pen on top of a picnic table. During the day they would go out and put her on the ground. She would walk or run a little way, or even fly, but she kept coming back.

More time passed. They began tossing her up into the air. She would fly short distances and then return to a convenient shoulder or hand.

And so it went. Bowser began to fly to the top of the carport, the top of the house, into trees, wherever—but she always flew back.

They moved her living quarters to a hanging nest in the carport, and for a while she slept there regularly. Now they don't know where she sleeps, but they sure as shooting know where she eats: Right there with them.

For a while they tried providing worms and insects from the yard. Bowser ate all they could find. Neighbors came visiting with insects of their own. Down the hatch, and impatient cheeping for more.

By now the whole thing has fallen into a sort of pattern. Bowser usually demands her first meal before the family breakfast, and then returns all through the day for seconds, thirds and fourths.

She wants everything done for her. The Hamiltons fixed up a bird bath for her in the back yard, but the other day when she had something sticky on her tail she came to Mrs. Hamilton to be bathed in a plastic butter dish and dried with a towel.

The Hamiltons have been reduced to buying worms from a store. And it goes on all day long. Even as she told me about the business, Mrs. Hamilton had to stop and let the bird in the back door for a bowl of milk, cheese and wild strawberries—all delivered by hand or through an eyedropper.

That bird, in short, has simply refused to grow up and take her place as a useful member of society.

Mrs. Hamilton worries about her, but not as much as she did before she talked to her husband about it the other day.

"Do you think she's retarded?" she asked him.

He gave her a wry look.

"Who," he asked, "is feeding whom?"

My Squirrels Turn Backflips

This could be one whale of a spring. Just the other day, a squirrel turned three backflips in my front yard.

Did you ever see a squirrel turn a backflip?

For that matter, did you ever even hear of such a thing?

Well, this one did. Among other equally exuberant if less startling stunts.

All this occurred within only a few feet of our breakfast table, just outside the window in an area that is primarily intended for birds.

There's a birdbath out there, and a large flat rock, and a feeding jar hanging from a tree limb. Every morning, I toss around a few handfuls of birdseed, and we are accordingly provided a nature show along with the cereal. We get the usual crowd of birds—a few cardinals and bluejays, an occasional junco or towhee or titmouse or chickadee, too many sparrows and blackbirds, that sort of thing—plus from one to four squirrels.

The squabbling, bullying, bluffing and greed demonstrated by our innocent little furred and feathered friends are enough to prepare anybody to face the day with the bitter cynicism required for survival.

But this day was different.

We first noticed this particular squirrel when he appeared to have got himself tangled in something. But he wasn't tangled at all.

He had a sweetgum ball in his paws, and he was playing with it the way a kitten plays with a roll of yarn. He went over on his back, holding it up in the air. He rolled this way and that, batting it back and forth.

And then he simply up and did a backflip. I nearly spilled crunchy granola all over the table.

By the time my wife and I were able to compare notes and agree he had really done a backflip, the squirrel had engaged in a kittenish tussle with a twig, leapt up and chased another squirrel into a nearby tree, jumped across to another tree, zipped back down to the ground and shot through a small congregation of birds, scattering them before him like chickenfeed.

And then, by golly, he did a second backflip. And a third.

If he had been Nadia Comaneci, the Olympic judges would have awarded him a gold medal on the spot.

Since then, I have consulted several squirrelly friends, none of whom had ever seen such a sight and at least one of whom reacted in typical contemporary fashion.

"Get a gun quick and shoot it," he advised. "You've got a mad squirrel on the loose. It could bite somebody."

Just to be sure about the matter, I consulted Charles Wilson, director of the Memphis Zoo, who remained calm.

That flip could have been some kind of courting display, he suggested, though it isn't described in the literature; or it could have been simply good spirits on the part of a young squirrel—play behavior, it's called. Assuming the yard hadn't been sprayed or treated recently, and assuming nobody had spilled a bottle of cologne or something else out there, he doubted that anything more than youth or romance was involved. Certainly no cause for alarm.

So what I say is, don't look a gift squirrel in the mouth. Generally, March comes in like a lion and goes out like a lamb. This March came in like a lamb and is going out with squirrels turning backflips. If it means fine weather ahead, squirrels can do backflips in my yard anytime.

Bite Brim, Not Bullet

Want to know how to avoid being bitten by a dog?

John W. Purvis Jr. has the answer. At least he says he does. He has been intending to tell me about it for five years, he said, but he's only now getting around to it.

After hearing his system, I can understand his delay.

"When you're threatened by a mean or vicious dog," he told me solemnly, "simply put the brim or visor of a hat or cap in your mouth and stare the beast down, showing no fear."

I told him he had to be kidding. He said no, it was a family technique that had been passed down through the generations since his forfathers roamed the Scottish moors in the early 1800s.

"The reason is simple," he said. "Animals are fearful of something they have never seen before. How many people go around with a hat or cap in their mouths?"

You run into all sorts of weird ideas in a job like this, but it's not every day somebody recommends biting a cap to keep a dog from biting you.

And if animals are fearful of something they have never seen before, how come they bite strangers?

But Purvis stood firm.

"I have seen this theory work beautifully on two occasions," he insisted.

So what were they?

"Some 20 years ago my father and I visited the fire tower on top of Round Top Mountain at Heber Springs, Ark.," he recalled.

"We were attacked by a vicious dog. I ran and got in the car, but my father simply put his hat in his mouth.

"That did it for the dog."

On the other occasion, he said, he himself was the hat-biter.

"About 10 years ago, down at Sardis Lake, we had outboard motor trouble. I lost the toss of the coin and had to walk to the car, some seven miles away.

"While walking down a remote gravel road, I was about to be attacked by about two dozen semiwild mixed-breed dogs.

"Once again, the old hat trick. In five seconds, the whole pack was demobilized. When I walked over a hill a hundred yards away, they were sitting on their haunches, staring in complete disbelief."

Purvis said he thought his revelation would be of great benefit to letter carriers, sanitation workers, meter readers, door-to-door salesmen, joggers and even burglars.

The only times it's not guaranteed to work, he went on , are (1) in the case of highly-trained "killer" dogs, (2) in the case of rabid dogs, and (3) when you forget your hat or cap.

Personally, I wouldn't touch the idea with a 10-gallon Stetson. If a dog doesn't think a typical jogger looks too outlandish to bite, why should it be bemused by a jogger with a mouthful of hat?

Besides, I have been bitten by a dog that came up behind me and never even saw my mouth. What, I asked Purvis, about that? I don't remember his exact words, but my recollection is that he suggested you can't blame the dog if the victim is foolish enough to be facing the other way.

"Maybe I should have just kept my cap in my mouth all the time," I suggested, trying to find some logic to the whole thing.

"In that case," he said sternly, "people would have thought you were crazy."

I suppose it's remotely possible that we have something big here. If biting the brim beats biting the bullet, the world needs to know.

Clothes Encounter Of Worst Kind

Things aren't as bad in this area as you might have thought. What if we had real furbearing skunks around here instead of just politicians?

That's the grim situation up in Minnesota, according to recent reports.

Well, actually they have skunks and politicians both, but it's the former that are causing the more pressing problems at the moment. Talk about smelly conditions.

The skunk population of Minnesota and several other upper-Midwest states "is riding the crest of a cyclical high," reports the Wall Street Journal, which keeps track records of significant cycles of all sorts.

And, it adds,"record numbers of Minnesota automobile drivers are finding their reveries interrupted by slow skunks in the fast lane."

Skunks often travel on the highways, and they pay no attention to traffic regulations, and they aren't afraid of anything. So all over Minnesota, one gathers, the aroma is overwhelming. It's caused by what Journal chooses to call "a close encounter of the worst kind."

Here in Memphis, by contrast, we haven't had a substantial skunk scare as long as I can remember. And when I called Charles Wilson, director of the Memphis Zoo, his comments couldn't have been more reassuring.

"We haven't had but two skunk calls this year, and one of those was about a pet," he told me. "I think you can say we're not going to experience a skunk winter."

Raccoons, yes. We have scads of raccoons. But anybody who ever tangled with a skunk will tell you a raccoon is a blessing by comparison.

Indeed, those raccoons may actually be protecting us from skunks, Wilson suggested.

It's a matter of competition. Both animals like to raid garbage cans and perform other scavenging jobs, and it's just possible that our large raccoon population has kept the skunks out. After all, they got here first and have the territory all staked out.

And when was the last time we had a real skunk problem in Tennessee? Well, Wilson said, that would have been in the 1950s. Animal populations go in cycles, just as the Journal report suggested, and back then the state had a lot of skunks and foxes.

In fact, there were so many cases of rabies among foxes and skunks that we made national headlines. But that, of course, was nigh onto a generation ago.

Still, the odd skunk does turn up, so you should know that the critters come in two types—the standard striped skunk and the Eastern spotted skunk, sometimes known as the polecat.

They're equally effective at any given range, Wilson warned, and innocent citizens shouldn't be misled by reports that a skunk will never go into action without giving you ample warning. It will if it's startled or scared badly enough. Never go around saying "Boo!" to skunks.

So what should the cautious skunk-avoider do? Check all around the foundations of the house for openings. If you don't want a skunk taking up residence at your place, then don't leave a place for it to enter.

And what if you already have one?

Don't—repeat, don't—go in after it. That way lies disaster.

What you should do is wait till around midnight, at which time the animal will almost surely be out foraging around, and then go barricade the opening it got in by.

Meanwhile, console yourself with this thought: As bad as conditions may get around here sometimes, we can at least be grateful
that we aren't in Minnesota, downwind from the interstate.

A Little Common Mule Sense

Mules are so smart you can't help wishing they could run for Congress.

The other day a reader recalled the glory days of those noble
creatures, now all but forgotten by a wretched and ungrateful
public.

And Walter Neal's account of how a mule refused, in the dark, to
cross a bridge that turned out to be unsafe has unlocked memories of
other mule lovers.

Many have commented generally on the wisdom, agility and loving
cussedness of the creature. Others have harked back to the mule-
trading days in Memphis and still others have recounted marvelous
mule tales of their own.

Lest future histories of the mule turn out to be as sterile as the
animal itself, it seems prudent to relay at least a couple of the
stories. Stand well away from those back legs, friends, and prepare
to be impressed.

The adventure recalled by Richard Barrett deals primarily with
the grace of the ungainly looking animal. It occurred down around
Camden, Miss., where Barrett was born and raised.

"My daddy would let us boys ride Bully to see our girls or
sometime to church," he said. "One of my brothers, Wesley, had a
girl across the creek two or three miles away.

"One afternoon he rode Bully to see his girl. It came up a big rain
about the time he was to leave, 9:30 or 10. Dark as a sack of black
cats . . ."

Together they set out, and soon they reached the creek. By then
the bridge was under water. But earlier, a big tree had blown across
the creek about 100 yards upstream, and the boys had trimmed off
the limbs on the upper sides and fixed some steps on the butt end so
they could walk across.

"Wesley and Bully got to the log and Wesley unfastened one side
of the bridle so he would have a long leash, and told Bully he would
have to swim.

"Wesley got up on the log, holding one hand out to the side to kind
of guide Bully . . ."

So the boy set out, not looking back. Gradually the leash tightened in his hand. Just as a big flash of lightning lit up the sky, he looked back to see what was keeping Bully.

"And there was Bully," Barrett said, "walking the log and doing it fine."

But it was as guardians to safety that the animals truly shone. Listen to G. Lee Weaver.

"In 1911, when I was real young, my father, mother, brother and I were on our way home in a wagon drawn by two beautiful mules when a thunderstorm came up.

"We were on an old log road in the woods.

"Suddenly the mules stopped and began to back the wagon.

"They had backed about 30 yards when a big tree came crashing down in front of us."

So mules could not only sense hazards they couldn't see, and they could not only walk watersoaked logs across raging streams, but they even knew when something bad was about to happen. In a land that has almost given up on people, let us not forget that there's still time to return to mulebreeding.

Bell Gets Nanny's Goat

Strange stories still come out of rural areas of the country, stories some city slickers find hard to believe.

There is, for example, the case of the terrified nanny goat. Jim Monroe has been telling Memphis friends about it lately, and it is safe to assume some of them are skeptical.

Can you scare a poor little goat to death with a bell? Hang on and we'll see.

Not long ago, Monroe, who is engaged to Miss Sarah Jones, went to visit his fiancee's parents and brother near Arkabutla, Miss. The brother told them the story.

Last spring he acquired a small black nanny goat which was allowed to roam at will over the family's property and in the general area.

That suited the goat fine. She ate virtually anything and everything, but she acquired an especial fondness for Miss Tommie's rose bushes.

Miss Tommie, by the way, is really Mrs. Bob Jones, Monroe's fiancee's mother. They call her Miss Tommie because Tommie is her name. Anybody knows that, and it has nothing to do with what happened to the goat.

"One day last summer," as Monroe relayed the story to me, "Miss Tommie noticed the goat lunching on her rose arbor. She decided to teach it a lesson.

"She took a cowbell, held onto the clapper, sneaked out the back door and surprised the goat at lunch with a furious ringing of the bell.

"The goat just gave it all up and fell over.

"Miss Tommie was distraught over scaring the goat to death and didn't know what to do. But fortunately the animal came to and managed to drag itself away from the bell ringer."

This is the sort of story calculated to mystify outlanders and outrage the tender-heated, but it is more.

It is also a classic example of a phenomenon too little known and and admired in our area.

The diagnosis, in short, is clear. Miss Tommie rang that bell at a nervous goat. Nervous goats are an unusual breed, or cross-breed, or something. Surprise them with a sudden loud noise and down they go, but only for a couple of minutes. Then they're as fit as ever.

Tales aren't told about them as often as they used to be, but reports trickle in from time to time, and I for one believe in the preservation of interesting oddities.

It's good to know about the wonders of nature all about us. And besides, you can win bets on nervous goats.

Or even more than bets. The story is still told in Middle Tennessee about a Brooklyn lieutenant in those parts during the early days of World War II. His job was to drive around in a Jeep, settling claims of farmers whose lands had been used in Army maneuvers. He would drive up to a farmhouse, let go a blast of his horn and ask for evidence of damages.

And they do say he paid one farmer half a dozen times, on successive days, for the same flock of nervous goats. Every time he drove up and blew his horn, the goats keeled over and the farmer collected. It pays to know about these things.

It's Raining Cats and Dogs

A nice woman with a problem has called on me to tell her what can be done about dogs.

She lives in a housing project occupied mostly by senior citizens, she says, and the dog situation has progressed from a mere vague threat to a present menace.

Uncollared and unleashed dogs roam the area, attacking letter carriers, biting children, terrifying elderly strollers. The complainant, whose name I won't use lest some vicious dog or dog-owner bite her in reprisal, says her calls to officialdom have been in vain. What can be done?

I hate to tell her, but the answer to that is simple. Not one blessed thing, ma'am. Nothing. Zilch. Go on suffering and hold out as long as you can. Help won't be coming.

The simple fact is that there's not a politician alive today with gumption enough to deal with the problem of dogs. Let alone the problem, almost equally maddening, of cats.

Neither animal has any place in city life, of course. Yet they continue to multiply. And mere humans, those who don't care to be plagued by other people's critters, suffer.

Do you grow flowers? A roaming dog can put the hex on them in less time than it takes to throw a shoe. Do you like chipmunks or birds? Your neighbor's cat will get them before you can yell "Scat." Do you jog, or take bike rides, or go for walks, or send your children out to play in their own front yards? Then prepare for the worst and keep the antiseptic handy.

No reasonable person will blame the animals themselves. They're only doing what comes naturally—or, considering the environment in which they have been thrust, unnaturally.

But, by golly, the city's not the place for them to do it.

Owners who speak of loving dumb animals and spend millions of dollars a year for pet food actually sentence those pets to lives of cruel restraint, either indoors (where the animals become sly, vengeful monsters or pathetic psychotic misfits) or turn them loose on the community, where pets and innocent citizens alike are endangered as a result.

Or, in the case of dogs, they fasten them at the end of chains, where they grow so frustrated it is painful to hear them.

In either case, the pets are the victims, not the villains. But that doesn't help matters in the least.

The obvious solution is to outlaw such animals from cities entirely, with the possible exception of those living in tremendous fenced yards beyond barking or yowling range of any human beings but the owners. And the fences would have to be of a sort hitherto unknown that can keep even a cat imprisoned.

But none of that helps the nice woman in the housing project, because none of it will ever be done. The right to own and mistreat small pets has become a part of the American dream. The fact that the dream has become a nightmare doesn't change matters a bit.

Stay in your apartment, ma'am, and keep the medicine chest well-stocked. It's raining cats and dogs outdoors.

Frog Dogs Self-made

As our space probes have proved, the wonders of the universe are almost beyond belief.

And you don't even have to go to Saturn to find them. Remember a recent column in which a woman asked if there really is such a thing as a frog dog?

Barry Saunders, a nationally known field trial judge, read that column with special interest.

You know why? He has, or had, a frog dog himself.

The question arose because a man down in Mississippi kept insisting to his friend in Tennessee that there really are frog dogs, and that he trains them. They catch bullfrogs, he said. She didn't know whether to believe him or not.

Saunders' frog didn't require any training. It learned all by itself.

As a matter of fact, Saunders never heard of a frog-dog trainer. He never even heard of a frog dog before his own dog became one, and he's an expert. He judges pointing dogs all over the country. In 1978, and again this year, he was a judge at the National Field Trials at Grand Junction, Tenn.

No, they don't have a classification for frog dogs. But still . . .

Saunders has this dog named Sam, a stylish pointer which he began to train two years ago when it was a puppy.

He was taking it for a walk around his farm at Grand Junction one day when Sam began dashing from pond to pond, pointing bullfrogs.

And that wasn't all. He retrieved 'em as well.

Oh, they were big bullfrogs, all right, and Sam didn't kill them. He just captured them carefully and brought them, intact, to Saunders.

(Think of that for a moment. Could you catch an adult bullfrog in daylight with your bare hands, let alone your mouth?)

This went on for a while. One day Sam retrieved four big bullfrogs, and Saunders gave them to some friends, who had frog legs for dinner. So he can, if necessary, produce witnesses.

There is no future in frog-pointing for field trial dogs, of course, so Saunders had to break Sam of the habit. How would it have looked in a trial if Sam had been found pointing a bullfrog? You don't win prizes that way.

But the possibility of frog-dogging as an art remains.

Saunders feels that a good bird dog is so intelligent it can be trained to do almost anything, and he has no doubt that includes pointing and retrieving frogs.

As for people who snort that nobody ever heard of a "frog dog," well, that's what Saunders' friends called Sam after they learned about his self-taught skill. And that's what startled him when he saw the inquiry in this column.

So we get back to the question asked by the woman whose friend said he trains frog dogs.

Maybe he doesn't. If Saunders hasn't heard of such an occupation, the chances are it isn't well known at the very least.

Indeed, maybe the fellow thought he was just pulling her leg when he talked about frog dogs.

If so, he was wrong. We now have the evidence.

And what, you may ask, can anybody do with it? What good does it do to know that a dog can point, capture and retrieve a full-grown bullfrog?

I don't know. But I don't really know what we're going to learn from the rings around Saturn, for that matter.

If revealing the existence of frog dogs adds to the sum total of human knowledge, that ought to be sufficient for the moment.

And besides, if the price of food goes much higher, we might even want to consider training a frog dog of our own.

A Case of the Frizzlies

Save this. Next time you mention frizzly chickens and somebody snorts, you'll have evidence.

They laughed when John Nassar sat down to discuss frizzlies, you may recall, so he asked the Sims Laboratory of Unusual Research Problems (SLURP) for support.

It's here. Consider the testimony.

"I'll have to stand up and be counted when frizzlies are brought into question," Mrs. W. C. Trotter Jr. of Greenville, Miss., told me stoutly.

Indeed, she said, her grandmother raised nothing but frizzlies. That was for easy identification. Chickens roamed a lot in those days, but nobody else in Coffeeville, Miss., had frizzlies.

As Mrs. Trotter remembers them, frizzlies differed from other chickens only in their curly feathers: "In every other respect they were like other chickens—they clucked, cackled, crowed, laid eggs, squawked, pecked and uprooted flower beds." What more could anyone expect of a chicken?

A more poignant report came from Reminiscer of Coldwater, Miss.:

"During my childhood there was a frizzly chicken in our henhouse. I named her Pulcharia and regarded her with interest and affection.

"Unfortunately, she became the victim of a chicken thief and met with an untimely end. All that remained of poor Pulcharia were frizzly feathers."

Others found them less enchanting. When she was a small child, Mrs. Pete Norowski of Memphis told me, she was given two baby chicks at Easter that grew up to be frizzlies. Bad frizzlies.

"Oh, they were mean," she said. "They would attack me in the back yard—they pecked blood out of my leg. We had a little collie puppy, and they attacked it, too."

At last her mother, Mrs. Louise Stults, decided the time had come to act. "She backed them up in the corner of the shed and shot them both in the head with a .22 rifle. They were too tough to eat."

An indication of the general public awareness of frizzlies came from an Alabama reader, who recalled:

"When I was in high school and had just gotten my first permanent wave, a friend said to me, ' You look just like a frizzly chicken'."

It was, I believe, a common jest in those days.

But what does science say on the subject? Arthur H. Prince checked frizzlies out in a book called The Principles of Heredity and found they are identified as "frizzled feathered creepers."

According to the book, frizzled feathered creepers have shortened and deformed wings and legs, and are never born to normal parents. When creepers mate with normal birds, equal numbers of creepers and normal progeny may be expected. When creepers are crossed, the offspring show a ratio of two creepers to one normal.

That's as may be. Old Timer offered a different explanation.

"Any dumbkopf knows," he told me, "that frizzly chickens are hatched from eggs laid on Easter Sunday."

Check it out, if you like. But don't tolerate jeers from anybody when frizzlies are mentioned.

Bury Those Jokes In The Mole, Mole Ground

One animal the world could well do without, I am now persuaded, is the mole.

Well, yes, I brought it all on myself with a column about a group of students who are collecting molish jokes, and a second column adding to the collection.

Too much, some readers cried at that point. Hah. They should have seen all the ones I got but didn't use. By now, every time I see a soft-looking lawn, I get an urge to burrow in.

So today marks the end: Molish jokes together again for the very last time.

There are, for example, the three educational questions from Edie Hill.

What do you call a mole that thinks it's superior to other animals? A mole chauvinist pig.

Why do frugal moles buy compact cars? To get better moleage.

What did the drunken mole beg for when the bar was closing? Just one mole for the road.

By now I'm not even sure when a repeat item turns up in a different setting. But Kate Hollingsworth's complaint is surely legitimate.

When we were listing the great mole capitals of the country, she asked, why did we leave out the most important of them all?

Moulton, Ala., of course. Sorry about that.

"I sat down and moled it over," Felicia Anderson noted by way of explaining her own entries, which include:

How does a mole heat its house? With moler energy.

What does a mole wear when it is cold? A molehair scarf.

What is a mole full of when it makes no sense? Molearky.

I tell you, it has been like that around here day after day. A fellow can go wild. Visions haunt my sleep at night, passing at a pace one reader tells me is preferred by drowsy moles: Slow moletion.

But the worst outrages in the lot were perpetrated by a university professor, Charles Treas, who teaches marketing at an institution he identified as Mole Miss., where he said the fall enmolement is expected to reach 10,000. Holy moley!

There is room for only a few of the professor's findings—the remainder will no doubt turn up in some learned journal—but I pass them on in an earnest effort to share the misery.

Students at Mole Miss have a lot of fun. Their favorite movie star is Mole Brooks, and those who go to the opera enjoy Wagner's Immolation of Brunhilde. Others look forward to the spring formoles.

But most prefer footmole, which is played in Memolial Stadium. The object of the game is to cross the mole line first, and the team hopes to play in the Sugar Mole or the Liberty Mole after the regular season ends.

It takes a lot of simoleons to run a university, and the coach gets the highest emoleument of any member of the staff.

There is a lot more that I could report," the professor concluded, "but I must get to class and take the mole to see who's absent."

And so, I trust, we say goodbye to moleish jokes forever. No mole! It is time to turn our thoughts to higher matters. Perpetrators are hereby warned. Any further outrages may be resented with a Moletov Cocktail.

The World Is
Falling Apart

Is This One All Right?

HERE AND THERE around the country, intrepid rebels have already arisen to denounce the massive overuse and misuse of that once-harmless phrase, "Have a nice day," known in some circles simply as "H.A.N.D."

Now a simmering citizen has launched a crusade against yet another phrase, the hallmark of restaurant cashiers everywhere:

"Was everything all right?"

And high time, by golly. That mechanical question, for which the cashier is programmed only to receive an affirmative reply, has been giving me indigestion for years.

"The phrase was originally used in the present tense by a waiter or waitress at the start of a meal, to expedite possible corrective action," said my anonymous critic, who prefers to be known by yet another dubious phrase—Your Faithful Correspondent.

"But now it is usually said after the meal, by the cashier.

"One finds this use of W.E.A.R. irritating, since no corrective action could be taken after the meal except a refund, an apology, or, in the worst case, directions to the nearest hospital.

"A couple of times, testing this post-prandial use of W.E.A.R., I replied honestly, 'No, it wasn't.'

"This only elicited a dirty look, not an apology or any other word."

I can testify to that too, having tried the same vain ploy.

Oh, there are exceptions, to be sure. But in most cases, when I have responded that the steak was too tough, the potato too rare or whatever, the cashier has assumed an expression of bemused distaste while looking in some other direction, as if someone has just committed some utterly repulsive social indiscretion.

And, as in the case of Your Faithful Correspondent, she offered no reply whatever, merely pushing out the change in a way that assured their hands wouldn't touch.

So a desperate experiment undertaken by our hero was of especial significance. What he decided, he told me, was to avoid the problem "by ignoring, or pretending not to hear, the cashier's bogus W.E.A.R."

Even he was not prepared for the result.

"I hereby relate the ensuing exchange, verbatim," he told me. And here it is, as he gave it.

Cashier: W.E.A.R.?
Your Faithful Correspondent: (silence, with averted gaze.)
C: W.E.A.R.??
Y.F.C.: (more silence, fiddling with pocket change.)
C.: W.E.A.R.?!
Y.F.C.: What do you want from me?
C.: I want to know if E.W.A.R.
Y.F.C.: What would you do if I said it wasn't A.R.?
C.: I would want you to give me a logical explanation.
Y.F.C.: I can't believe my ears. (Departs)
C. (calling after): Have a nice day!
Our critic, who is clearly a man of great learning, called attention
to "the skillful conjunction of H.A.N.D. and W.E.A.R.—which, when
used together, yield a sort of synergistic effect."

I'm not entirely sure what synergism is, but I do hope it can be
cleared up with a toothpick. Otherwise it is doubtful whether, for him
at least, everything was ever all right.

Whatever Happened To Small?

In this summer of constant trials and tribulations, one puzzling problem has not yet been commented on by the social scientists or
economists.

It's a small matter, literally, but it appears to be bothering more
and more people who order soft drinks in disposable cups at movie
houses and fast-food establishments.

The question: Whatever happened to small?

Small, they report, is disappearing. In many places you can no
longer order a small Coke, or Pepsi, or whatever.

And in places where you can order small, you get large.

Here and there, it is true, small is still available. But the price is
large. What happened?

It appears to be part of a pattern in the entire soft-drink industry.
The day is long gone, for example, when you could buy a small bottle
of your favorite soda or cola. Only the oldtimers remember when one
firm's advertising jungle boasted that its "12 full ounces" was
"twice as much for a nickel, too."

Twice as much? Nowadays you generally begin with 12 full ounces
and work up to a liter, or above. And some people say the new metric
system isn't a threat to us all.

But in the world of plastic or cardboard cups, the confusion is even
worse.

I have just completed a consumer survey—limited, it is true, but highly unscientific—that indicates the chief complaints:

Small has disappeared. Large has become small. Medium has disappeared. And besides the only way you can tell which drink is which is to watch which machine the syrup is squirted from. Mostly, you get ice, water and a touch of color.

A couple I know went to a Memphis movie recently and ordered two small colas. The friendly young woman behind the counter got out a pair of cups that could have held family-sized orders of fried chicken.

"Wait," said the wife. "We wanted small."

"This is small," said the young woman, smiling. "That'll be 60 cents each, please."

The two customers went into the movie so puzzled over what large would have been that they couldn't follow the plot. But they did notice that the floor was drenched with spilled colas that had been ordered by people who couldn't finish them.

But an example cited by one observer summed up the situation better than all the generalized complaints of the others. It went like this.

He and his wife visited a barbecue establishment this week. Sometime during their stay therein, they noticed a sign on the wall advertising soft drinks in three sizes: 25 cents, 30 cents, and 40 cents.

They ordered two small drinks. The waitress reached for two giant cups.

"Wait," said the wife. "We wanted small."

"This is small," said the waitress.

They shrugged. The drinks were handed over. The husband gave the waitress 53 cents.

"No," she said. "That's 64 cents."

"But we ordered small. That's supposed to be 25 cents each."

"No, when people order small this is what we give them. The 30-cent size."

The husband looked again at the three prices listed on the wall.

"Well," he asked desperately, "what do you call the 25 cent sizes?"

She smiled at him. "We don't call them anything. Nobody ever orders them."

Maybe President Carter ought to try that one on his council of economic advisers.

Cat Named MOZART

People get themselves into the darndest messes. I know a woman, for example, who tried recently to order a phonograph album by phone.

There are places where you can do that. The shop she called, one that concentrates on rock music, clearly wasn't one of them. She was almost hysterical, and not entirely from glee, when she told me about it.

Her daughter in another city had sent her money for a gift, along with specific instructions. She was to get a certain album she wanted, and she was to get it from a certain shop. Thus directed, our heroine began the effort.

Because of bad weather, she decided to call first. That way, if they didn't have it, they could order it. Innocently, she dialed.

What she described as "a piping young voice" came on the phone, along with an incredible blast with a disco beat, and announced the name of the shop.

"I want to order a record," she said.

"Howzat?" The noise in the background was overwhelming.

"I want to ORDER a RECORD."

Silence, except for the beat. Our lady realized, she told me later, that anyone who wanted to order a record was expected to have a bullhorn.

"What kind of record?" the boice finally asked querulously. In the background, a calf or some animal was bawling, "You wanta run a-WAY, but you know you gonna STAY, oh, WHOAH."

Torn between running away and staying, oh whoah, our lady had an idea.

"Could you go somewhere quieter to talk to me?"

"No, I have to stay out here on the floor. What was it you wanted?"

Suddenly she felt ashamed. "The way it is," she shouted guiltily, "I want to order a CLASSICAL RECORD."

(Members of her family, she reported, had fled that area by now and were huddled under blankets in nearby bedrooms, trying to escape the noise emerging, from the telephone.)

"What's the name of it, lady?"

"The Magic Flute," she cried despairingly. "Cat named MOZART."

"We'd have to order that, lady."

"That's what I WANT YOU TO DO," she shrieked.

The calf in the background continued to ponder going or staying.

"I'll see what I can do, lady. You call me back."

She begged the gift of his name before he cut her off, and assured him she was prepared to pay real money. He said sure, they'd look into it. She gave him her own name and phone number. He said fine, lady.

The days passed. At last she called back for information.

Another piping voice answered, over yet another disco beat. She asked for her former clerk.

"You want who?"

She repeated the name.

"Nobody by that name works here."

After only a half-hour of debate, she got the manager, who said if somebody there had taken an order and if they had located the record, it would be at the front desk. Our lady pleaded to be given the front desk. The front desk had never heard of her. Head thumping wildly, she gave up, oh whoah.

She has learned her lesson, she told me. She has figured out the only way to order by phone. Now she remains glued to her television set, waiting for the day when the Wolfgang Memorial Special is advertised and they give the number you call to order the Golden Album of Mozart Biggies.

Middle Name Victims, Fight Back!

About the only oppressed people in this country who still don't have an organization to fight their cause are those unfortunates who are known by their middle rather than their first names.

It's generally not their fault, but they suffer all the same. Oh, how they suffer.

In a moment of parental ecstasy, for example, some couple may name a child Throckmorton Robert Jones. Later they will realize what they have done and, to make up for it, they'll call the kid Bob.

So he will grow up as Bob or Robert, and all will be well . . .

Until he has to fill out a name form for the first time.

The people who construct name forms make absolutely no allowances for anyone who wants to keep a first name hidden, or even for those who don't care all that much but simply have grown accustomed to using their middle names.

"Last name," every form demands. "First name. Middle initial."

This is in a democracy, mind you, where individual freedom is supposed to mean something.

In form-filling it doesn't. As far as the form-makers are concerned, everybody in this country is given a last name, and that's it.

The resulting trauma can be tremendous in some cases. In others, it's merely a matter of confusion—but confusion that lasts a lifetime.

Sooner or later, poor Bob Jones will find himself listed on official forms, in school or military records, in the Social Security files and elsewhere as Throckmorton R. Jones.

His banker will demand his first name and middle initial. So will his medical insurance company, and his employer, and all the rest.

Snide friends will begin calling him Throckmorton, or Rockbottom, or something equally cruel. His social life will fade. Young women will shun him, feeling certain that nobody named Throckmorton can show them a good time, let alone provide for them properly in the event of a marriage. And who would want to be the mother of a child named Throckmorton Jr.?

(If there are any Throckmortons in the audience, let me apologize profusely. It is a fine name; it's simply out of fashion. Having been christened Linus Lydel myself, I can ill afford to make sport of anyone's name—but, having been called by my middle name since infancy, I can understand the frustration suffered by all victims whose names are parted in the middle.)

But all this is not merely a surly complaint. It is instead a preface to the stirring story of R. Stephen Smith, who has found a way out of the dilemma.

Smith is not his last name. He asked that it be withheld. But he is R. Stephen, and he has had a terrible time fighting for that Stephen and keeping the "R," which stands for Robert, under wraps.

"My campaign began when I first got my driver's license," he said. "I was told that I must have Robert S. on my license unless I could show that I had legally changed my name. Not wanting to argue the matter further, and confused as to what I would have to change to get what I wanted, I left defeated."

Since then he has managed somehow to get himself listed as R. Stephen on his checking, saving and charge accounts, and even his paycheck is made out the same satisfying way. The driver's license problem remained.

"Recently when it came time to renew my license," he told me triumphantly, "I had an idea—and it worked.

"On the back of the form where they have the change of address or name spaces, I simply inserted in the first name slot, 'R. Stephen,' and left the middle initial blank.

"My license came to me a week or so later just the way I had requested."

It may not work for everyone. It may indeed be no more than a computer foul-up. But at least it can give hope to millions of us. Someday, somehow, first initials and middle names may become as acceptable as vice versa.

The Loneliness of the Short-Distance Walker

It's strange how physical fads—and adulation for the faddists—come and go without relation to prowess, skill, or even the inspired dedication of the participant.

Crowds roar their approval of tennis players in their cute little outfits. Joggers are legends. Golfers are glamorous.

But who has paused to chronicle the loneliness of the short-distance walker?

I leave the front door a few minutes before the hour, grim determination etched in every steely line of face and frame. The walk around the block is about to begin.

I am dressed in the colorful costume of short-distance walkers everywhere: Old pants, a slightly ragged shirt, last year's good shoes. Not for me the colors, the racing stripes, the padded foam rubber, the exotic fabrics. An inner compulsion drives me.

As always, I stride across the street and then turn right, well-versed in the lore learned by all short-distance walkers in areas without sidewalks: One must walk on the left side of the street, so if one turns right from the starting point, subsequent turns in the long, weary block will all be to the left. That means no crossing of streets at corners and a clear saving of 20 or 30 steps in the circuit.

To the hardbitten short-distance walker, every step counts.

I breathe deep gulps of pollen-infested air, stoking my lungs for the journey ahead. I am aware, as no motorist or jogger is, of birds singing in the neighborhood. It doesn't particularly help, but I'm aware.

Past one house, and a second and a third, and my pace has only now begun to falter. I set my lips grimly to the task ahead.

A horn sounds in my ear and a driver whooshes past from behind, driving on the left side of the street, the better to startle me. A sly leer rides his vapid face. I smile to myself, thinking how that leer would disappear if he could hear the rich assortment of titles with which I am adorning his person.

The first corner approaches. Somewhere deep within me, summoned up by sheer force of will, my second wind is arriving. I make the turn at a pace that would impress a drill sergeant.

Before me rises a hill of dimensions no car driver would believe. I toil upward, gasping for breath. There is a wrinkle in my left sock. Beads of perspiration stand on my temples. I am an unsung saga.

The hill begins to flatten out. The down-side stretches before me. I coast with it, breathing regularly again, the great chest rising and falling silently, the iron legs moving, moving, moving.

I am at the second corner.

The agony and the ecstasy continue. I walk around parked cars,

past barking dogs and piles of dead shrubbery. Flowers wink at me
from nearby yards. I see no point in winking back. What do they
know about walking?

Abruptly, the skies grow cloudy. Tiny drops of water explore my
hair. I increase my pace. The shower attacks. Within minutes I am
dripping wet. My shoes squush when I walk; my shirt sticks to me.

But the inexorable walk continues. The barrel-like chest continues
to function like a mighty engine. An exultation is upon me. Could a
tennis player possible understand? Hah.

The skies are sunny again when I turn into my own driveway. I
check my watch; the grim lines of my face relax.

Almost a mile, in only about 15 minutes.

Incredible? For the average person, perhaps. But not for the in-
domitable short-distance walker. And there are thousands of us.

Some day we, too, may take our places among the physical culture
symbols of our time. Some day people will shout for us, weep for us,
award us trophies, try to sell us gaudy and expensive walking gear.

Meanwhile, we endure. For the dedicated short-distance walker,
that is all that counts.

With A Little Help From Our Friends

With the world falling apart all around us, it is good to know that
some of the sturdy, simple virtues like concern for one's neighbor
still abide in parts of the country. And Memphis, whatever its faults,
can justly lay claim to a share.

I was fortunate enough to hear a moving example the other day,
and it is a privilege to pass it on.

Our two heroines, whose names I must withhold, are close
neighbors. One is a widow; the other, the wife of a retired engineer.
Between the two households—and indeed, all up and down the
street—the spirit of mutual concern and helpfulness prevails.

So it was not especially unusual when Mrs. A, the widow, called
Mrs. B in some agitation on a recent morning to report her concern
about Mr. C, another neighbor.

Mr. C's wife was away on a trip, and he was all alone in his house.
It was well known in the neighborhood that his habits were the sort
you could set your watch by. Every morning, rain or shine, he
emerged on the stroke of the hour (I'm not clear which hour) and got
into his car to drive to work.

"I'm worried about Mr. C," Mrs. A told her friend. "It's an hour past time for him to leave for work, and there hasn't been a sign of him. His car is still parked in the drive."

"Maybe he overslept," said Mrs. B.

"No it can't be that. I called and let the phone ring a long time, and got no answer. I'm concerned about him."

So was Mrs. B. She agreed to go over to Mrs. A's and talk it over.

(It should be noted here, in the interest of fairness, that not all citizens are so openhearted and ready to be of service. Mrs. B's husband urged her to stay at home and mind her own business. That, of course, is the curse of today's culture. We don't want to "get involved." Fortunately, Mrs. B ignored him.)

So the two ladies met in Mrs. A's yard and cast concerned eyes at the C household.

Nothing stirred.

"Something must be wrong," said Mrs. A. "You suppose he's had a heart attack?"

"I don't know," said Mrs. B. "But we'll certainly have to find out."

There are those who would say that two little ladies faced with such a potential crisis would be utterly helpless. They don't know the mettle of the true American.

Mrs. A and Mrs. B went over to the C house and walked around it. Still no sound.

"What are we going to do?" asked Mrs. B.

Mrs. A was already scouting around for the answer. "Look," she said, "here's a ladder. If we set it up right over there we can get a look into the bedroom."

And so they did. They dragged the ladder painfully to the window, set it in place, and made sure it was firm.

Then Mrs. A held it and Mrs. B resolutely prepared to mount.

It was a precarious climb, but she made it. And sure enough, when she reached the top she was able to look into the bedroom . . .

Just in time to see Mr. C emerge, joyous and dripping from his morning shower.

And that is why I have had to withhold their names. It is their fervent hope, even yet, that Mr. C has never quite figured out the source of the little screech and scramble outside his bedroom window on the morning he slept late.

Green Gobbler Can't Curb Appetite

If some member of your family is out in the yard working one of these days and suddenly disappears, don't panic.

Before you send out search parties, just look in the garbage can. Chances are you'll find your relative languishing right there.

Reports are spreading that, in Memphis, garbage cans are consuming people faster than a hound dog eats hushpuppies. It could happen to you.

All this began, of course, with the advent of the giant green plastic containers with little wheels on them, provided by a benevolent city so you can wheel your refuse out to the street twice a week for the sanitation crews.

The first cans had scarcely been dropped off the trucks before people began having hair-raising experiences with them.

In the beginning, it was a matter of reaching down for the instruction sheets telling you what the city expected you to do with the things. The sheets were in the bottoms of the cans.

And, as thousands have learned, it's a long way from the top of one of those cans to the bottom. Reach in too unwarily and over you go.

But that series of crises has passed, at least for those who have had the new containers a while, and now a new series has begun.

Gardeners have discovered the cans are a great help in collecting leaves, grass clippings or whatever. They hold amazing amounts, far more than you can get into a garden cart or a plastic bag.

So now we have gardening-related mishaps, which brings us to the case of Mrs. Blanche Harper, who was gobbled up by her can the other day.

She was weeding flower beds, she told me, and rolling the can along with her.

"I was thinking how much easier it was to toss the grass in the can rather than use plastic bags—and then lightning struck," she recalled.

It wasn't literal lightning.

She had opened the hinged lid and let it drop all the way back. The rim of the lid hung there, just a few inches above the ground, like a giant lip.

And, as she pushed the can, she accidentally stepped on the lip.

Whereupon, the whole can simply flipped over, shut its mouth, and swallowed her.

"I guess I went in all the way," she told me. "My forehead hit the top rim of the can, and I went straight in. I got a knot on my forehead, two black eyes, two skinned knees, a cut on my arm—and I'm sore all over."

Well, she finally crawled out and went on with her weeding, and she told me she still loves her new can, but from now on she plans to be more careful around it. It doesn't pay to turn your back on a garbage can these days.

What especially struck her about the incident, she said, was the response of a friend when she told her about it that night.

"I just talked to another friend," her friend said, "and she fell into her garbage can today. I can't imagine two people on the same day having a run-in with a garbage can."

It can happen here, and you'd better believe it. The good green Memphis garbage can is the Venus flytrap of the human world. Don't say you haven't been warned.

Do Not Ask For Whom the Cold is Carried

We are rapidly approaching the season when people acquire bad colds and then go bravely out to inflict them on all their friends. Some chronic victims think it's time somebody did something about it.

Indeed, a few early outrages have been reported already. A Memphis woman was complaining to me only the other day.

Her husband is just out of the hospital after an operation, she said, and she took him with some misgivings to a dinner to which they had been invited.

And there, sure enough, was a brave guest who was simply determined her cold wouldn't get her down.

The air was full of sneezes and sniffles, my informant told me, and she had to endanger her own health outrageously to be sure that her husband was never close to the brave sniffling guest, and it was an ordeal all around.

When, she asked, are people going to learn they ought to stay home if they're carrying all those germs?

It is a question all America ought to be asking. Year after year, people come down with colds and then don't actually come down. Instead of going to bed where they ought to be, they go right on out to spread their vicious little viruses all over the continent.

The advertisers of cold remedies are, of course, delighted with this sort of arrangement. They encourage it in every way they can.

Don't let your cold keep you from your job or your pleasure, they advise us. Take one of our pills and you'll feel as good as new.

So you take the pill and go to work and feel miserable and a dozen other people come down with colds within a few days as a result.

And all the new victims go out and buy cold remedies so that they, too, can go courageously on with thieir lives as if nothing had happened.

The speed with which colds can be transmitted is startling. One person, sneezing and sniffling industriously, can infect an entire school, church, office, movie, social gathering or store. And all the while, the victims themselves will be praising the culprit for "not letting it get you down."

Some of the offenders don't even bother to sneeze into handkerchiefs, for Pete's sake. What kind of culture do we live in, anyhow?

If I had my way, they'd take some of those vice-squad policemen off the job of raiding topless bars and set them to work detecting and arresting public carriers of the common cold.

A damp handkerchief would be prima facie evidence of a crime, or at least a potential crime, against the public. The offender would be released on bail, taken home in a squad car and warned that future public appearance before recovery would result in a severe fine or, in extreme cases, lengthy incarceration with people suffering from even worse infectious ailments.

But it won't work out that way, of course. Faithful, loyal employees will turn up sniffling and snuffling and sneezing on the job and be praised for their dedication to duty. Movie houses will echo to the sound of wracking coughs. Oafs at social gatherings will assure all comers that no little old cold is going to keep them from the fun.

And by the middle of the winter, everybody in the whole country will either have a cold or be starting one. When is somebody going to put an end to this sort of thing?

Warning—They Always Start with "Two"

It's the little things, the nagging things, that drive you up the wall.

Like what happened to Mrs. George R. Thompson's other dollar.

Something's wrong, but what?

Here is her story, just as she told it to me.

She stopped at a service station to buy two packs of cigarets. Noting that she had only a $20 bill, she asked if making change would be any problem.

The attendant shook her head.

"If you don't mind 19 ones, I can handle it," she said.

Mrs. Thompson said that would be fine. She handed over the $20 bill.

The attendant gave her the two packs of cigarets.

"That's one, she said. Then she reached for her supply of dollar bills.

"That's two," she said, putting down the first single. "That's three . . . four . . . five . . ."

She counted to 19 and handed over the stack of bills.

A tiny bell tinkled in Mrs. Thompson's head as she turned away. She stoppped, counted the bills and returned to the attendant.

"Pardon me, but I think I'm a dollar short. You only gave me $18."

The attendant was concerned and polite. "I'm sorry," she said as Mrs. Thompson handed over the bills. "You have $19 coming, don't you?"

"That's right. $19."

"Let's see," said the attendant. "The cigarets were $1."

"That's right."

She put down a dollar. "This makes two . . . and three . . . and four . . ."

The count continued.

"There," said the attendant looking at her customer somewhat suspiciously. "That's $19."

Mrs. Thompson was at a loss. "But you didn't go to $20."

"That's because you have only $19 coming."

"But the cigarets were a dollar."

"That's right."

"But this is only $18."

With elaborate patience, the attendant picked up the stack of bills once more.

"The cigarets were $1," she said. "Here's two . . . three . . . four . . ."

For the third time, the count was completed.

"There. That's $19."

Dazed, cowed and confused—her own words—Mrs. Thompson went meekly away.

She knows what happened. At least she thinks she knows what hapened. The cigarets were $1, right enough. And she watched the money being counted three times.

Still, she confessed, she keeps wondering. What happened to the other dollar?

Maybe it . . . or on the other hand, perhaps it . . . but never mind. Let us all agree to leave it one of those unsolved mysteries of the universe. It's best that way.

Today's Bargain: Less = More

Shoppers tend to get carried away by the prospect of a bargain, Mrs. Phillip R. Cox figures, so it doesn't hurt to be a little cautious.

Sometimes, she observes, more isn't as much less as you might think. Indeed, it may not be less at all. And if you can keep your head when all about you are losing theirs, then you just might save a few pennies.

There is, for example, the case of a special proclaimed at her market the other day.

There was a table full of ears of corn, she told me—white corn on half the table, yellow corn on the other.

And there was a sign proclaiming the price:

18 cents each . . . or 5 for 99 cents.

And people were going for it like crazy.

After thinking it over for a while, Mrs. Cox went to the cashier, and asked if she could buy fewer than five ears.

Why yes, said the cashier, but they would have to charge her a straight 18 cents each if she did.

Mrs. Cox said that was all right with her, so she completed her shopping and checked out. And when she did, the checkout clerk noticed only three ears of corn in her basket.

The routine was, more or less, repeated.

The cashier pointed out that she could get five ears for only 99 cents. Mrs. Cox said no, thanks, she only wanted three. The cashier said well, in that case she would have to charge 18 cents each for the ears. Mrs. Cox said all right.

"As I left the store." she told me, "a man was gleefully picking out 15 ears. He said he was getting them while the special was on."

But Mrs. Cox was not deterred.

"To me, " she said sturdily, "five ears for 99 cents is 9 cents more than five ears at 18 cents each."

Which, if you stop and think about it, is correct.

But you have to be careful both ways. Not only can more fail to be less, but in some cases less can actually be more.

A fellow gave me an ideal example of that a number of years ago—one of those cases with a logic so eerily unanswerable that you just can't forget it.

This happened in the spring, and he had driven out into Shelby County in search of some kind of flowers—daffodils, maybe—to transplant.

He came to a house with a display of just what he wanted, and a sign that advertised the plants at 35 cents a dozen or 50 for a dollar.

(I told you this was a number of years ago.)

"I need three dozen," he told the lady. "They're just what I was looking for."

So she counted out 36 plants and handed them over, and he handed her a dollar bill and started to leave.

"Just a minute," she said pleasantly. "You owe me a nickel more."

"Why?"

"They're 35 cents a dozen and you bought three dozen. That's $1.05."

"But I could hve bought 50 for a dollar," he protested. "How can you charge me $1.05 for only 36 when you're offering me 50 for a dollar?"

She gave him a stern look.

"We have to draw the line somewhere,"

Well, they settled the matter to their mutual satisfaction. He asked for 14 more plants and she counted them out, and that way he didn't have to pay the extra nickel. But it does go to show you have to keep your wits about you when you're looking for a bargain.

The Sims Monday Re-Entry Plan

Now and then a simple but dazzling idea occurs to an ordinary citizen and, once adopted, makes the world a better place.

Such an idea occurred to me yesterday.

It concerns the return by millions of persons to a standard work week after a standard weekend holiday, and its potential is breathtaking.

It can be summed up in a sentence:

On Mondays, no work should begin before noon.

The fact that today is Tuesday may be considered evidence, of a sort, that the world has survived the energy drain of yet another back-to-work Monday.

But flesh and blood have their limits. Like our oil supplies, our Monday morning energy reserves are certain to run out in time. When the world collapses (and it will unless the Sims Monday Re-Entry Plan is adopted) it will be on a Monday, as surely as snow falls in Buffalo.

Consider the barbaric way we treat our bodies and nervous systems under present custom.

On Mondays, all over the country, millions rise sleepily to alarm clocks in the predawn hours and struggle their way to semiconsciousness.

Like zombies they grope through the usual get-up-and-get-ready routine. Like snails they creep unwillingly to their transportation. And like sleepwalkers, once they have arrived at their places of employment, they go about their jobs.

Tuesdays are spent in trying to rectify the errors committed on Monday.

By Thursday or Friday, people have begun to get the hang of the thing. They have learned to fall into bed early and sleep soundly. Some of the more offensively well-adjusted ones actually arise bright, chipper and full of what is known deplorably as pep or vigor.

Then comes Friday afternoon and the beginning of another weekend. And instantly the routine changes.

For two nights and mornings, people stay up late and sleep even later. Their metabolism adapts to the change in habits. They grow accustomed to a life-style of gracious sleeping.

And then, another Monday morning.

The harm done to nervous, let alone physical, systems is catastrophic as well as cumulative. The vicious circle is repeated: Misery, numb acceptance, slowly growing adaptation, sudden release and then back to misery again.

If we are serious about energy conservation in this country, we will turn at once to consideration of the energy in the human system. And a Monday workday that begins at or after noon is the answer.

It will provide the re-entry program we need for readjustment of our sleeping habits. A Monday afternoon given over to work will remind us once again that there's more to life than pleasure, but a late beginning for the day will make the remainder endurable.

And more: The work done on half a Monday will almost surely exceed, in quantity as well as quality, the work done during the entire, endless, unprofitable Mondays of the present.

Let the employer consider. The sooner we get this new system going, the sooner our economy as well as our personal well-being will recover. In terms of profit alone, is not half a Monday better than no bread?

Good Ol' American Know-How

The energy crisis is producing a new breed of heroes and heroines, and it's high time they were recognized.

Today, for starters, we give you the inspirational cases of (a) the clothes-washing fisherman, (b) the cost-conscious dishwasher and (c) the lawn-mowing great grandmother.

I am indebted to a fellow columnist and former Memphian, Linton Weeks of the Arkansas Sun at Heber Springs, Ark., for the first example. It should make fishermen everywhere proud.

A fellow over there, Weeks reported, was left to do his own housekeeping recently when his wife went on an extended visit to help care for their new grandchild.

He did fine until he ran out of clean clothes.

If he could only get one pair of coveralls washed, he figured, he could make it until his wife got home. But how could he, a grown man, wash a pair of coveralls?

In the end, American know-how triumphed. He tied the coveralls to the stern of his fishing boat, knotted the sleeves and legs, dumped in some flakes and headed off down the Little Red River for an afternoon's fishing. By the time he got home, the job was done.

"My coveralls were cleaner that night than they had been in a year," he assured Weeks. And he hadn't used one kilowatt of washing-machine power.

Our second case is that of a Memphis woman who convinced her husband that they needed to buy an electric dishwasher in order to conserve power.

He objected. The old-fashioned method of washing by hand was bound to save energy and money both, he insisted.

"Ah," she shot back, "but you use a lot more hot water when you wash by hand. And that takes more power and costs more money than running an electric dishwasher."

And, by golly, her statement was supported—with various qualifications, of course—by Mrs. Emma Page, chief home economist of the Memphis Light, Gas & Water Division.

A lot of variables are involved, Mrs. Page told me, but generally speaking, if you wash dishes by hand three times a day and let the hot water run, it costs more and consumes more energy than if you run an electric dishwasher once a day.

On the other hand, you could always dump all the dishes into a pair of dirty coveralls and go fishing.

Finally, there is the sterling energy-saving example of Mrs. Mable Williams, a great-grandmother five times over.

After reading here about a citizen who had rediscovered the delights of a hand-pushed lawn mower, she called to say she had never lost them in the first place.

"I've been using a push mower for 15 years," she told me. "I'm 70 years old and weigh 94 pounds, and I mow my own lawn every other week."

How big a lawn? Pretty good-sized, she said.

"And I have a neighbor who's 88," she added, "so I mow her yard too."

The only trouble she has, she said, is getting the mower back in-doors when she's through. It's bigger than she is.

But she likes it?

"I wouldn't take a pretty for it," Mrs. Williams declared. It could be she hasn't even heard of an energy shortage.

The Price of Being Backward

Every time humanity takes a giant step forward, somebody gets a foot in his face.

Right here in Memphis, for example, there's a man who has been sorely wounded in spirit by hand-to-wrist conflict with a digital watch.

The poor fellow, who doesn't want his name used—by now he's afraid gadgets have it in for him and might punish him if he squeals—was telling me about his experience just the other day.

"Recently I bought a battery-operated quartz digital watch at a leading discount store," he said.

"You kow the kind I mean. It tells time, minutes, seconds and all that, serves as a stopwatch, has an alarm that plays 'Stars and Stripes Forever,' gives the date of the month, the year, and so on.

"Well, try and figure out how to set the monster."

The answer to that sounded simple enough. Why didn't he read the directions?

"I read the directions," he said, "and decided the thing couldn't be set."

So why not get help from the store?

"I took it back to the store. Twenty minutes and three watches later, the poor clerk said, 'Sir, I can't set it.' "

So what did he do next?

"I got my money back and went to another store, but they told me, 'We only sell 'em, we don't set 'em.'

"Then to another store. This time the clerk says, 'I can't set them but it has directions.'

"I tell her to read the directions and explain it.

"She laughs.

"It made me so mad I wanted to quit keeping up with time."

I am as progressive a fellow as the next one, I hope, but I have never got around to digital watches and never expect to. What's the point in having a watch that can do all sorts of things you don't even want done?

I'll admit I may be a little on the conservative side there, but shucks, I've done enough pioneering in watches. Back when I got my first wristwatch, my father was thoroughly put out with me. Men of his generation considered wristwatches sissy.

When you have defied your elders' opinion to the extent of putting a watch on your wrist, you don't feel the need to prove yourself later by buying a watch that plays "Stars and Stripes Forever."

But I do know a man who pants eagerly after every new gadget that comes on the market, so I called him. Did he have a digital watch?

Of course, he said, with that smug sense of superiority that is a part of what you buy with the latest gadgetry. Matter of fact, he had more than one. Wonderful things. Tell you what day it is, even.

"But I've heard from a fellow who couldn't set his digital watch," I told him.

He snorted. "Tell him to read the directions. It's simple."

"You've read the directions," I said. "You tell me."

"Well, you just push a button."

"Which button?"

"It depends. You can push one button to change the hours and another one to change the minutes."

"How many buttons are there?"

"I don't know how many," he said, getting exasperated. "But all you have to do is read the directions."

Further talk revealed that his own watch, the one he uses regularly, is an hour off because he has never gotten around to resetting it since the time change. I said that made setting a digital watch sound pretty complicated. He said not at all, he had just misplaced his directions.

He's probably right, at that. To enjoy progress, you have to have knowledge. Meanwhile, some of us will struggle on in the Dark Ages, winding our watches and looking at calendars. It's the price we pay for being backward.

What Makes a Judge Smile?

If you have nothing better to do with your time these hot, inflated days, you may wish to consider visiting the courthouse to watch a trial. Any trial. The chances are good that someone will say something interesting.

I still remember the first murder trial I covered, many years ago in another city. The defendant, a squat redfaced man with an angry scar, was determined not to give an inch in his claims of innocence.

Time after time during cross-examination, the prosecuting attorney was unable to get beyond blanket denials of everything.

"Well, anyhow," he said wearily, "we can agree that, unfortunately, your wife was killed on the day in question."

The defendant thought it over, spotted the trap so cunningly laid, and shot back triumphantly:

"I don't know whether it was unfortunate or not."

That memory was called up by some items of courtroom testimony passed along by Fred Denison. Some years ago, he told me, members of the National Shorthand Reporters Association began collecting tidbits from trial transcripts of various court cases. They turned up from time to time in various publications, and Denison clipped them out and saved them.

"They are all factual and authentic, not contrived," he told me. And in truth they don't sound like the responses—or even the questions—of persons speaking under some emotional or professional pressure.

There is, for example, the case of the attorney who asked a witness: "You say that she shot her husband at close range. Were there any powder marks on him?"

"Sure," the witness answered promptly. "That's why she shot him."

And there is the interesting defense offered in what must have been a routine city court case somewhere.

"You have been charged with habitual drunkeness," the judge intoned. "What's your excuse?"

The transcript doesn't show whether or not the defendant paused to consider, but his answer was convincing:

"Habitual thirst, your honor."

A few other exchanges from various transcripts:

1. Attorney: Are you acquainted with the parties to this action?
Witness: Oh, yes. I went to all of them.

2. Judge: Do you want to poll the jury?
Defendant: Yes, I do. Just give me that pole for two minutes!

3. Attorney: And what parts of your body were injured in the collision?
Plaintiff: Well, it was my right front leg.

4. Attorney: What organization was sponsoring the bake sale?
Witness: The Mother's Club.
Attorney: I take it they were all women?

5. Attorney: Are your parents living?
Witness: My mother is.

Attorney: Was she living in 1960 also?

6. Attorney: Before the ambulance came, did you see a police officer?

Witness: Yes.

Attorney: Did you speak to him?

Witness: No, because I was unconscious.

And finally, what may be one of the most convincing bits of testimony on record anywhere turned up in the following question and answer.

Judge: Officer, what made you suspect the defendant was drunk?

Officer: Well, your honor, when I first noticed him, he was standing in front of the call box at Fourth and Jackson. He pushed a penny in the key slot, then looked up at the clock on the King Street Station, and said, "Holy smoke, I've lost 15 pounds."

It beats reruns on television, anyhow.

Fooling Around
With
Mother Nature

Of Mice and Pachyderms

ILLUSIONS ARE TUMBLING these days faster than the balance in your savings account. You know what we've believed all these years about elephants?

It ain't so. Elephants aren't one bit afraid of mice.

And for that matter, they don't even go to a secret graveyard to die. And they don't bear grudges against people who give them chewing tobacco.

There is, in fact, not much anybody can believe in anymore.

What led me to this disheartening discovery was a batch of letters from St. George's School in Clarksdale, Miss., one of which read as follows:

"Hi! My name is Elizabeth Carson. I go to St. George's School. I am nine years old and in the fourth grade.

"In social studies we are studing Africa. You will probably think I am crazy, but are elephants afraid of mice?

"That was mainly why I wrote you to see if you think elephants are afraid of mice. If so why? But don't get me wrong. I doubt it and so does my teacher Mrs. Robinette.

" But we are very curious. So if you get a chance, if you can print a few of our letters and answer us."

There were 18 other letters, but mostly they just asked the same question.

A few threw in additional details. Reba Gayle and others said they had heard that mice get up in the elephant's ears and bother him. Jobe said he had heard that elephants are afraid of mice "like women are," a clear case of early male chauvinism. Chad and Bret speculated that the whole thing may be just "an old wise tale."

What really spurred me to nervous action, though, were the drawings that acompanied many of the letters. One showed a mouse saying "Boo!" to an elephant, which was quavering, "Get it away." Other mice in other drawings said things like "Squeak" and "Watch out buddy," while elephants roared "Eek!" and "Yikes!" and "Oh no! Help" and "Get that mouse out of here."

A few books I checked didn't mention the matter of mouse phobia among elephants, so I talked to Wayne Carlisle, chief curator at the Mempis Zoo, and he cleared the matter up in a hurry.

No, he said. Elephants aren't afraid of mice at all. In fact, a mouse occasionally scurries across the floor of the pachyderm house at the zoo, and the elephants don't squeak, squeal, trumpet or leap onto stools. They just ignore the little critters.

If that word had got out earlier, an entire generation of cartoonists would have been out of business.

Fuurthermore, he confirmed what I had been reading about elephant graveyards and tobacco-chewing.

Remember all those Tarzan movies where the villains sought, and even found, the fabled land where elephants went to pack it in? All that ivory lying around?

Forget it.

As one source I checked explained it, perhaps the legend arose from the fact that a big grassland fire could cause the death of a whole elephant herd.

And similarly, you can forget those tales about rustic wits who fed chewing tobacco to elephants, who always remembered the affront and later found ways to get even.

Matter of fact, it turns out, an elephant sort of likes a chaw now and then.

I trust all this information will be of some aid to Mrs. Robinette's fourth graders down in Clarksdale, but it doesn't increase my own happiness one bit.

Elephants not afraid of mice? Next thing you know, somebody will be claiming that hares can outrace tortoises.

Love Apples Are High-Stakes Gamble

Every summer I keep hearing from people who have grown giant tomatoes on mile-high plants and are willing for the world to know about it.

I don't blame them. If I had fallen so deeply into the tomato-growing trap as to have produced a giant tomato—or indeed a tomato of any size—I would feel the same. I'd probably be carrying the plaguey thing around with me.

But that doesn't mean I'm willing to encourage such practices.

It's a matter of conscience with me. I believe the road to hell is paved with tomato planting. I am convinced an idle tomato patch is the devil's workshop.

So I always have to say thanks, but no thanks. I don't ever want to be blamed for encouraging anybody to plant tomatoes, let alone to grow big tomatoes on mile-high plants.

Man is weak and temptations lie all about him, so it is not surprising that so many of our fellow creatures succumb to the vice of tomato-planting.

They are encouraged by fallen associates. They are egged on by green-thumbed neighbors and even by photographs in seed catalogs. They actually come to believe, for heaven's sake, that there is something wholesome and uplifting about working in what has been called "the good earth."

Good earth, my foot. All earth is evil, and the earth in a tomato patch is probably more evil than most.

The poor soul who is tomato-tempted beyond his powers of resistance is doomed to one of two fates.

The first is relatively mild: He—or she, as the sad case may be—will fail miserably.

In this case, hope remains. After weeks of loathsome labor, the tomatoes will poop out entirely or produce three or four pathetic fruits about the size and consistency of golf balls, and our victim will have learned the error of his ways. There will then be time for him to repent, turn away forever from the glittering lures of the tomato patch, and take the high road to idleness.

But the second fate is terrible indeed: A jolly harvest of fat red tomatoes hanging from plants shoulder high.

It's like gambling, a remarkably similar vice: Once you win, you're hooked. Like as not, such a pathetic victim will then go through life planting tomatoes year after year.

And what does success with tomatoes produce? Why, such things as overweening pride, feelings of superiority, a compulsion to talk incessantly about tomato-growing, and even worse. If anything could be worse.

In the past, tomatoes were often known as love apples. In view of the evils they can cause, I wouldn't be a bit surprised if that famous apple in the Garden of Eden was a tomato, and if Adam had been bragging about his tomato-growing ability just before he and Eve were thrown out.

But for those who can resist the annual urge to get out and plant tomatoes, all sorts of uplifting benefits await.

Instead of toiling in the tomato patch or boring their friends, these fortunate people will be free to:

Sit out on the terrace in the cool of the evening with a nice glass of cold lemonade or something.

Go about their business without thought of lugworts, or whatever they call those splendid insects that attack tomatoes.

Drive down to the ice cream store for a sundae.

Read a good book.
Lie on the couch.
And so on. The rewards of the righteous are endless.
I know not what others may choose to do, but as for me and my
house, we will never grow tomatoes. If erring friends want to give us
some of theirs, now, that's another matter entirely.

You Bet Your Yams

Do sweet potatoes bloom?
You can bet your yams they do.
And that's not all. You wouldn't believe what plant they're kin to.
Morning glories. Who would have thought it?
All this is in answer to Bill Donahoe, who asked the Sims
Laboratory of Unusual Research Problems (SLURP) to settle a con-
troversy that had been raging where he worked. And the answers
have come pouring in.
One fellow had said he had seen sweet potatoes blooming. Another
one, who grew up somewhere in Mississippi where they raise sweet
potatoes, said they don't bloom, and he'd give a farm to anybody
who could prove they did.
Later, Donahoe told me the fellow didn't really have a farm to
give, so we can take that part of the argument as rhetoric. But if it
hadn't been, the guy would have been short a farm.
There was, for example, the response of Paul Ashley, who actually
has a photograph of a sweet-potato plant in radiant bloom right here
in Memphis.
A friend of his had raised it, he told me, and the friend said he had
been raising potatoes for years and never saw a blossom on one
before. So when this plant bloomed, he got Ashley to take a picture
of it.
And there was the testimony of Sidney C. Smith of Milan, Tenn.,
who learned a lot about sweet potatoes more than 40 years ago when
he visited an agricultural researcher down in Louisiana. This man
told him the vine will continue to live for years and will bloom after
the third year.
Smith saw some blooms himself, so it wasn't just hearsay.
Another witness of sweet potato blooms is B.L. Jackson of Steele,
Mo., who noted that it's not an annual occurrence, only now and
then.
He described the blooms as orchid and white.

And Jackson proved he is a man of great judgment by his con-
cluding remark:

"I don't want no one's farm. Just stating a fact."

These days, almost anybody is better off stating facts than working a farm.

Al Gwyn consulted his partner, an accomplished gardener, who
said that sweet potatoes do indeed have blooms and that they're
very similar to those of a morning glory.

Dan Shil, who has grown sweet potatoes and thinks he remembers
occasional blooms, checked the encyclopedia and found that they are
a member of the morning glory family. He even called his grandmother, and she did some more checking and reported that they did
have rose-colored pink or purple blooms.

Well, color descriptions vary. The Encyclopedia Britannica, it
develops, describes the blooms as funnel-shaped and tinged with
pink or rose violet.

But don't let anybody tell you otherwise: Sweet potatoes are kin to
morning glories, and from time to time they bloom.

And such information could save you a lot of trouble on occasion,
as Joe Arwood pointed out to me.

He has a garden with sweet potatoes in it, so he knows about
blooms. But a while back he was visited by a friend who had just
bought a farm with a lot of sweet potatoes in cultivation.

She had been having a terrible time, she said. She had almost worn
herself out, cutting all the morining glory vines out of those sweet
potatoes.

Dowsing, Anyone?

More work remains to be done on the subject of dowsing for ripe
watermelons.

Can it really be that there's something to the method, after all?

The question came up recently when a Memphian was told by an
Arkansan that the way to tell if a watermelon is ripe is to set a short
straw on it lengthwise.

Then, he said, if the straw swings around, it means the melon is right.
And by golly, they tried it on a melon, and the straw swung around, and
they cut into it, and it was ripe. Coincidence?

Investigators in the Sims Laboratory of Unusual Research Problems
(SLURP) were invited to study the problem.

But there was no need for Travis Taylor of Como, Miss., to study it,
he told me.

"I have known the secret of watermelon testing for 10 years now," he said, "but I must admit that the way I learned it was a little different."

According to the Taylor system, which was passed on to him by a fellow-townsman now dead, the straw ought to be the other way.

"You take a broomstraw about six inches long," he said, "and balance it crossways on a suspected ripe melon.

"If the melon really is ripe, it will turn the straw until it points toward the end of the melon.

"Through extensive testing of my own, I find this method to be true and foolproof."

So much for firsthand experience. Mrs. L. G., a former teacher of general science, called to report a remarkable coincidence.

On the very day the question was put here, she heard two people in different localities explain how you test watermelon ripeness with a straw.

She was taking a melon from Memphis to her mother's home in Lawrenceburg, Tenn. Before she left Memphis, she stopped at a gasoline station.

The attendant looked into the car and commented that surely was a pretty watermelon in there.

Mrs. G. said she didn't know whether it was ripe or not.

"Well, I'll tell you," said the man. "If you take a straw and balance it on it, you can find out."

Bemused by the long arm of coincidence, Mrs. G. proceeded on her way. At Bolivar she stopped at a wayside stand to buy another melon.

She found one she liked, and thumped it. "This sounds ripe," she said. The man nodded. "If we had a straw," he told her, "we could tell."

Lacking a straw, she listened to his directions, bought the melon and continued to Lawrenceburg. When she got there, she tried the system for herself, following the man's instructions to the letter.

You don't set the straw firmly on the melon, she said. You just sort of ease it down, very lightly, almost as if you were dropping it. And you don't line it up with the length of the melon; you set it crossways.

And that's what she did, and the straw quivered and then swung around lengthwise. So she tried it a time or two more, just to be sure, and then she cut the melon. Beautiful.

We may have this whole matter wrapped up, except for positioning the straw, but it's not scientific to go off half-cocked. A few more tests ought to do it. Watermelon, anybody?

It's Raining Fishes

A recent question about rains of fishes hit Dr. Ross E. Hutchins, prolific author and emeritus professor of entomology at Mississippi State University, smack in the middle of one of his favorite subjects.

"This has smoked me out again," he told me.

Hutchins has a whole file on rains of fishes, including a remarkable report by an established authority who just happened to be present while one was going on.

That was on Oct. 23, 1947, and biologist A. D. Bajkov was in Marksville, La., conducting biological investigations for the Department of Wildlife and Fisheries.

So Hutchins relayed to me portions of Bajkov's report of that memorable day.

"In the morning between 7 and 8 o'clock," Bajkov wrote, "fish ranging from 2 to 9 inches in length fell on the streets and in yards, mystifying the citizens.

"I was in the restaurant with my wife, having breakfast when the waitress informed us that fish were falling from the sky. We immediately went to collect some of the fish."

Well, sir, they were all over the place. A bank director said hundreds had fallen in his yard and the yard next door. Two businessmen had been hit by falling fish as they walked toward their places of business. Some spots on Main Street had an average of one fish per square yard.

What kinds? Bajkov reported there were largemouth bass, goggle eye, sunfish, hickory shad and several species of minnows.

He went out and collected quite a few himself, including a largemouth bass that measured more than 9 inches.

And what about weather conditions?

"The actual falling of the fish occurred in somewhat short intervals during foggy and comparatively calm weather. The New Orleans weather bureau had no report of any large tornado or updraft in the vicinity of Marksville at the time."

On the other hand, the presence of numerous small tornadoes or "devil dusters" had been noted the day before.

Hutchins himself has collected many other accounts of rains of fishes and other critters, including the case of a gopher turtle, encased in ice, which landed in a town near Vicksburg, Miss., during a hailstorm in 1894.

And hundreds of small trout, perch and a catfish fell at Tilliers Ferry, S.C., during a heavy rain in 1901. And worms and turtles rained on Iron Hill, Md., in 1900, and tadpoles fell on Fourth Avenue in New York City in 1901. That's just a sampling.

The list goes on and on—but what about an explanation broad enough to cover all cases?

Hutchins himself, in an article he wrote in 1957, said people simply don't realize how much power the wind has.

If a tornado can move a church steeple 17 miles, he observed, "it can also pick up fish." So can a monsoon, or a waterspout. And he thinks waterspouts are responsible for many rains of fishes.

But how about other cases, such as the one at Marksville?

The answer to that one appears to be, nobody can say for sure. But fortunately for all the people who tell tales about seeing fish fall from the sky, a trained observer happened to be on the scene that day at Marksville.

So if you ever saw, or expect to see, little fishes paddling about in the puddles or your yard, you'd better clip this. Somebody's sure to call you a liar. A little documentation never hurt anybody.

Raker, Spare That Leaf

All over town you can feel the tension mounting as grim citizens prepare to deal with the crisis ahead.

The leaves, the fabulous leaves of autumn, are beginning to fall. And we can't tolerate that, can we?

So rakes and shredders, drop-cloths and giant garbage sacks, are being made ready to deal with this terrible affront to dullness.

And a letter signed "Grass and Leaf Lover (Uncut and Unraked)" reminds me it is time for this column's annual public service message:

Relax, friend. Who says you have to rush out and rid your lawn of the crackling multi-colored glories of nature?

But there you are. The belief, among great segments of the population, has deepened into a sort of superstitious dread. Leaves are evil; when they fall, man's duty is to gather them up and dispose of them.

And for what? Well, simply for the principle of the thing. Or in order to try to make winter grass grow, during a season when grass wasn't intended to grow anyhow. How did this weird cult get started?

As yet we haven't reached the staggering peak of the autumn-color season. Most of the leaves that have fallen thus far are brown. But already amongst them are yellow and peach and a little orange, and a whole rainbow of colors will follow shortly.

And as they fall, conscientious householders everywhere will rush out to sweep them into proper piles, push them onto the property line, or stuff them into sacks. It is as if we can't endure the sight of natural beauty any more in a land lurid with the colors of fast-food palaces and neon signs.

Some earnest rakers will tell you it's not good for the lawn to leave the leaves where they fall. Well, that's debatable. In many cases, the leaves will do a lawn more good than harm. And if you have an erosion problem, they can be a great help indeed.

And so we toss away one of the splendors of the changing seasons.

Whole generations are growing up without any knowledge of the sensual pleasure of walking through leaf-falls, feeling the crunch, watching the bounce, looking for glowing specimens to collect. Aside from a few kindergarten teachers, who ever teaches kids how to press leaves between sheets of wax paper and save their colors and shapes to brighten all the winter that follows?

If some company with a big advertising budget announced that it had hit on a scientific technique to transform ordinary leaves into miracles of color, and it it packaged the results and offered them at discounts with coupons, everybody in town would be rushing out to buy a carload to decorate their lawns.

But, alas, autumn leaves are free. Therefore they must be attacked the moment they fall from the trees. In the weeks ahead, not one golden slice of yesterday's sunshine will be allowed to remain where it disturbs the ordered desolation of browning bermuda.

So the sanitation trucks will work overtime, and in less than a couple of months the dash and splash of fall will be tidily carted away, and no doubt thousands will feel better about it.

But you don't have to be one of them. Raker, spare that leaf. Get out and kick it around. Admire its contours and its colors. Then go indoors and sit down and take it easy. There are enough problems in life already. Nobody says you have to make war on natural beauty.

Courage Overcomes Temptation For Snow Job

The following communication is one of eight, all dealing with the same problem, that I have received from some very young scholars at St. George's Episcopal Day School in Clarksdale, Miss. It summarizes succinctly a question often debated on miserable winter days.

The letter is signed by an earnest young fellow named Clint, and it reads:

"Dear Lydel Sims,

"I want to know if it gets to cold to snow.

"Because I thought it would snow won night. But my daddy said it wouldn't because it was too cold.

"Well when I went to school the next day and asked my teacher. She said, 'Well how does it snow at the North Pole.'

"I went home that afternoon and said, 'Daddy my teacher said, 'How does it snow at the North Pole?' He said, 'It's in a different continent and atmosphere'."

"When I went back to school I told Mrs. Robinette. She asked everybody in the class to ask there parents. They asked them. Mrs. Robinette asked everyone.

"Some said yes some said no. And this is what I am asking you about. I want you to answer this question somehow."

Other letters from Clint's classmates only emphasized the problem. Parents, friends, fellow-townspeople gave differing answers to the question.

Some of the young seekers after truth confessed that they had considered asking a television forecaster for the answer, but changed their minds. They were wise. Instead of a straight answer, they would probably have been given a lecture on high-pressure zones, low-pressure zones, fronts coming out of Canada and all that rot.

My only hesitation in giving a straight answer is that it might be resented by Clint's father, who could well be larger and stronger than I am. So I want to say at the outset that I agree, at least in part, with what he said.

The North Pole is on a different continent, just as he noted. As for whether it has a different atmosphere—well, maybe. I wouldn't want to argue about that, but some of our January days would indicate that the atmosphere in the Mid-South is the same as the one that delights the polar bears at the top of the world.

But dedication to truth leads me to say flatly, and without fear of successful contradiction, that it is never too cold to snow, just as things are never so bad that they can't get worse.

It is painful to say that. If indeed there were times when it got too cold to snow, we might find some fleeting consolation in winter.

We might be able to say to ourselves, "Well, cold is a bad thing, but at least it keeps the snow away."

Unfortunately, it's not true.

I quote no authorities. Once, years ago, I did indeed seek out a meteorologist in order to get a definitive and attributable answer, and he almost fell down laughing at me. I have forgotten his name.

But the possible size and pugnacity of Clint's father continues to bother me. Let me add, then, that it can conceivably get so cold you don't know whether it's snowing. There is even a chance that it can get so could you don't care. But too cold to snow? The only place such a phenomenon exists is in the land of the Tooth Fairy.

Maybe that's where your father meant, Clint. If you can stay in that world, do so. At least until spring.

Clear Mandate for Flaky Rhyme

As any one of the presidential candidates will tell you, when you get a mandate you've got a mandate.

And the mandate in this case is clear.

"What about the snow poem?" people have kept asking me. "It's time for the snow poem."

I said aw, shucks, no.

People kept asking.

"What about the snow poem?"

So, after two whole people demanded it, I figured, what can you do? What the public wants, the public gets.

It was 30 years ago, to the best of my faltering memory, when some mighty poetic spirit overwhelmed me and, under its direction, drove me to artistic creation of the highest order.

> *I think that I shall never see*
> *A snowflake that appeals to me.*

That was the beginning—a beginning born of the agony and suffering and contempt and hatred and revulsion from which all great poetry comes. It was, in short, during weather like this.

Little did I dream that, 30 years later, the public would be clamoring for a rerun. But the sentiments so boldly expressed back in 1950 have been embraced by more and more intelligent persons through the years.

It was simply my modest function to put what they were yet to feel into words.

> *A flake that quickly turns to ice—*
> *You get up once, you slip down twice.*

Well, sure, I guess it was a masterpiece. But I take no credit for it. Now and then across the centuries, these things happens. Look at Shakespeare.

> *Upon my bosom snow has lain*
> *It causes me no little pain.*
> *In all my knowledge there is no*
> *Good thing at all to say for snow.*

And the spirit moved me further, and the words continued to come.

A snow that may in Memphis lie
On sidewalks till you can't get by.
Your car won't start, the bus runs late
You stand and curse your frosted fate . . .

And then at last came what we poets call L'Envoi. At least I think that's what we call it. It's something like that.

Ah, let the nature-lovers gush—
Some day the stuff will turn to slush.
A snow may bring the Yankees glee
But not for me, in Tennessee.

So there it is, and I wouldn't have repeated it except for that overwhelming demand.

And let me say right now, before it is too late, that since then this column has outlawed the use of verse in any form.

Snow-lovers, then, should refrain from forwarding copies of their own masterpieces in praise of the miserable stuff. We have a rule against it.

And besides, poetry should contain the highest truth. Nothing good about snow could qualify.

Kids

Still Water Doesn't Run

LITTLE PITCHERS HAVE big ears, but they don't always hear all the words in old sayings.

So, on the theory that a stitch in time saves nine, Bettye Gibson tried an experiment with her eighth grade English students at Annie Camp Middle School in Jonesboro, Ark.

She gave them a special assignment on proverbs.

"Each student drew from a box a famous proverb that had the ending removed," she told me.

Half a loaf is better than no bread, no doubt, but her idea was to have the scholars complete the sayings.

It didn't work out that way.

"As I had suspected," she told me, "almost no one had heard of these sayings."

So then she invited them to write their own endings.

New brooms sweep clean, and rolling stones gather no moss. There wasn't even a smattering of lichen on the results she got.

One student, for example, undertook to complete the expression that begins, "You can catch more flies . . ."

The result:

"You can catch more flies in the dog's pen."

And there was the proverb quoted here earlier, the one about little pitchers.

As one eighth grader completed it:

"Little pitchers should play shortstop."

Remember what they say about still water? Now there's a new version, and it makes a lot more sense than the old one:

"Still water doesn't run."

That's a minimum maxim, Mum.

Any oldtimer can tell you what people are known by, and where fools rush in. But might there be truer proverbs waiting to be proclaimed?

Might be and are:

"You are known by your smell."

"Fools rush in to school."

And what's that they say about having your cake, and when to make hay, and what haste makes?

New truths await us there as well:

"You can't have your cake until you're through eating your dinner."

"Make hay while you're in the barn."

"Haste makes you late."

The new realism is apparent in some of these revised versions of tired old sayings.

Nobody really believes any more, for example, that you can become healthy, wealthy and wise just by getting up early. But let us settle for more modest advantages:

"Early to be and early to rise makes a person not sleepy when he wakes up."

A good sociologist could surely see in these modern rewrites of proverbs (these new sees to old saws, as it were) a refreshing readiness to face reality, a declaration of expectations appropriate to our age, a no-nonsense impatience with the empty promises of phrase-makers.

It's good, it's healthy, and most of all it's practical.

It even notes that some metaphors have become realities, and gives appropriate guidance as a result.

"People who live in glass houses," wrote one young sage, "shouldn't walk around in their underwear."

Yeah. Why didn't Aesop or Ben Franklin or somebody warn us about that?

Court is Adjourned

City folks are so smart you can't blame them for getting impatient with country bumpkins.

And lawyers, of course, are smarter than other city folks. Which brings us to a recent adventure involving two Memphis lawyers, a flat tire and a country bumpkin.

Weary from their legal labors, the two men decided to drive over to Horseshoe Lake in East Arkansas for a spot of fishing. The trouble began on a narrow gravel road near Lehi.

The flat was on the boat trailer. Changing a flat on a trailer is no fun, as any authority on tires and torts can tell you.

The baffled barristers were standing there scratching their heads when a boy about 10 years old appeared in the distance, ambling along the road in their direction.

They waited. At last he came within hailing distance.

"Son," one of the lawyers called, "do you live around here?"

The boy reached them, halted and looked the situation over.

"Yep," he said after a while.

"Is your daddy home?"

"Yep."

"Then how about going and getting him?"

The lad looked at them curiously.

"Why?"

The lawyers exchanged glances. Here, their eyes agreed, is a real live one.

"Because," one of them explained patiently, "we want him to go to the nearest service station and get a man to come help us with this flat tire."

"I don't know," said the boy after suitable consideration. "He's working."

"We'll pay him for his time."

"I don't know."

Such rustic reluctance was almost too much for the gentlemen from the big city.

"Well," said one of them, "will you just go try?"

"All right. But . . ."

"But what?"

The boy looked again at the tire, the trailer, the car.

"Well, it just seems to me you could save yourselves some money if you'd unhitch that trailer and go get your own help."

He paused long enough for either attorney to enter exceptions. Hearing none and assuming court was adjourned, he continued his meandering way along the road while the light dawned slowly in the city slickers' eyes.

Little Connie's Halloween Stew

Any night now, maybe even tonight, it'll be cold and rainy and you'll be wondering what to have for supper, and you'll say to yourself:

"Gee, I wish I had a good recipe for Witches Stew."

And you won't have one. Unless you save Connie's.

Connie Martin is 8, and she set down her recipe before Halloween, but her proud grandmother, Mrs. Maisie Smith, just got around to sending it to me the other day. And who needs Halloween to enjoy a good stew?

Macbeth's Witches, you may recall, enjoyed stew often at their cookouts, but Shakespeare, for all his admitted merits, just wasn't very good with recipes.

Fillet of a fenny snake, for Pete's sake. In the cauldron boil and bake. Which do you do—boil or bake? Eye of newt and toe of frog. How many? On such details the Bard of Avon is silent.

Not so Connie. The recipe her grandmother sent me is as terse and specific as any I have ever seen anywhere. Are you ready?

Witches Stew:

1½ cups of blood
900 bats
5 cups of little snakes
200 bird wings
7½ cups of glitter
500 eyeballs
9 cups of wood
600 tennis shoes
20 cups of glasses
80 tennis rakets
50 cups of metal
10,000 cups of mud
70 cups of rocks
20 pices of possum
100 scoops of sand
30 frog legs
300 cups of ink
40 snails
700 lizard guts

Compare precision like that with the vague adder's fork and blind-worm's sting, lizard's leg and howlet's wing recommended by the First Witch in Macbeth, and you'll see what I mean.

Here is a list of ingredients, in short, that commands respect.

And the instruction? Again, precision is the key:

"Let it boil till it says 'och.' "

There you have it, then—something different to spring on the family one of those cold dreary nights when everybody is expecting some prepackaged delight alleged to taste like you'd cooked it yourself.

Whip up this delicacy and they'll know darned well you cooked it yourself.

Wait Till It Exploeds

And now, friends, get ready for some real Christmas goodies.

Just in time for seasonal feasting, Mrs. Andrea Farrell's second grade girls at St. Agnes Academy have brought out their annual cookbook, this one entitled "Merry Cooking."

And you have to agree it's nothing if not merry. Follow any recipe written by one of these 7-year-olds and you simply can't escape the Christmas spirit.

There is, for example, that ever-popular Yuletide specialty, lasagne. Deanne's recipe sounds like just what you've been waiting for:

"25 meatballs. 28 cups spagetee saos. 18 green pepers. 20 nuduls. A big pan.

"Put luzzonyu in uven and cook it in uven for 60 min. at 50 dugees and take it out."

"Servings: 20 pepela. Now clen up the mes you made."

You prefer pizza? You got pizza, with Kristine's own culinary secrets to guide you:

"1 pound cheass. 1 haff pound sacig. 2 pounds dow. Tomat sose. 2 pizzee pans.

"First play with the dow. Then get the pan and put the dow in. Then put the tomato sose. Slice the cheass. After the cheass, put on the sacig. Bake from 5:00 too 6:00 at 100 degrees."

And after that, how about a nice cheesecake with Bridget guiding your every move?

"1 vanila waffer. 1 box vanila cake mix. One bottle cheeries. Cups.

"First you put in the paper cups. Then put the cookie in each cup. Then put the cake mix in. Put in the fridgerader. Then it has to be done. I hope so."

Or would you like to sink your teeth into a wonderful cherry pie? Laura's your authority for that.

"2 cups cherries. 1 cup flour. 1 cup cooking oil. Some sugar. Globs of dough. A huge pan.

"Put cherries in pan. Take all the rest of the ingedce. Put them in. Then stire it up. Take the blender and mix it. O.K. That's that. Let it cook for about 50 minits, then take it out. Cook at 40 dagrese."

But there will be times when you long for something simple. Try Carol's Irish hamburgers:

"1 ouneon. 4 handfuls hambragr meat.

"Get the 4 handfuls of hambragr meat. Put the hambragr meat into a patty. Cut up the ouneon in little peses. Put it in the patty. Put in for 60 minetes at 100 degrees."

After which, you should be feeling just right for some of Jana's marshmallow treats:

"50,000,000,000 rice crespes. 20 marmelos. 5 cups oil.

"Mix in a pan. Put in the oven. Let it cook for 6 minutes. Cook for 5 mines at 6 tegres."

See how simple cooking can be when you know how?

I wish there were room for Rachel's sukiyaki ("Their nodoles are not like ors") and for Theresa's spinach pie, which you make without any spinach, and for all the others.   But we need something solid, satisfying and explosive to close with. How about Christina's spaghetti?

"10,000 noodles. 600 meetballs. Ragoo's spagetee sauce. Big pot.

"Now put everything in the big pot. Then put it in the oven. Put it at 600 degrees. Wait till it exploeds."

(If that won't give you a bang-up Christmas, nothing will.)

I Wont To Be A Dennis

Children still have all those bright eager traditional dreams you remember from your own childhood—and then some.

Mrs. Barbara Segal's second graders at Raineshaven School, for example, have been dreaming like crazy.

They got the chance in their creative writing lessons, times when second graders may properly be allowed to forget the cares of spelling and the like and let their imaginations soar.

The other day they asked, and answered, the familiar question: What do I want to be when I grow up?

"I want to be a cheerlead," wrote Rosyln. "And I want to be a Teacher. And I want to be a nurse. And I will be good."

To be all those things she'll have to be good. As will Steven, who wrote boldly: "I want to be a boxer so I can knock people down and make good money."

But it is natural to dream only of success. "I want to be a policeman," wrote Oliver, "because they driv cars fast and because they catch people esay. And I want to be a waiter because they smeel the food the people have and it smeels very good."

Who but a second grader would link police work with food-smeeling?

"I want to be a teacher," wrote Casandra, "and I coud teach the class and the children to read an write and they could have a colering sheet." A natural-born teacher, Casandra, as any observer can note. In a single sentence she taught herself how to spell "could."

"I am going to be a Nurse," wrote Karen. "I will make a lot of money. My doctor will tell me what to do. And what to bring him. I will work with pations. And When I go home, I will rest and go to bed."

Tina, too dreamed of working with pations:

"I wont to be a Dennis. I will like to be a Dennis very must. It will be fun to be a Dennis. I Can see people tooht."

Basically, then, the dreams haven't changed much through the years.

Cheerleader, boxer, policeman.

Waiter, teacher, nurse.

Even a tooht-Dennis.

So where is the unexpected?

Lisa provided that. Lisa has an ambition shared by almost nobody, but if she ever achieves it she will be envied by many.

And when that day comes, thousands of us will say to ourselves, why in the world didn't I ever think of that?

"I," wrote Lisa, "want to be a ice cream parlor."

Goerge Washington Wore Wooden Teeth

As George Washington's birthday is celebrated by calendar-confused citizens all over the country, legends about the great man continue to grow.

And that is as it should be. If his birth date can be shifted around for the sake of convenience, why shouldn't the stories be embellished, adorned, revised?

Now a third-grader named Carol Ann, at Central Academy in Macon, Miss., has done what may be the definitive job in bringing the myth and the facts up to date. Her teacher, Mrs. Mary A. Thomas, is so proud of the result that she has passed it along for others to share.

Let us review the great man's exploits as detailed by Carol Ann.

"Goerge Washington's father was planting cherry trees one evening. The first tree that grew Goerge's father was proud of.

"But Goerge was angry one day. He was so angry he chopped the tree down.

"When his father was going to water the other trees. He saw the chopped tree. He asked Goerge if he chopped it down.

"Goerge said, 'Yes father I did. I'm very sorry. I guess I lost my temper.'

"'I'm proud of you son,' Mr. Washington said. 'And I didn't say that becuse you chopped it down. I said it because I know my son doesn't lie.' And as Goerge grew older he began to get smarter.

"One day in school they read about something in science. And when Goerge went home he wanted to learn more about the human body. So he asked his father if he could walk to the library.

"He said he could. So Goerge walked two miles to get the book.

"Goerge studied very hard and learned alot. Goerge was a smart boy. His father and mother was very proud of him. They were glad to have a smart son tha obaied pretty good. The bigger he grew the smarter he grew too.

"Goerge needed some good teeth. His daddy took him to the doctor's office. The doctor said Goerge was going to have to wear false teeth.

"But they didn't have false teeth as we do. Goerge had to wear wooden teeth.

"When Goerge grew up he married a girl named Martha. She could sew very good. She made alot of things for her friends. Goerge got elected prceidant.

"Two men came to Goerge and asked him is his wife could make an American flag. Goerge said yes. When Goerge got home he told Martha what they had said.

"She said she can make one. He told her to have it ready by next week.

"She put red and white stripes and wite stars. The colors was red white and blue.

"The men came to get it. The men told her is was the best he had ever saw. The men was happy. Goerge and Martha was too.

"And they lived happily ever after."

It's too bad she wasn't able to find room for the part about that campaign slogan, "Tippecanoe and Washington, too," or about the time Goerge sent that immortal message, "Sighted sub, sank same," but you can't have everything in one short essay by a third-grader.

So let us be grateful for this new biography of the Father of His Country and seek to pattern our lives after his. Perhaps we, too, can reach the point where people will say we never lie, and perhaps like Goerge we can grow older and begin to get smarter. It is a goal for us to cherish on this important day.

No Mache For A Dragon

It's hard to understand in this best of all possible worlds, but youngsters are growing cynical.

Remember all those stories about knights slaying dragons?

It doesn't work that way anymore. At least, not in the practical minds of some third graders at Gardenview School whose teacher, Mrs. Betty Nicholas, gave them a shot at story writing on their own.

It was in one of those exercises call word challenges. The teacher showed the children a picture of knights and dragons and a castle and told them to write a story about what might have happened in such surroundings.

Happy endings were as hard to find as dragon's teeth. Evil flame-throwers kept winning.

Consider the grim version dreamed up by Tonia:

"Once there was a young princess. She lived in a casel with a king. And one day the dragon came up to her and killed her.

"The king told one of his knight men that the dragon must be kill-ed so the knight men went to kill the dragon.

"The knight found the dragon and the dragon let out fire at the knight men. The knight men tryed to stick the dragon but he mist and the dragon struck the knight and killed him. And thats the end."

Patrick was equally pessimistic about the whole affair:

"One day a king said to one of his knight. I wait you to go kill the dragon for killing my prince in my best knight.

"The said I shall kill the dragon. So the whith to kill the dragon. Then the knigth heard hot breath on him. The dragon ran after him so the knight jump off his horse. The knigth got bruned.

"After a hour or so the dragon bruned up the knight so now that the King know that no knight is no mache for a dragon."

And it wasn't any better the way Cedric saw it:

"Once upon a time there was a fire breathing dragon he burned one city and that city sent a massage to the King the said thee fire breathing dragon is coming to your city to burned it up.

"The King sent one of his arme knights he thought that the knight could kill the dragon when they meet the knight grabed his sword and hit the dragon the dragon blowed fire and meatled the knight armer then he ate him up and the dragon burned up the kings city a few years later the dragon died."

At least we have it on Cedric's authority that the dragon finally got his. Meanwhile, the world being what it is, it behooves all of us to take Patrick's advice. When fire-breathing dragons are around, let no knight light the first mache.

Hawk In The Name Of The Law

"If I were police chief," 13-year-old Alex pledged, "I would drive up and down street looking for trouble.

"If I would find it I would look them up and down and say, 'Get in the car, let's go, let's go, let's go.'

"And if they try to get away I would say, 'Hey, come back here,' and if he don't come back I say, 'Hawk in the name of the law, man'."

Hawking in the name of the law was only one of many splendid plans proposed by more than 5,000 sixth-grade boys and girls in public, private and parochial schools who've been competing for the title of Junior Police Chief.

The annual contest—sponsored by the Memphis Park Commission and the Memphis-Shelby County Exchange Clubs—was, as usual, a whopping success. Winners will be honored at the annual Crime Prevention Luncheon.

But we mustn't let all the fine suggestions of the losers go unnoticed, must we?

The proposal, as summed up by a boy named William: "I would stop crime and it wouldn't pay a dime to be doing time. If you know about this, don't make a fist."

That's too general for you? Then consider Derrick's terse pledge to rid the city of white-sheeted bigots:

"I will stop the Clu Club Clan."

Personnel problems were on the minds of many contestants.

"I would start an Adopt-a-Policeman program," wrote John.

"I would hire more policemen," Angie promised. "Tha would drop unemployment."

Renita was prepared to head off trouble before it started: "I would make sure the men policemen wouldn't mess around with the women policemen."

Jail conditions weren't overlooked, either.

Terence promised to "have carnivals for people in jail and they would never want to leave."

Mario, on the other hand, pledged to "feed them cornbread and milk every two days."

Sheila was more selective: "I would put the people with hard crime in hard sails."

The legislative powers of a police chief received wide attention.

"I would make prices go back down to the 1700s so this could be a happy world," Lashonda promised.

"I," wrote Jeff, "would make a rule that you can cross the street without getting his."

"I would try to stop rape," Gregory offered, "by putting more men in the neighborhoods."

A few other no-nonsense specifics:

"I would put children in jail for cursing and not bathing."—Dana.

"I would close all Discoes that have Nude Dancing in them and turn them into homes for little orphans."—Treccia.

"I would make more streets so not as many people will get in a crash."—Mike.

"I won't bend rules for handsome pimps, and money paying prostitutes."—Angela.

"I would stricken the laws on drugs. Require that every person have a bargular alarm. Stricken laws on vandelisim. Reqire that people have money in more than one place."—Bryan.

But even a sixth grader can recognize that all work and no rest makes anybody a dull police chief. A lad named James sumed up the philosophy of leadership through delegation of power.

"I would drive around and see if the police is on there duties," he promised.

"And then I would go back to the office and sits back and relax my heavy bones."

Well, he wasn't named honorary police chief, but who knows? Some day that boy may grow up to be president.

Yes, Virginia, There Is A Farrah Fawcett

At 6, Louis Burgess of Germantown is beginning to re-examine some of the glorious illusions of childhood.

Cynical and disenchanted colleagues in the first grade have fed his skepticisms. That is the way of the world.

As early as last Christmas he almost asked some awkward questions of his mother, Mrs. Bill Burgess. She could see them in his eyes, she told me.

But he held off.

Easter came and went. Louis and his friends held more discussions, but he kept his peace.

Then, for some reason, the time came for him to break his silence.

He came running home from school with a touch of sadness in his eyes.

"Mama," he asked, "is there really a Santa Claus?"

Mrs. Burgess braced herself before the plunge. When her children ask questions, she feels, she must tell them the truth—gently and lovingly, to be sure, but faithfully.

She told him about Santa Claus and mothers and fathers and the spirit of Christmas.

Louis thought about it a while.

"And the Tooth Fairy?" he asked.

She told him about the Tooth Fairy.

"And the Easter Bunny, and all that?"

She told him about the Easter Bunny, and all that.

Then he smiled. It was a good smile, Mrs. Burgess told me, a smile of understanding and acceptance. And when he spoke, his first words were of his little brother and sister.

"I'll have to keep it a secret for Neal and Jennifer," he said.

Mrs. Burgess said yes, they must all do that.

After that there was a comfortable silence. Mrs. Burgess looked at her little boy with pride. He's growing up, she thought.

But as she watched him, what she was to describe later as "a sudden, panic-stricken look came over his face.

He had, it developed, thought of one more question.

"Mama . . ."

"Yes?"

"Mama, is there really a Farrah Fawcett-Majors?"